ON STRATEGY

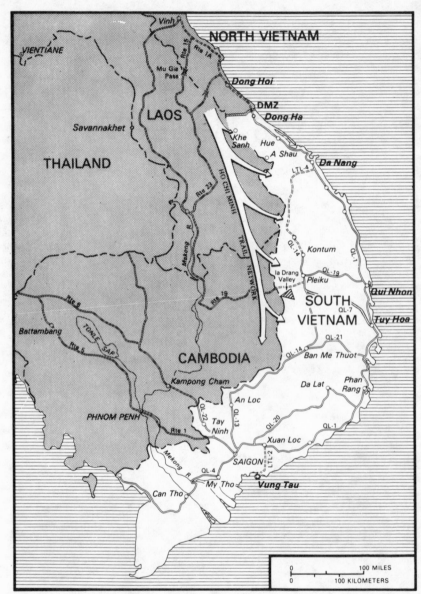

Adapted from Map 6, *Vietnam from Cease-Fire to Capitulation* by Colonel William E. LeGro, USA. Washington, U.S. Army Center of Military History, 1981, p. 37.

ON STRATEGY

A Critical Analysis of the Vietnam War

HARRY G. SUMMERS, JR.
Colonel of Infantry

PRESIDIO

Introduction, epilogue, and revisions to basic text
copyright © 1982 by Presidio Press
Third printing 1983

Published by Presidio Press
31 Pamaron Way, Novato, CA 94947

Library of Congress Cataloging in Publication Data

Summers, Harry G.
    On strategy.

    Bibliography: p.
    Includes index.
    1. Vietnamese Conflict, 1961–1975—United States.
2. Strategy. I. Title.
DS558.2.S95   1982   959.704'33'73   82-7498
ISBN 0-89141-156-9   AACR2

Jacket Design by Kathleen A. Jaeger
Book Design by Lyn Cordell

Printed in the United States of America

To
GENERAL WALTER T. KERWIN, JR.
(United States Army, Retired)

whose deep and abiding concern for the
future of the United States Army and the Nation
it serves was the original inspiration for this work.

Contents

Acknowledgments

This book could not have been written without the active support and encouragement of the senior leadership of the Army. They not only provided the time and the means to research and write the book, but also widely distributed the original paperback edition throughout the Army and the Defense establishment. This early edition is now being used as a student text at the Army War College, the Army Command and General Staff College, and the Marine Corps Amphibious Warfare School, and for selected seminars at the National Defense University, the Air and the Naval War Colleges.

It also could not have been written without the help of a number of Army officers, both here at the War College and throughout the Army, who had been involved in the articulation, formulation and execution of military strategy. Among those who provided comments and suggestions were Chairman of the Joint Chiefs of Staff (then Army Vice Chief of Staff) General John C. Vessey, Jr., Army Chief of Staff General Edward C. Meyer, Commander of the Army Training and Doctrine Command (then Chief of Operations and Plans) General Glenn K. Otis, retired Generals Andrew P. O'Meara, Bruce Palmer, Jr., and Richard G. Stilwell; former Army War College Commandants Lieutenant Generals Jack N. Merritt and DeWitt C. Smith, Jr., Lieutenant General Richard L. Prillaman, retired Lieutenant Generals John H. Elder and William B. Fulton; Major Generals Dave R. Palmer and Dale R. Vesser; Brigadier General Dallas C. Brown, Jr., Colonel Donald P. Shaw, Director US Army Military History

Institute; Chaplain (Colonel) Charles Kriete, Colonels Keith Barlow, Sanders Cortner, Zane Finkelstein, Charles Hines, Thomas Leggett, Donald Lunday, Henrik Lunde, Dandridge (Mike) Malone, Lloyd Matthews, Ramone Nadal, Andrew Remson and Joseph Sites, Major David Russell and Captain James Waters of the Army War College Staff and Faculty; Colonel Roger MacLeod and Lieutenant Colonels Creighton Abrams, Ronald Griffith, William Orlov and Thomas Rhen of the Army War College Classes of 1980 and 1981; Colonel William Stofft and the members of the Combat Studies Institute US Army Command and General Staff College; and Colonel Andrew P. O'Meara and Major Charles Scribner of the Army General Staff.

In addition to the Army reviewers, comments were also received from former Secretary of State Dean Rusk, Oxford University Professor Michael Howard, Georgetown University Professor Edward N. Luttwak, Congressional Staffer William S. Lind, author and strategist John M. Collins and Herbert Y. Schandler, as well as Department of State Representative Frank E. Cash, Central Intelligence Agency Representative James Dimon and Mrs. Marianne Cowling of the Army War College Staff and Faculty.

Particular thanks goes to Colonel Wallace P. Franz, United States Army Reserve. A former member of the consulting faculty of the US Army Command and General Staff College now on active duty with the Army War College faculty, he served as an infantry company commander in the Korean war and as a district advisor in Vietnam. Colonel Franz, an avid military historian and student of military tactics and strategy, was the source of much of the detailed information on the evolution of military theory. His critical page-by-page review of this work added much to the clarity of the final product.

Thanks must also go to my wife, Eloise, and our two sons, Captain Harry G. Summers III and Captain David C. Summers, United States Army, whose comments provided a unique perspective and who were the inspiration for this attempt to help make their Army of the future a more effective instrument for national security.

A final word of thanks to Colonel Robert V. Kane (U.S. Army, Retired), publisher of Presidio Press, who not only provided the means for this analysis to reach a wider public audience, but also made it possible for royalties to accrue to the Army War College Foundation, a nonprofit organization dedicated to enhancing the War College's education mission . . . in former Secretary of War Elihu Root's words, "not to promote war but to preserve peace."

In expressing my thanks to those who provided comments and advice I must add that the conclusions and such errors as this book contains are solely my responsibility.

H.G.S.
Carlisle Barracks, Pennsylvania
6 May 1982

Foreword

At the turn of the century, Secretary of War Elihu Root established the Army War College to, among other things, instruct senior Army officers on "the science of war . . . in all matters pertaining to the application of military science to the national defense" and then to "present, by written papers and reports . . . the results of their investigations, explorations, reflections and professional scientific work."

At that time, the major problem at hand was sorting out the debacle of the Spanish-American War, particularly the failures in management, administration and logistics—what Clausewitz called the art of preparation for war. The War College's efforts in this endeavor are reflected in the unparalleled successes in logistics and management which projected and sustained our Army around the globe during the World Wars, Korea and Vietnam.

But, as Clausewitz warned, war preparation is only half of the art and science of war. In Vietnam it appeared that our failings were in the other half of that equation—the conduct of war proper. Once again, the Army War College, in the person of Colonel Harry G. Summers, Jr., was tasked to examine what went wrong. The results of his "investigations, explorations, reflections and professional scientific work" is the book at hand, *On Strategy: A Critical Analysis of the Vietnam War.*

It is important for the reader to understand what this book is and what it is not. It is not, nor was it intended to be, a history of the Vietnam war. It is not a detailed account of day-to-day tactical operations or an examination of the many controversies of the war. What was intended was a narrow focus on the war in the area of major concern to the Army War College—"the application of military science to the national defense." Using Clausewitzian theory and the classic principles of war, the book attempts to place the Vietnam war in domestic context as well as in the context of war itself. Its central thesis is that a lack of appreciation of military theory and military strategy (especially the relationship between military strategy and national policy) led to a faulty definition of the nature of the war. The result was the exhaustion of the Army against a secondary guerrilla force and the ultimate failure of military strategy to support the national policy of containment of communist expansion.

As a critical strategic analysis, I believe that this book is firmly on the mark. This conviction is reinforced by the overwhelmingly favorable comments that the War College has received since the book was originally published in paperback in the spring of 1981. They came not only from the current leadership of the Army (who, it must be remembered, were captains, majors and colonels during the 1960's, primarily concerned with tactical operations), but also from many retired general officers who were intimately involved in the strategies and plans of the war at the highest level.

The purpose of this analysis was not to find fault or to identify villains but rather, by drawing from the lessons of the past, to prepare today's senior Army officers to meet the challenges that will face our country in the future. By incorporating this book into our course of instruction here at the War College and at the Army Command and General Staff College at Fort Leavenworth, I believe the Army has taken a major step in improving its ability to implement, through force of arms, the national policies of the United States when called upon to do so.

Moreover, improving strategic understanding within the Army is only part of the answer. If the Army is to be used wisely, the American people should have some idea of military strategy. This is especially so since, under the Constitution, the American people through their elected representatives not only raise, support, and regulate the Army but also determine the very battlefields upon which their Army must fight.

One hundred and fifty years ago, in his classic study of the dynamics of war, Carl von Clausewitz warned that the military must always be subordinate to political policy. This was no news to Americans, for we had written that very premise into our Constitution fifty years earlier. But Clausewitz went on to say that this subordination rests on the assumption that "policy knows the instrument it means to use." By making the Army War College's critical analysis of Vietnam war strategy available to a wider audience, this edition should help the American people to know the nature of their Army and to appreciate how it can be used to provide for the common defense and to protect and secure the national interests of the United States.

JACK N. MERRITT
Major General, USA
Commandant, U.S. Army War College

Carlisle Barracks, Pennsylvania
6 May 1982

TACTICAL VICTORY, STRATEGIC DEFEAT

"You know you never defeated us on the battlefield," said the American colonel.

The North Vietnamese colonel pondered this remark a moment. "That may be so," he replied, "but it is also irrelevant."

Conversation in Hanoi, April 1975[1]

ONE OF THE most frustrating aspects of the Vietnam war from the Army's point of view is that as far as logistics and tactics were concerned we succeeded in everything we set out to do. At the height of the war the Army was able to move almost a million soldiers a year in and out of Vietnam, feed them, clothe them, house them, supply them with arms and ammunition, and generally sustain them better than any Army had ever been sustained in the field. To project an Army of that size halfway around the world was a logistics and management task of enormous magnitude, and we had been more than equal to the task. On the battlefield itself, the Army was unbeatable. In engagement after engagement the forces of the Viet Cong and of the North Vietnamese Army were thrown back with terrible losses. Yet, in the end, it was North Vietnam, not the United States, that emerged victorious. How could we have succeeded so well, yet failed so miserably? That disturbing question was the reason for this book.

At least part of the answer appears to be that we saw Vietnam as unique rather than in strategic context. This misperception grew out of our neglect of military strategy in the post–World War II nuclear era. Almost all of the professional literature on military strategy was written by *civilian* analysts—political scientists from the academic world and systems analysts from the Defense community. In his book *War and Politics*, political scientist Bernard Brodie devoted an entire chapter to the lack of professional military strategic thought.[2] The same criticism was made by systems analysts Alain C. Enthoven and K. Wayne Smith who commented: "Military professionals are among the most infrequent contributors to the basic literature on military strategy and defense policy. Most such contributors are civilians. . . ."[3] Even the Army's so-called "new" strategy of flexible response grew out of civilian, not military, thinking.

This is not to say that the civilian strategists were wrong. The political scientists provided a valuable service in tying war to its political ends. They provided answers to "why" the United States ought to wage war. In like manner the systems analysts provided answers on "what" means we would use. What was missing was the link that should have been provided by the military strategists—"how" to take the systems analyst's *means* and use them to achieve the political scientist's *ends*.

But instead of providing professional military advice on how to fight the war, the military more and more joined with the systems analysts in determining the material means we were to use. Indeed, the conventional wisdom among many Army officers was that "the Army doesn't make strategy," and "there is no such thing as Army strategy." There was a general feeling that strategy was budget-driven and was primarily a function of resource allocation. The task of the Army, in their view, was to design and procure material, arms and equipment and to organize, train, and equip soldiers for the Defense Establishment.

These attitudes derive in part from a shallow interpretation of the Army's mission. While it is true that the National

Security Act transferred operational command to the Department of Defense, leaving the Army with the task to "organize, train, and equip active duty and reserve forces," the Army General Staff is still charged with "determination of roles and missions of the Army and strategy formulation, plans and application; Joint Service matters, plans, and operations. . . ."[4] In addition, Army officers assigned to the Office of the Joint Chiefs of Staff and to operations and planning positions in unified commands also have responsibility for Army (i.e., land force) strategy. Further, to argue as some do that in our democracy only the President can "make" strategy is to confuse the issue, since in most cases the President does not formulate military strategy but rather decides on the military strategy recommended to him by his national security advisors, both military and civilian.

Unconsciously, such attitudes reflected a *regression* in military thought. As early as 1971 then Lieutenant Colonel Albert Sidney Britt III, Department of History, United States Military Academy, noted that "the modern philosophy of limited war derives in part from the practice of the 18th century."[5] Colonel Britt's observations were borne out in the classic critique of 18th century warfare, Carl von Clausewitz's *On War*. His 150-year-old description of "the art of war" closely paralleled the conditions bitterly attacked by such critics as Richard Gabriel and Paul Savage in their widely quoted book *Crisis in Command* (New York: Hill & Wang, 1978)—an army more concerned with management than with military strategy. Describing these conditions, Clausewitz said:

> [In the 18th century] the terms "art of war" or "science of war" were used to designate only the total body of knowledge and skill that was concerned with material factors. The design and use of weapons . . . the internal organization of the army, and the mechanism of its movements constituted the substance of this knowledge and skill.[6]

Using this criterion for the art and science of war, it can be argued that the system worked, that it did everything that it was asked to do. Such arguments are the Army's version of

Leslie H. Gelb and Richard K. Betts' analysis of the Vietnam-era political-bureaucratic system. Examining the structure of the system, they found that it did everything that it was designed to do.[7] If the Army is, as some would have it, merely a logistics and management system designed to "organize, train, and equip active duty and reserve forces," it was an unqualified success.

The illogic of such an analysis springs from a faulty understanding of military theory. In his clarification of military theory Clausewitz said, "The activities characteristic of war may be split into two main categories: those *that are merely preparation for war*, and *war proper*." All that is required from the first group, he said, is "the end product"—trained and equipped fighting forces. "The theory of war proper, on the other hand, is concerned with the use of these means, once they have been developed, for the purposes of the war."[8] During the Vietnam war we confused these two activities. There are those who would have it that the reason was that there were so many conflicting definitions of "strategy" that we lost our way. But such an excuse is not supported by the facts. According to the Joint Chiefs of Staff *Dictionary of Military and Associated Terms*, the official definition of military strategy is "the art and science of employing the armed forces of a nation to secure the objectives of national policy by the application of force, or the threat of force."[9] As we saw earlier, the "missing link" in strategy was the failure to address the question of "how" to use military means to achieve a political end. Yet this missing link is contained in our own definition of military strategy—*employing* the armed forces . . . to secure *the objectives of national policy*.

To find where we went wrong, Part II, *The Engagement*, will examine our military strategy in Vietnam in detail. For now, suffice it to say that, by our own definition, we failed to properly employ our armed forces so as to secure U.S. national objectives in Vietnam. Our strategy failed the ultimate test, for, as Clausewitz said, the ends of strategy, in the final analysis "are those objectives that will finally lead to peace."[10]

Seeing war in 18th century terms not only had an influence on the battlefield, it also influenced the actions of the government and the perceptions of the American people. As we will see, this latter effect may have been the more deadly of the two. On the battlefield the effect was confusion between the administrative requirements of war preparation and the operational requirements of war proper. In the political domain the difference was between seeing the Army as an instrument of the government and seeing it as an instrument of the people. According to Clausewitz:

> In the eighteenth century . . . war was still an affair for governments alone, and the people's role was simply that of an instrument . . . the executive . . . represented the state in its foreign relations . . . the people's part had been extinguished . . . War thus became solely the concern of the government to the extent that governments parted company with their peoples and behaved as if they were themselves the state.[11]

Such a neo–18th century outlook goes a long way toward explaining why the government decided not to mobilize the American people and why it did not seek a declaration of war. It also explains why to many Americans the Vietnam war was "Johnson's war" or "Nixon's war" or "the Army's war" rather than the American people's war.

The task of the military theorist, Clausewitz said, is to develop a theory that maintains a balance among what he calls the trinity of war—the people, the government, and the Army. "These three tendencies are like three different codes of law, deep-rooted in their subject and yet variable in their relationship to one another," he says. "A theory that ignores any one of them or seeks to fix an arbitrary relationship between them would conflict with reality to such an extent that for this reason alone it would be totally useless."[12] Part I, *The Environment*, will examine the relationship between the Army and the American People. It will emphasize how public support must be an essential part of our strategic planning, and how Congress has the Constitutional responsibility to legitimize that support. It will then examine the natural friction that exists between the American people and its

Army, the friction inherent in our national security bureaucracy and the friction caused by our own doctrine.

It might seen incongruous that much of the analysis in
both Parts I and II will be drawn from a 150-year-old source
—Clausewitz's *On War*. But the fact is that this is the most
modern source available. In economics one does not have to
return to Adam Smith but can read Milton Friedman, John
Kenneth Galbraith, or Paul Samuelson for an understanding
of economic theory. In political science one does not have to
return to Plato but can gain an understanding of the political
process from a variety of contemporary scholars. In military
science, however, *On War* is still the seminal work. As the
late Bernard Brodie observed, "Clausewitz's work stands out
among those very few older books which have presented profound and original insights that have *not* been adequately
absorbed in later literature." Addressing the question of
pertinency, Brodie notes that "most of the contemporary
books [do] not, as Clausewitz does, have much to say of
relevance to the Vietnam war."[13]

Clausewitz can also assist us in understanding North
Vietnam's actions. Although we usually ascribe their actions
to Mao's "people's war" theories, it is important to note that
as an avowed Marxist-Leninist state they also drew from
Clausewitz. In September 1971, Illinois State University Pro-
fessors Donald E. Davis and Walter S. G. Kohn drew attention to the influence of Clausewitz on V. I. Lenin and detailed
Clausewitz's contribution to Marxist-Leninist military
thought.[14] More recently in June 1980, Wilhelm von
Schramm, one of Germany's foremost authorities on Clausewitz, noted Clausewitz's influence on the founders of world
communism, Karl Marx and Friedrich Engels, as well as on
Lenin. He goes on to say that as a result Clausewitz's theories
(in distorted form) "became part of the dogma of Leninism."
"Thus," he says, "Clausewitz attracted more and more interest—first in Moscow, where the study of his works was made
a compulsory subject at the Frunse Military Academy. From
there, his fame radiated to most other orthodox communist
countries, including the China of that time. When [Federal

Republic of Germany] Chancellor Helmut Schmidt visited Peking he was told of the high esteem which Mao Tse-tung held for the German philosopher of war."[15]

By analyzing the Vietnam war against a source untainted by today's bias, we should arrive at a better understanding of the deficiencies in military theory that led to our problems there, and the changes necessary for the future. "The primary purpose of any theory," said Clausewitz, "is to clarify concepts and ideas that have become, as it were, confused and entangled."[16] The purpose of this book is to lay out such a theory, using our Vietnam war experience as the vehicle.

NOTES

1. Conversation on 25 April 1975 in Hanoi between Colonel Harry G. Summers, Jr., then Chief, Negotiations Division, U.S. Delegation. Four Party Joint Military Team and Colonel Tu, Chief, North Vietnamese (DRV) Delegation.

2. See chapter 10, "Strategic Thinkers, Planners, Decision Makers," in *War and Politics* by Bernard Brodie (Macmillan: New York, 1973).

3. Alain C. Enthoven and K. Wayne Smith, *How Much Is Enough: Shaping the Defense Program 1961–1969* (New York: Harper & Row, 1971), p. 90.

4. *US Government Manual, 1979–1980* (Washington, D.C.: USGPO, 1979), p. 202.

5. Lieutenant Colonel Albert Sidney Britt III, "European Military Theory in the 18th and 19th Centuries," *Supplemental Readings for Advanced Course in the History of Military Art* (West Point, New York: USMA, 1971), p. 10.

6. Carl von Clausewitz, *On War*, edited and translated by Michael Howard and Peter Paret with Introductory Essays by Peter Paret, Michael Howard, and Bernard Brodie and a Commentary by Bernard Brodie (Princeton, New Jersey: Princeton University Press, 1976), II:2, p. 133 [Afterwards, "Clausewitz, *On War*." The roman numerals represent the book, the arabic numerals the chapter.]

7. Leslie H. Gelb and Richard K. Betts, *The Irony of Vietnam: The System Worked* (Washington, D.C.: The Brookings Institution, 1979), p. 353.

8. Clausewitz, *On War*, II:1, pp. 131–32.

9. *JCS Pub. 1: Dictionary of Military and Associated Terms* (Washington, D.C.: The Joint Chiefs of Staff, 1979), p. 217.

10. Clausewitz, *On War*, II:2, p. 143.

11. *Ibid.* VIII:8, pp. 583, 589–91.

12. *Ibid*, I:1, p. 89.

13. Bernard Brodie, "The Continuing Relevance of *On War.*" *Ibid*, p. 51.

14. Donald E. Davis and Walter S. G. Kohn, "Lenin as Disciple of Clausewitz," *Military Review*, September 1971, pp. 49–55.

15. Wilhelm von Schramm, "East and West pay homage to father of military theorists," *The German Tribune*, 8 June 1980, pp. 4–5.

16. Clausewitz, *On War*, II:1, p. 132.

PART I

The Environment

Political purposes and military aim in warfare serve together to define and limit its scope and intensity, the number of national actors, the limits of geographic involvement, and restrictions on employment of weapons and choice of targets, as well as other factors. *The interactions of military operations and political judgments, conditioned by national will,* serve to further define and limit the achievable objectives of a conflict and, thus, to determine its duration and conditions of termination.

Department of the Army Field Manual 100–1, *The Army* (Washington, D.C.: USGPO, 1978), p. 10. [Emphasis added]

CHAPTER 1

THE NATIONAL WILL:
THE PEOPLE

Vietnam was a reaffirmation of the peculiar relationship between the American Army and the American people. The American
Army really is a people's Army in the sense that it belongs to the
American people who take a jealous and proprietary interest in its
involvement. When the Army is committed the American people are
committed, when the American people lose their commitment it is
futile to try to keep the Army committed. In the final analysis, the
American Army is not so much an arm of the Executive Branch as it
is an arm of the American people. The Army, therefore, cannot be
committed lightly.

General Fred C. Weyand
Chief of Staff, U.S. Army, July 1976[1]

ONE OF THE more simplistic explanations for our failure
in Vietnam is that it was all the fault of the American people
—that it was caused by a collapse of national will. Happily
for the health of the Republic, this evasion is rare among
Army officers. A stab-in-the-back syndrome never developed
after Vietnam.

By an ironic twist of fate, the animosity of the Officer
Corps was drained off to a large extent by General William C.
Westmoreland. On his shoulders was laid much of the blame
for our Vietnam failure. According to a 1970 analysis, "For
the older men, the villains tend to be timorous civilians and
the left-wing press; for the younger men, they are the tra-
dition-bound senior generals and the craven press. For one

11

group, it is the arrogance of McNamara; for the other the rigidity of Westmoreland."[2] Those then "younger men" now make up the majority of the Army's senior officers. For example, the Vietnam experience of the Army War College Class of 1980 was mostly at the platoon and company level. As will be seen in subsequent chapters, placing the blame on General Westmoreland was unfair, but, unfair or not, it did spare another innocent victim—the American people.

The main reason it is not right to blame the American public is that President Lyndon Baines Johnson made a conscious decision not to mobilize the American people—to invoke the national will—for the Vietnam war. As former Assistant Secretary of Defense for Public Affairs Phil G. Goulding commented, "In my four-year tour [July 1965–January 1969] there was not once a significant organized effort by the Executive Branch of the federal government to put across its side of a major policy issue or a major controversy to the American people. Not once was there a 'public affairs program' . . . worthy of the name."[3] Having deliberately never been built, it could hardly be said that the national will "collapsed." According to his biographer, President Johnson's decision not to mobilize the American people was based on his fears that it would jeopardize his "Great Society" programs. As he himself said:

> . . . History provided too many cases where the sound of the bugle put an immediate end to the hopes and dreams of the best reformers: The Spanish-American War drowned the populist spirit; World War I ended Woodrow Wilson's New Freedom; World War II brought the New Deal to a close. Once the war began, then all those conservatives in the Congress would use it as a weapon against the Great Society. . . .

> And the generals. Oh, they'd love the war, too. It's hard to be a military hero without a war. Heroes need battles and bombs and bullets in order to be heroic. That's why I am suspicious of the military. They're always narrow in their appraisal of everything. They see everything in military terms.[4]

What the military needed to tell our Commander-in-Chief was not just about battles and bombs and bullets. They needed to tell him that, as Clausewitz discovered 150 years earlier, "it would be an obvious fallacy to imagine war between civilized peoples as resulting merely from a rational act on the part of the Government and to consider war as gradually ridding itself of passion."[5] They needed to tell him that it would be an obvious fallacy to commit the Army without first committing the American people. Such a commitment would require battlefield competence and clear-cut objectives to be sustained, but without the commitment of the American people the commitment of the Army to prolonged combat was impossible.

Unfortunately, this fallacy was not obvious to either the military or its Commander-in-Chief, for the limited war theorists had excluded the American people from the strategic equation. With World War II fresh in their minds, they equated mobilizing national will with total war, and they believed total war unthinkable in a nuclear age. Even as astute a military strategist as General Matthew B. Ridgway saw dangers in mobilizing the American people for a limited war.[6] Unfortunately nuclear weapons had obscured the realities of American military history. With the exception of the two world wars and the Civil War, all of our wars had been limited wars. They had only to hark back to the turn of the century when America was swept with war fever by cries of "Remember the Maine!" Yet, even though America was aroused, we fought the Spanish-American War without invading Spain or seizing its capital.

For most of our history, the support of the American people was built into our very force structuring. The Army consisted of a rather small standing force, backed up first by the reserve forces of the National Guard and Army Reserve, and ultimately by nationwide conscription. The American people had to give their approval through their elected representative in Congress before this Army could be mobilized and deployed. As recently as 1939 the Army's *Field Service Regulations* stated as the first principle of operations, "The Congress determines the strength and composition of the peace and war establishments and decides what citizens are available for military service." The regulation defined the Army as including not only the Regular Army, the National Guard, and the Army Reserve, but also the *"unorganized militia* [which] comprises all persons . . . who have been or may be declared by the Congress to be liable to perform military duty in the service of the United States.''[7]

As *The Federalist Papers* clearly show, the Founding Fathers deliberately rejected the idea of an 18th century–type Army answerable only to the Executive. They wrote into the Constitution specific safeguards to ensure the people's control of the military.[8] These safeguards would ensure civilian control of the military, and, in so doing, guarantee that the United States would not go to war without the initial support of the American people. This secondary effect is often overlooked. Contrary to popular mythology, maintaining public support was a constant problem during the Revolutionary War. As Brigadier General Dave Palmer pointed out in his book on American strategy during the American Revolutionary War, the delegates to the Constitutional Convention were "mostly men who had served in Congress and the Army during the Revolution." They knew from bitter experiences the difficulty of maintaining public support throughout the conduct of a war. "Drawing on their successful wartime experiences, they not surprisingly formally incorporated into the new constitution the informal but effective relationships developed in that war."[9] The Constitutional requirement for a congressional declaration of war served a dual purpose. It insured public support at the outset, and through the legal sanctions against dealing with the enemy, it created impediments to public dissent.

After World War II this connection between the Army and the people was weakened in the name of insuring more rapid response to threats of American security. For the first time in our history a large standing military was maintained in peacetime and our reserve forces declined in importance. The unwitting effect of this was the creation of a neo–18th century–type Army answerable more to the Executive than to the American people. In June 1950, the President—without asking the Congress for a declaration of war—committed this Army to combat in Korea. The reaction to this action in the Congress should have warned us, as General Weyand put it, that the American people take a jealous and proprietary interest in the commitment of their Army.

During what General Matthew Ridgway called "The Great Debate" on the Korean war (the 1951 Joint Senate Armed Forces and Foreign Affairs Committee Hearings), one of the major topics was the issue of Constitutional control over the military. In their findings the committee emphasized that "the United States should never again become involved in war without the consent of the Congress."[10] They were particularly concerned that the Korean war not set a precedent for the commitment of the Army without congressional consent.

Presaging what was to follow in the Vietnam war, the military witnesses did not see the criticality of this point. For example, Senator Wayne Morse of Oregon asked General MacArthur, "Do you believe that we should have declared war against the Koreans or against the Chinese?" MacArthur answered that we were in fact practicing war—a limited war to which he objected but a war nonetheless. When asked about the constitutionality of the war he replied that "the actions of the United Nations might well be regarded as [the] declaration of war."[11] Senator Harry P. Cain of Washington later raised the same question and MacArthur answered, "I have never given special consideration to the *technical question* of whether a declaration of war should be made or not."[12]

Senator Cain later asked then Secretary of Defense George Marshall, "Tell me what modern day factors require a formal declaration of war against our enemies?" General Marshall agreed it was an important question but evaded the issue and laid the blame on the complications of collective action.[13] During the questioning of General of the Army Omar Bradley (then Chairman of the Joint Chiefs of Staff) by Senator William Knowland of California and Senator Cain, General Bradley said, "Someone might question whether technically or not [the Korean war] was a war because normally Congress declares war and I don't believe Congress has declared a war. . . . The question of when you declare a war in this case, how you do it, and how you explain to the people the exact nature of it I don't know."[14]

It is often forgotten that the attempt to fight without mobilizing the American people and without a declaration of war by the Congress almost came to grief in Korea. As General Maxwell D. Taylor wrote:

> The national behavior showed a tendency to premature war-weariness and precipitate disenchantment with a policy which had led to a stalemated war. This experience, if remembered, could have given some warning of dangers ahead to the makers of the subsequent Vietnam policy. Unfortunately, there was no thorough-going analysis ever made of the lessons to be learned from Korea, and later policy makers proceeded to repeat many of the same mistakes.[15]

With all the warnings that the Korean war provided about the importance of mobilizing the national will and legitimizing this mobilization through a declaration of war, how could we go so wrong in Vietnam? Part of the answer is in the temper of the times.

The Vietnam war coincided with a social upheaval in America where the old rules and regulations were dismissed as irrelevant and history no longer had anything to offer. There were those who proclaimed it a new age—the "Age of Aquarius." Even the term sounds banal today, but in the mid-1960s respected speakers at Leavenworth and Carlisle were warning the Army that we were entering a new phase—"post-industrial society," "Consciousness Three"—and "relevancy" was the watchword.

In December 1979, social commentator Tom Wolfe was asked about the collapse of these notions. He answered by saying that in the 1970s the flower children in Haight-Ashbury began appearing in health clinics with diseases unknown since the Middle Ages. They had learned the hard way why there were rules on personal hygiene and regulations about public sanitation. He prophesied that in the decade ahead, Americans will relearn the necessity for the societal rules that were ignored or abandoned in the late 1960s and early 1970s.[16]

Like the flower children, the Army and the military establishment went through its own version of the Age of Aquarius. We thought the rules for taking America to war were hopelessly old-fashioned and out of date. Like society, we became confused between form and substance. Legalistic arguments that the form of a declaration of war was out of date may have been technically correct, but they obscured the fact that this form was designed to be an outward manifestation of a critical substance—the support and commitment of the American people.

A formal declaration of war was seen as a useless piece of paper, in much the same light as many saw the marriage certificate. In the 1960s and early 1970s, there were many, especially among the trendy and sophisticated, who saw marriage as an antiquated institution. By avoiding marriage they thought they could avoid the trauma of divorce, just as some thought that by avoiding a declaration of war they could avoid the trauma of war. But thousands of years of human nature and human experience are not so easily changed. By the late 1970s, it had become obvious that formal institutions had societal value. This reaction was summed up by *Washington Post* writer Judith Martin in her "Miss Manners" column. Some wrote questioning the worth of a marriage certificate, since it was just a piece of paper. She replied, "Miss Manners has a whole safety deposit box full of pieces of paper."

Pieces of paper *do* have value. A marriage certificate— or a declaration of war—legitimizes the relationship in the eyes of society and announces it to the world. It focuses attention, provides certain responsibilities, and creates impediments to dissolution. While neither a marriage certificate nor a declaration of war are guarantees for staying the course, these legal forms are of immense value to society.

But in the early 1960s, we were under the delusion that we could disregard not only the *form* of a declaration of war but also its *substance*—the mobilization of the American people. Secretary of Defense Robert S. McNamara was quoted as saying:

> The greatest contribution Vietnam is making—right or wrong is beside the point—is that it is developing an ability in the United States to fight a limited war, to go to war without the necessity of arousing the public ire.[17]

But "right or wrong" was not beside the point and neither was the intangible of "public ire." Vietnam reinforced the lessons of Korea that there was more to war, even limited war, than those things that could be measured, quantified and computerized. A bitter little story made the rounds during the closing days of the Vietnam war:

> When the Nixon Administration took over in 1969 all the data on North Vietnam and on the United States was fed into a Pentagon computer — population, gross national product, manufacturing capability, number of tanks, ships, and aircraft, size of the armed forces, and the like.
>
> The computer was then asked, *"When will we win?"*
>
> It took only a moment to give the answer: *"You won in 1964!"*

The story had a bite, for by every quantifiable measurement there was simply no contest between the United States, the most powerful nation on the face of the earth, and a tenth-rate backward nation like North Vietnam. Yet there was one thing that did not fit into the computer—national will, what Clausewitz calls the moral factor. We have seen earlier that President Johnson deliberately avoided mobilizing the national will so as not to jeopardize his Great Society programs. The North Vietnamese, after their experience with the French, had every reason to believe that American morale could be our weak strategic link. Knowing they did not have the military means to defeat us, they concentrated on this weakness. It was not a new strategy. "When we speak of destroying the enemy's forces," Clausewitz wrote, "we must emphasize that nothing obliges us to limit this idea to physical forces: The moral element must also be considered."[18]

The failure to invoke the national will was one of the major strategic failures of the Vietnam war. It produced a strategic vulnerability that our enemy was able to exploit. Consider this explanation of Tet 1968, written by Clausewitz 150 years earlier:

> Not every war need be fought until one side collapses. When the motives and tensions of war are slight we can imagine that the very faintest prospect of defeat might be enough to cause one side to yield. If from the very start the other side feels that this is probable, it will obviously concentrate on bringing about this probability rather than take the long way round and totally defeat the enemy.[19]

NOTES

1. "Vietnam Myths and American Realities," *CDRS CALL* (July-August 1976); also reprinted in *Armor* (September-October 1976). General Weyand was the last commander of the Military Assistance Command Vietnam (MACV) and supervised the withdrawal of U.S. Military forces in 1973.

2. Ward Just, *Military Men* (New York: Knopf, 1970), p. 186.

3. Phil G. Goulding, *Confirm or Deny: Informing the People on National Security* (New York: Harper & Row, 1970), pp. 81–82.

4. President Lyndon B. Johnson, quoted in Doris Kearns, *Lyndon Johnson and the American Dream* (New York: Harper & Row, 1976), p. 252.

5. Clausewitz, *On War*, I: 1, p. 76.

6. Matthew B. Ridgway, *The Korean War* (Garden City, New York: Doubleday, 1967), p. 245.

7. *War Department Field Manual 100—5, Field Service Regulations* (Washington, D.C.: USGPO, 1 October 1939), p. 1.

8. *The Federalist*, edited by James E. Cooke (Middletown, Connecticut: Wesleyan University Press, 1961). See particularly the essays of Alexander Hamilton (No. 8, 24, and 29) and James Madison (No. 41 and 47).

9. Dave Richard Palmer, *The Way of the Fox: American Strategy in the War for America 1775–1783* (Westport, Connecticut: Greenwood Press, 1975), pp. 76, 148.

10. 82nd Congress, 1st Session, Hearings Before the Committee on Armed Services and the Committee on Foreign Relations, United States Senate, *Military Situation in the Far East* (Washington, D.C.: USGPO, 1951), Part 5, pp. 3600, 3605. It is interesting to note that these committees included then Senators Lyndon B. Johnson of Texas, J. W. Fulbright of Arkansas (who introduced the Tonkin Gulf Resolution in the Senate in 1964), and Wayne Morse of Oregon (one of two senators who voted against the Tonkin Gulf Resolution).

11. *Ibid*, Part I, pp. 227–28.

12. *Ibid*, Part I, pp. 305–6. (Emphasis added.)

13. *Ibid*, Part I, pp. 614–15.

14. *Ibid*, Part II, pp. 794–95, 852, 1065–66.

15. General Maxwell D. Taylor, *Swords & Plowshares* (New York: Norton, 1972), pp. 135–36.

16. Interview on the Today Show, NBC Television, 20 December 1979. Tom Wolfe was the author who coined the phrase "The Me Decade" to describe the 1970s. For the origins of this phrase see *Mauve Gloves and Madmen, Clutter and Vine* (New York: Farrar, Straus, and Giroux, 1976), pp. 153–67.

17. Quoted in Douglas H. Rosenberg, "Arms and the American Way: The Ideological Dimension of Military Growth," *Military Force and American Society*, edited by Bruce M. Russett and Alfred Stepan (New York: Harper & Row, 1973), p. 170.

18. Clausewitz, *On War*, I:2, p. 97.

19. *Ibid*, I:2, p. 91.

CHAPTER 2

THE NATIONAL WILL:
THE CONGRESS

The officers tend to get sardonic when civilians forget where the larger responsibility for the war lies. *"I don't choose the wars I fight in,"* says crew-cut Lt. Col. Wallen M. Summers, 38, a social-science instructor at West Point. *"When people ask me why I went to Vietnam I say, 'I thought you knew. You sent me.'"*

. . . To a man, the officers I talked with are committed to civilian control of the Army. But they are puzzled by the civilian sector's growing refusal to take responsibility for the kind of army it needs.

Newsweek, 1971[1]

ONE OF THE continuing arguments about the Vietnam war is whether or not a formal declaration of war would have made any difference. On the one hand there are those who see a declaration of war as a kind of magic talisman that would have eliminated all our difficulties. On the other hand there are those who see a declaration of war as a worthless anachronism. The truth is somewhere in between. A declaration of war is a clear statement of *initial* public support which focuses the nation's attention on the enemy. (Continuation of this initial public support is, of course, contingent on the successful prosecution of war aims.) As we will see, it was the lack of such focus on the enemy and on the political objectives to be obtained by the use of military force that was the crux of our strategic failure.

Further, a declaration of war makes the prosecution of the war a shared responsibility of both the government and the American people. As Colonel Wallen Summers' remarks above illustrate, without a declaration of war the Army was caught on the horns of a dilemma. It was ordered into battle by the Commander-in-Chief, the duly elected President of the United States. It was sustained in battle by appropriations by the Congress, the elected representatives of the American people. The legality of its commitment was not challenged by the Supreme Court of the United States. Yet, because there was no formal declaration of war, many vocal and influential members of the American public questioned (and continue to question) the legality and propriety of its actions.

This dilemma needs to be understood. It transcends the legal niceties over the utility of a declaration of war. It even transcends the strategic military value of such a declaration. It should not be dismissed as a kind of sophisticated "stab in the back" argument. As will be seen, the requirement for a declaration of war was rooted in the principle of civilian control of the military, and the failure to declare war in Vietnam drove a wedge between the Army and large segments of the American public.

It is not as if we did not know better. We knew perfectly well the importance of maintaining the bond between the American people and their soldiers in the field, and that this bond was the source of our moral strength. As early as the Revolutionary War this moral strength was a primary factor in our defeat of the British, then a major world power. As a result of this experience we wrote the rules for invoking the national will into our Constitution. Article I, Section 8 states them clearly:

> The Congress shall have Power . . . To declare War . . . To raise and support Armies . . . To make Rules for the Government and Regulation of the land and naval forces . . .[2]

Implicit in this rule was the rejection of an 18th century–type army answerable only to the Executive. The American Army would be a people's Army to be committed only by the will of the people. As Alexander Hamilton explained:

> The whole power of raising armies [is] lodged in the *Legislature*, not in the *Executive*; This Legislature [is] to be a popular body, consisting of the representatives of the people, periodically elected . . . a great and real security against the keeping of troops without evident necessity.[3]

> . . . The power of the President would be inferior to that of the Monarch. . . . That of the British King extends to the *Declaring* of war and to the *Raising* and *Regulating* of fleets and armies; All which by the Constitution . . . would appertain to the Legislature.[4]

Hamilton's remarks highlight a critical distinction. In other nations a declaration of war by the chief executive alone (emperor, king, premier, party chairman) may or may not represent the *substance* of the will of his people. By requiring that a declaration of war be made by the representatives of the people (the Congress), rather than by the President alone, the Founding Fathers sought to guarantee this substance and insure that our armed forces would not be committed to battle without the support of the American people. Ironically, President Johnson seemed to know that. In a peculiar passage in light of what was to follow, he said:

> I believed that President Truman's one mistake in courageously going to the defense of South Korea in 1950 had been his failure to ask Congress for an expression of its backing. He could have had it easily, and it would have strengthened his hand. I made up my mind not to repeat that error . . .[5]

Like President Truman in 1950, President Johnson could probably have had a declaration of war in August 1964 after the Gulf of Tonkin incidents when two American destroyers were attacked by North Vietnamese patrol boats. Instead of asking for a declaration of war, however, President Johnson asked Congress for a resolution empowering him to "take all necessary measures to repel an armed attack against the forces of the United States and to prevent further aggression."

This Southeast Asia Resolution (better known as the Gulf of Tonkin resolution) passed the Senate by a vote of 88–2, and the House by a unanimous voice vote of 416–0.[6]

Commenting on this resolution, Senator Jacob Javits of New York acknowledged congressional complicity on Vietnam.

The language of the Gulf of Tonkin resolution was far more sweeping than the congressional intent. In voting unlimited presidential power most members of Congress thought they were providing for retaliation for an attack on our forces; and preventing a large-scale war in Asia, rather than authorizing its inception. . . .

Whatever President Johnson's position, however, Congress had the obligation to make an institutional judgment as to the wisdom and the propriety of giving such a large grant of its own power to the Chief Executive . . .

. . . The power of decision . . . had not been stolen. It had been surrendered.[7]

All this may have been avoided by a declaration of war, but there was a kind of Catch-22 working against it. When the President could have had it he didn't think he needed it, and when he needed it he couldn't have it. As the distinguished historian Arthur M. Schlesinger, Jr. commented, "[President] Johnson could certainly have obtained congressional authorization beyond the Tonkin Gulf resolution for a limited war in Vietnam in 1965. He might even, had he wished (but no one wished), have obtained a declaration of war."[8] The reason why neither the President nor the Congress (nor the military either, for that matter) seemed to think a declaration of war was necessary and why the President deliberately did not seek to mobilize public support for such a proposal was that initially no one envisioned a 10-year war, the massive commitment of American ground troops, nor the ground swell of American opposition. It was hoped that the use of U.S. tactical air power in South Vietnam, the "Rolling Thunder" air campaign against North Vietnam, and the limited use of U.S. troops to protect air bases and logistics installations would cause the North Vietnamese to halt their aggression.

By the spring of 1965, it was obvious that such a limited response was not effective, and the decision was made to commit U.S. ground combat troops to the war. Rather than go back to the Congress and ask for a declaration of war, "efforts were made to make the change as imperceptible as possible to the American public . . ."[9] In retrospect this was a key strategic error. Failure to make this crucial political decision led to fear of making the political decision to mobilize the reserves. Failure to mobilize the reserves led to failure of the military leadership to push for strategic concepts aimed at halting North Vietnamese aggression and led to campaigns against the symptoms of the aggression—the insurgency in the South—rather than against the aggressor itself. These effects will be examined in greater detail in Part II. For now, we will limit our analysis to the question of why a declaration of war was not requested prior to the commitment of U.S. ground combat forces.

One reason was that it would have seemed ludicrous for a great power like the United States to declare war on a tiny country like North Vietnam. War sanctions, both foreign and domestic, were deemed too massive to be appropriate. Another reason was the desire not to risk a Korea-style intervention by threatening Chinese security. There was also the danger that a formal declaration of war against North Vietnam might have triggered the implementation of security guarantees by China and the Soviet Union. Yet another reason may have been the fear that Congress would not approve such a declaration. This refusal would have caused an immediate halt to U.S. efforts in South Vietnam (a preferable result, given the final outcome). A final reason may have been our use of the enemy's terminology to describe the nature of the war. In his analysis of our failure to declare war, University of California Professor Chalmers Johnson commented:

> [The label "People's War"] made it harder for a counterinsurgent state, such as the United States, to clarify for its own citizens exactly

whom it was fighting when it defended against a people's war. Steeped in the legalistic concept that wars are between states, the American public became confused by its government's failure to declare war on North Vietnam and thereby identify the *state* with which the United States was at war. . . .[10]

While there is no evidence the military insisted on a declaration of war at the time, General Westmoreland did say in his autobiography that:

> President Johnson erred in relying on the Gulf of Tonkin resolution as his authority from the Congress to do what he deemed necessary in Southeast Asia. When dissent developed in 1966 and 1967, he would have been well advised to have gone back to the Congress for reaffirmation of the commitment to South Vietnam, a vote either of confidence or rejection. . . . President Johnson . . . should have forced the Congress to face its constitutional responsibility for waging war.[11]

As a matter of practical politics General Westmoreland's recommendation was simply not feasible. A declaration of war undoubtedly would have been obtainable in 1964 and may even have been possible in the spring of 1965, but by the time the protests started in 1966–1967 even a statement of continued congressional support, much less a declaration of war, would have been a difficult if not impossible endeavor. It was made more difficult because President Johnson was caught up in a contradiction of his own making. Stirring up the American people in support of the war would have been the surest way to insure continued congressional support, but as we have seen, this was precisely what President Johnson did not want to do.

Instead of seeking further congressional support for the war, President Johnson took the opposite tack and fell back on his authority as President. In March 1966, the Legal Advisor to the Department of State told the Senate Committee on Foreign Relations:

> There can be no question in present circumstances of the President's authority to commit U.S. Forces to the defense of South Vietnam. The grant of authority to the President in Article II of the Consti-

tution extends to the actions of the United States currently undertaken in Vietnam.[12]

Emphasizing this point in a news conference on 18 August
1967, President Johnson said, "We stated then, and we repeat
now, we did not think the [Gulf of Tonkin] resolution was
necessary to do what we did and what we're doing."[13]

The only other time a declaration of war was politically
feasible was when Richard M. Nixon assumed the Presidency
in January 1969. He could have demanded that Congress
either affirm our commitment with a declaration of war,
giving him authority to prosecute the war to its conclusion,
or reject the commitment, allowing him to immediately with-
draw all American troops from Vietnam. But President
Nixon had foreclosed this option with his campaign promises
to bring the war to a close. Within weeks after assuming
office, "Johnson's war" had become "Nixon's war." Like
President Johnson, he fell back on his position as Commander
in Chief as authority to prosecute the war.[14]

Commenting on this, the Senate Committee on Foreign
Relations said:

> The issue to be resolved is the proper locus within our constitutional
> system of the authority to commit our country to war. More, per-
> haps, than ever before, the Executive and Congress are in disagree-
> ment as to where that authority properly lies. It is the Executive's
> view, manifested in both words and action, that the President, in his
> capacity as Commander in Chief, is properly empowered to commit
> the Armed Forces to hostilities in foreign countries. It is the commit-
> tee's view—*conviction* may be the better word—that the authority
> to initiate war, as distinguished from acting to repel a sudden attack,
> is vested by the Constitution in the Congress and in the Congress
> alone. . . .
>
> From the Executive's standpoint, repeal of the Tonkin resolution will
> in no way impair what it believes to be its authority to conduct the
> present war. The Executive branch has already . . . disavowed a
> reliance on the Gulf of Tonkin resolution as authority or support for
> its conduct of the war in Indochina. From the standpoint of the com-
> mittee, on the other hand, repeal of the Tonkin resolution will leave
> the Executive in the legal position of continuing to conduct an
> unauthorized war . . . The committee does not regard the Tonkin

resolution as a valid legal authorization for the war in Indochina. This being the case, repeal of the resolution will not create but simply confirm and clarify the existence of a legal vacuum.[15]

Into this so-called "legal vacuum" fell the U.S. Army, caught in the middle between the executive and the legislative branches. This was a dangerous position for both the Army and for the Republic. It was dangerous for the Army because in failing to mobilize the national will the United States lost what Clausewitz called the strength of the passions of a people mobilized for war.[16] Instead of the passions of the American people strengthening and supporting us, the more vocal and passionate voices were too often raised in support of our enemies.

More importantly, it was dangerous for the Republic. The Army became the focus of anti-war sentiment. While such sentiment is not unusual in American history, and there has been public dissent against many of our wars, this dissent was usually directed primarily against the government rather than against the military. During the Vietnam war, however, many of the protestors focused their attention on the military itself and attempted to subvert it through public demonstrations, underground newspapers, teach-ins and infiltration. For example, the so-called "American Servicemen's Union" called for soldiers to disobey their orders and to refuse to fight in Vietnam.[17] By attacking the *executors* of U.S. Vietnam policy rather than the *makers* of that policy, the protestors were striking at the very heart of our democratic system—the civilian control of the military. As former Chief of Staff General Fred C. Weyand commented:

> During the Vietnam war there were those—many with the best of intentions—who argued that the Army should not obey its orders and should refuse to serve in Vietnam. But their argument that soldiers should obey the "dictates of their conscience" is a slippery slope indeed. At the bottom of this slope is military dictatorship.[18]

In the later stages, when the Vietnam war became a partisan political issue, the Army was placed in the untenable position of becoming involved in domestic politics solely because it was obeying its orders. As General Westmoreland observed:

> I recognized that it was not the job of the military to defend American commitment and policy. Yet it was difficult to differentiate between pursuit of a military task and such related matters as public and congressional support and the morale of the fighting man, who must be convinced that he is risking death for a worthy cause. The military thus was caught in between.[19]

This impasse continued as long as U.S. troops were committed to Vietnam. It was not until November 1973 that Congress, over the President's veto, passed the War Powers Resolution in an attempt to increase congressional control. The purpose of the Resolution was:

> . . . To fulfill the intent of the framers of the Constitution of the United States and insure that the collective judgment of both the Congress and the President will apply to the introduction of United States Armed Forces into hostilities, or into situations where imminent involvement in hostilities is clearly indicated by the circumstances, and to the continued use of such forces in hostilities or in such situations.[20]

The Resolution requires the President to consult with the Congress before military forces are committed. Military involvement can continue for 60 days, and for another 30 days thereafter if the President certifies in writing that the safety of the force so requires. Unless Congress specifically authorizes it by a declaration of war, resolution or legislation, the involvement cannot be continued beyond the 90 days. As one observer noted:

> The law forces Congress to take a decision after two or at the most three months of confrontation. A vote to continue operations signifies the sharing of responsibility with the Executive; a vote to terminate signifies an assumption of responsibility by Congress alone.[21]

Although the War Powers Resolution is a step toward solving the legal issues involved, it does not necessarily solve the moral and psychological issues so important to the Army. It raises the appalling specter of taking soldiers into combat and then being forced to disengage under fire because congressional approval was not forthcoming. As Senator Thomas F. Eagleton of Missouri warned:

> The President, under this measure, could deploy [troops] wherever he wanted, tomorrow. There is a 60-day period but the troops are there. They are deployed, being shot at, dying, and the flag is committed . . .[22]

Practical political concerns will probably provide a safeguard against this first shortcoming. After the experience with Vietnam, no President is liable to commit the Army unless he is reasonably sure the mood of the Congress and the Nation will support such an involvement.

The War Powers Resolution has another deficiency. It does not provide the full public sanctions that a declaration of war provides against treason, giving aid and comfort to our foes, subverting the armed forces, and all of the other rules that are—as history proves and the Vietnam war emphasized—essential to guarantee a united front in the face of the enemy. This is a shortcoming that must be addressed at the time troops are committed. A request to invoke the wartime laws that are already on the statute books must be part of the package that the President submits to the Congress under the War Powers Resolution.

We saw earlier that the congressional safeguard of a declaration of war had fallen out of fashion after World War II. But fashions change. Testifying before the Senate Foreign Relations Committee in March 1980 on the Iranian crisis, the distinguished scholar and diplomat George F. Kennan argued that the correct U.S. response should have been a declaration of war.[23] Not only would it have given the President clear-cut military authority, but it also would have provided nonmilitary options—e.g., internment of Iranian citizens, seizure of funds. U.S. public concern would have been fixed and focused, and a clear signal would have been sent to the international community.

As columnist William F. Buckley observed:

> To declare war in this country would require a researcher to inform the President and Congress on just how to go about doing it. Declaring war is totally out of style. The post-Hiroshima assumption being that the declaration of war brings with it the tacit determination to use every weapon necessary in order to win that war. Thus we didn't go to war against North Korea, North Vietnam, or Cuba. But . . .
>
> To declare war is not necessarily to dispatch troops, let alone atom bombs. It is to recognize a juridically altered relationship and to license such action as is deemed appropriate. It is a wonderful demystifier . . . [leaving] your objective in very plain view.[24]

As we will see in Part II, one of the primary causes of our Vietnam failure was that we did not keep our "objective in very plain view." If a declaration of war could have accomplished that one task it would have been worth the effort.

NOTES

1. Karl Fleming, "The Troubled Army Brass," *Newsweek*, May 24, 1971, pp. 21–23. (Emphasis added)
2. *US Government Manual, 1979–1980* (Washington, D.C.: USGPO, 1979), p. 12.
3. *Federalist* (No. 24), p. 153.
4. *Ibid* (No. 69), p. 465.
5. Lyndon Baines Johnson, *The Vantage Point: Perspectives of the Presidency 1963–1969* (New York: Popular Library Edition, 1971), p. 115.
6. *Ibid*, pp. 116–19.
7. Senator Jacob K. Javits, *Who Makes War: The President Versus Congress* (New York: Morrow, 1973), pp. 260–61.
8. Arthur M. Schlesinger, Jr., *The Imperial Presidency* (Boston, Massachusetts: Houghton Mifflin Company, 1973), p. 181.
9. Herbert Y. Schandler, *The Unmaking of a President: Lyndon Johnson and Vietnam* (Princeton: Princeton University Press, 1977), pp. 20–22.
10. Chalmers Johnson, *Autopsy on People's War* (Berkeley, California: University of California Press, 1973), p. 22. Dr. Fred Ikle calls such terms "semantic infiltration."
11. General William C. Westmoreland, *A Soldier Reports* (Garden City, New York: Doubleday, 1976), p. 412. In a 4 August 1981 letter to the

author former Secretary of State Dean Rusk said, "Incidentally, I do think that we should have gone to the Congress each year for a vote up or down on the Tonkin Gulf Resolution. You will be interested that it was the Congressional leadership who strongly urged President Johnson not to do that; they pointed out that the Resolution would readily pass again but with diminished majorities and that this alone would have a negative effect both internationally and at home. Nevertheless, in retrospect I think we should have held the feet of Congress to the fire and required them to make up their minds."

12. 91st Congress, 2nd Session, Committee on Foreign Relations, United States Senate, *Termination of Middle East and South Asia Resolutions*; Report to Accompany Senate Concurrent Resolution 64, May 15, 1970 (Washington, D.C.: USGPO, 1970), p. 7.

13. *Ibid.*

14. *Ibid.*

15. *Ibid*, p. 3.

16. Clausewitz, *On War*, III:5, p. 188.

17. For an example of the anti-war agitation directed against the Army, see Andy Stapp, *Up Against The Brass* (New York: Simon and Schuster, 1970), especially the "demands" on pp. 88–91.

18. Weyand, *CDRS CALL*, May-June 1976.

19. Westmoreland, *A Soldier Reports*, p. 417.

20. 94th Congress, 2nd Session, Committee on International Relations, United States House of Representatives, *The War Powers Resolution* (Washington, D.C.: USGPO, 1975), p. 1.

21. Richard Haass, "Congressional Power: Implications for American Security Policy" *Adelphi Papers* No. 153 (London: The International Institute for Strategic Studies, 1979), p. 22.

22. Senator Thomas F. Eagleton, *War and Presidential Power: A Chronicle of Congressional Surrender* (New York: Liveright, 1974), p. 219.

23. William F. Buckley, "George Kennan's Bomb," *National Review*, April 4, 1980, p. 432.

24. *Ibid.*

CHAPTER 3

FRICTION: THE PEOPLE

Militarism [is] an evil from which it has been our glory to be free. [While] we deplore the sacrifice of our soldiers and sailors, whose bravery deserves admiration even in an unjust war, [we believe] the United States cannot act upon the ancient heresy that might makes right. . . .

We deny the obligation of all citizens to support their Government in times of grave National peril applies to the present situation. If an Administration may with impunity . . . deliberately create a condition of war anywhere on the face of the globe . . . representative government itself is imperiled.

American Anti-Imperialist League, 1899[1]

ONE OF THE most important contributions Clausewitz made to the theory of war was his concept of "friction."

Everything in war is very simple, but the simplest thing is difficult. The difficulties accumulate and end by producing a kind of friction that is inconceivable unless one has experienced war . . . Countless minor incidents—the kind you can never really foresee—combine to lower the general level of performance, so that one always falls far short of the intended goal . . . Friction is the only concept that more or less corresponds to the factors that distinguish real war from war on paper.[2]

Clausewitz was talking about the battlefield, but there is also a kind of friction that exists between the American people and its Army. As General Fred C. Weyand observed,

"Americans have a long and proud tradition of irreverence toward and distrust of their military."[3]

American antimilitarism springs from a variety of causes —historical, cultural and social. It has been a constant since the beginning of the Republic. As far as the Regular Army went, it was even true in wartime. Someone once remarked that the old British doggerel about the professional soldier, *"It's Tommy this, and Tommy that, and chuck him out, the brute . . . But it's 'Savior of his Country,' when the guns begin to shoot,"* never applied here in America. It was the "citizen soldier"—the National Guard and the Army Reserve —not the regular who fought America's wars and who was the traditional "Savior of his Country."

Antimilitarism then was not something unique to Vietnam. It is part of what makes Americans what they are. "There is no use agonizing over it," General Weyand said. "If we cannot be loved, we can be trusted and respected."[4] But not only were we not "loved" during the Vietnam war, even trust and respect were denied by a great many Americans. This was a crucial failing, for, as Chaplain (Colonel) Charles F. Kriete observed:

> [War] requires for its successful pursuit the mobilization of a moral consensus of the legitimacy of both the objectives of violence and the means by which these objectives are pursued . . .
>
> Societies in which communication is open, which safeguard pluralism with legal sanctions, and which normally tolerate a high degree of political dissent find it much more difficult to develop and maintain a consensus of commitment to the legitimacy of strategic objectives. Yet the maintenance of that consensus is one of the key objectives of national strategy, in both a political and a military sense, for when it fails, the war is lost.[5]

Instead of building this moral consensus and taking action to smooth the natural friction that exists between the American people and their Army, Vietnam war policies tended to aggravate it. One of the most damaging aggravations was the decision to grant draft deferments for students. As General Westmoreland wrote, "The policy contributed to anti-war militancy on college campuses in that young men feeling twinges of conscience because they sat out a war while others fought could appease their conscience if they convinced themselves the war was immoral."[6]

The student draft deferments, along with the decision not to ask for a declaration of war and not to mobilize our reserve forces, were part of a deliberate Presidential policy not to arouse the passions of the American people. The effect of this was that we fought the Vietnam war *in cold blood*. This cold-blooded approach to war was not unintentional. It was an outgrowth of the limited war theories that reduced war to an academic model. As we go back and read the writings of the political scientists and systems analysts on limited war, they are noteworthy for their lack of passion. The horror, the bloodshed and the destruction of the battle-field are remarkably absent. Clausewitz warned about those who would "exclude all moral factors from strategic theory and . . . reduce everything to a few mathematical formulas."[7] The academics could be excused for this omission, but we in the military knew better. It was the job of those of us who had seen war firsthand to add this missing dimension to their academic theories. We knew the true nature of war. We knew the truth of Clausewitz's observation that:

> Kindhearted people might . . . think there was some ingenious way to disarm or defeat an enemy without too much bloodshed, [but] pleasant as it sounds, it is a fallacy that must be exposed . . . It would be futile—even wrong—to try and shut one's eyes to what war really is from sheer distress at its brutality.[8]

But through fear of reinforcing the basic antimilitarism of the American people we tended to keep this knowledge to ourselves and downplayed battlefield realities. In order to smooth our relations with the American people we began to use euphemisms to hide the horrors of war. We became the Department of the Army (not the *War* Department) and our own terminology avoided mention of the battlefield. We did not kill the enemy, we "inflicted casualties"; we did not destroy things, we "neutralized targets."[9] These evasions allowed the notion to grow that we could apply military force in a sanitary and surgical manner. In so doing we unwittingly prepared the way for the reaction that was to follow.

We had concealed from the American people the true nature of war at precisely the time that television brought its realities into their living rooms in living color. As a result, to many Americans Vietnam became the most destructive, the most horrible, the most terrible war ever waged in the history of the world. This viewpoint has persisted in the face of all historical evidence to the contrary.

Professor Peter L. Berger of Boston College recently re-examined his opposition to the Vietnam war in a thoughtful and introspective article.[10] He observes that the anti-war movement was a primary causal factor in the American withdrawal from Indo-China, and acknowledges that Hanoi's victory was a "human catastrophe of monumental dimensions." He notes U.S. political and military decline as a result of the war and a "world situation in which totalitarianism has grown stronger and in which peace is more precarious." Finally he observes that Vietnam has left America 'a sick society.' "Anyone who participated in the anti-war movement in any public form," he says, "must ask himself about his responsibility for these events."

Having said that, however, he still defends his opposition. "I continue to believe that the war was marked by a distinctive brutality which cannot be subsumed by some general statement that 'all war is hell,' " he says. Noting what he calls the "exceptional cruelty" of the methods of warfare, he condemned the "systemic and intrinsic . . . free-fire zones, napalm bombing of villages, the generation of refugees, defoliation and kindred destruction of the countryside, the torture of prisoners, the assassination of political suspects. . . . I found it morally intolerable that my country should be engaged in [such actions] . . . It was this outrage that originated and sustained my opposition to the war. I believe that very similar sentiments motivated a very large number of Americans . . . I am not prepared to repudiate this moral response now . . . despite the disastrous consequences to which my own and many others morally motivated actions contributed, I cannot now indulge in confessions of guilt."

As Professor Berger said, his views are widely shared. To many civilians it is axiomatic that the Vietnam war was the cruelest ever waged. To those of us who experienced war firsthand, this is hard to understand. To the evidence of Vietnam cruelty portrayed by the horrible picture of the little girl running down the road seared with napalm, one asks about the tens of thousands of little girls incinerated in the fire bomb raids on Dresden and Tokyo in World War II only to be told, *"But that was different."* To the terrible picture of the Saigon police chief shooting the Viet Cong terrorist, one asks about the summary justice of the French Maquis or the Italian partisans and their photographs of Mussolini and his mistress strung up by their heels, only again to be told, *"That was different."* To those condemning the remark of the Army captain in the Delta that "we had to destroy the town in order to save it," one quotes the Continental Congress's orders, "If General Washington and his council of war should be of the opinion that a successful attack may be made on the [British] troops in Boston, he [may] do it in any manner he may think expedient, notwithstanding the town and the property in it may thereby be destroyed."[11] Yet again the answer, *"That was different."* And the critics were right. It *was* different. All of America's previous wars were fought in the heat of passion. Vietnam was fought in cold blood, and that was intolerable to the American people.

We should have known better. The lessons were there in the Korean war. But, as General Taylor commented earlier, we never learned those lessons. We proceeded to make the same mistakes again in Vietnam. The repugnance of the American people toward a war of attrition, with its grisly measurement by body count was spelled out in 1951 in the minority report of the Joint session of the Senate Committees on Armed Services and Foreign Relations on the Korean war:

The policy of the United States in Korea, as outlined in the testimony of the Secretary of State and the Secretary of Defense and others is that of destroying the effective core of the Communist Chinese armies by killing that government's trained soldiers, in the hope that someone will negotiate. We hold that such a policy is essentially immoral, not likely to produce either victory in Korea or an end to aggression. At the same time such a policy tends to destroy the moral stature of the United States as a leader in the family of nations.

War in any form is abhorrent. War means other humane ways of settling disputes have failed. Only a nation without regard for the sanctity of human life could be committed to a policy of prolonged war with no intent at winning a victory. American policy, in every war in which this Nation has engaged, has been designed to win the conflict at the earliest possible moment with the least possible loss of human life—especially American life, but also the lives of those who oppose us.[12]

Change "Korea" to "Vietnam" and "Chinese Communists" to "Vietnamese" and this statement could have been reissued 20 years later. As we should have foreseen, our statement of progress in Vietnam given in terms of people killed did not reassure the American people. Instead it inflamed American idealism and further eroded public support for the war.

The North Vietnamese were quick to seize the strategic advantage provided by this erosion of public support. Author Tom Wolfe commented on what he called "the Johnson Administration's attempt to fight a 'humane' war and look good in the eyes of the world":

There was something out-to-lunch about it, however. The eyes of the world did not flutter for a second. Stories of American atrocities were believed by whoever wanted to believe them, no matter what actually occurred. . . . If the United States was seriously trying to win the battle of world opinion—well, then, you had a real bush-league operation. The North Vietnamese were the uncontested aces.

After describing a raid on the Iron Triangle in North Vietnam, Wolfe notes that:

The North Vietnamese [were] blessed with a weapon that no military device known to America could ever get a lock on. As if by magic . . . in Hanoi . . . appears . . . Harrison Salisbury! Harrison Salisbury—

writing in *The New York Times* about the atrocious American bombing of the hard-scrabble folks of North Vietnam in the Iron Triangle! If you had real sporting blood in you, you had to hand it to the North Vietnamese. They were champions of this sort of thing. . . . it seemed as if the North Vietnamese were playing Mr. Harrison Salisbury of *The New York Times* like an ocarina, as if they were blowing smoke up his pipe and the finger work was just right and the song was coming forth better than they could have played it themselves.

"And yet," Wolfe concludes, "it couldn't simply be blamed on Salisbury. No series of articles by anyone, no matter what the publication, could have had such an immediate strategic effect if there weren't some kind of strange collapse of will power taking place back in the States . . ."[13] Wolfe's closing comments are important. There is a tendency in the military to blame our problems with public support on the media. This is too easy an answer. Certainly there were some like Salisbury who reported enemy propaganda, but the majority of on-the-scene reporting from Vietnam was factual — that is the reporters honestly reported what they had seen firsthand. Much of what they saw was horrible, for that is the true nature of war. It was this horror, not the reporting that so influenced the American people.[14]

There is an important lesson in this for the Army. Any future war will more than likely be as bloody as the war in Vietnam. It will probably also be carried into American living rooms by television reporters, for that is the nature of their craft. As we have seen earlier, attempts to hide the realities of war from the American people only inflame the problem. Censorship is not the answer. How then do we square the circle of the battlefield and the idealism of the American people?

In his analysis of the Vietnam war General Weyand pointed out the conflict arising out of American idealism and counseled what we must do in the future:

As military professionals we must speak out, we must counsel our political leaders and alert the American public that there is no such thing as a "splendid little war." There is no such thing as a war fought on the cheap. War is death and destruction. The American way of war is particularly violent, deadly and dreadful. We believe in using "things"—artillery, bombs, massive firepower—in order to conserve our soldiers' lives. The enemy, on the other hand, made up for his lack of "things" by expending men instead of machines, and he suffered enormous casualties. The Army saw this happen in Korea, and we should have made the realities of war obvious to the American people before they witnessed it on their television screens. The Army must make the price of involvement clear *before* we get involved, so that America can weigh the probable costs of involvement against the dangers of uninvolvement . . . for there are worse things than war."[15]

NOTES

1. "Platform of the American Anti-Imperialist League," October 18, 1899, in Henry Steele Commager (ed), *Documents of American History*, Vol. 2 (New York: Appleton-Century-Crofts, 1963), pp. 11–12.

2. Clausewitz, *On War* I:7, p. 119.

3. General Fred C. Weyand, "Serving The People: The Need For Military Power," *Military Review*, December 1976, p. 8.

4. *Ibid.*

5. Chaplain (Colonel) Charles F. Kriete, "The Moral Dimension of Strategy," *Parameters, Journal of the US Army War College* (Vol. VII, No. 2, 1977), p. 67.

6. Westmoreland, *A Soldier Reports*, p. 297. That student draft deferment policy continues to poison U.S. civil-military relations. As Arthur T. Hadley reported in an April 1980 article, "Those who avoided Vietnam through loopholes (or more correctly, loop-highways) in the draft, being in the main honorable men, now feel guilty. They relieve these feelings either by venomous attacks on all things military, including the draft; or, becoming 200 percent American, make Attila the Hun sound like Mother Goose and advocate colossal military expenditures." (Arthur T. Hadley, "The Draft Debate: A Special Section," *The Washington Post*, April 6, 1980, pp. E1–E5).

7. Clausewitz, *On War* III:1, p. 178.

8. *Ibid*, I:1, p. 76.

9. This tendency still persists. For example, note the use of the bland phrase "Target Servicing" in our training literature to describe the destruction of an enemy attacking force.

10. Peter L. Berger, "Indo-China and The American Conscience," *Commentary*, February 1980, pp. 29–39.

11. Palmer, *The Way of The Fox*, p. 103.

12. 82nd Congress, 1st Session, *Military Situation in the Far East*, Part 5, p. 3598.

13. Wolfe, *Mauve Gloves*, pp. 42–44.

14. But see former *Newsweek* and *Los Angeles Times/Washington Post News Service* correspondent Robert Elegant's analysis of the quality of Vietnam reporting, "A Reporter Looks Back at the Vietnam War," *Encounter*, August 1981, pp. 73–90.

15. Weyand, *CDRS CALL*, July-August 1976, pp. 3, 4.

CHAPTER 4

FRICTION:
THE BUREAUCRACY

In a bureaucratic dispute the side having no better argument than its
hierarchical right is likely to lose. Presidents listen to advisors whose
views they think they need, not to those who insist on a hearing
because of the organizational chart.

Henry Kissinger, 1979[1]

IN THE SPRING of 1980, a reporter for one of the country's
leading newspapers asked an Army War College faculty
panel what he believed to be a key question about the Vietnam war. "How many times," he queried, "did the Chairman of the Joint Chiefs of Staff demand to see the President?"
The answer he received, "Almost never," was distressing
enough, but it would have been more disturbing if he had
asked the question in another way—not how many times did
the Chairman demand to see the President, but the more
important question of how many times did the President
demand to see the Chairman, or any of the other of his uniformed military advisors. As Secretary Kissinger said, "Presidents listen to advisors whose views they think they need."
The answer to how much the President thought he needed
advice from military professionals on the war in Vietnam
would have been most revealing, for it would appear that our
civilian leadership in the Pentagon, the White House, and in

the Congress evidently believed the military professionals had no worthwhile advice to give.

The reason for this grew out of the fundamental fault discussed in the introductory chapter. By default the military had allowed strategy to be dominated by civilian analysts — political scientists in academia and systems analysts in the defense bureaucracy. This had come about in a curious way. While the costs of maintaining military forces were always an important factor, they became even more important after World War II when for the first time in its history the United States maintained a large standing military in peacetime. Sidelined for a time by the Korean war, the economics of national defense was a critical issue for the Eisenhower Administration. The answer appeared to lie in "strategic" nuclear weapons and a policy of "Massive Retaliation." Explaining the rationale for this policy in 1954, Secretary of State John Foster Dulles said:

> The Soviet Communists are planning for what they call "an entire historical era," and we should do the same. They seek, through many types of maneuvers, gradually to divide and weaken the free nations by overextending them in efforts which, as Lenin put it, are "beyond their strength, so that they come to practical bankruptcy."
>
> . . . In the face of this strategy . . . it is not sound to become permanently committed to military expenditures so vast that they lead to "practical bankruptcy." . . . We want . . . a maximum deterrent at a bearable cost.[2]

The impact of this was particularly hard on the Army. As historian Russell Weigley commented:

> A national military policy and strategy relying upon massive nuclear retaliation for nearly all the uses of force left the Army uncertain of its place in the policy and strategy, uncertain that civilians recognized a need even for the Army's existence and uncertain therefore of the service's whole future. . . . The Army . . . needed a newly defined *raison d'être*, it joined with the civilian strategists in creating the strategy of limited war and flexible response.[3]

In justifying strategy in civilian strategist terms, the Army surrendered its unique authority based on battlefield experience. This authority was already weakened by a general lack of appreciation for military art within the officer corps. Instead of concentrating attention on military strategy which had become unfashionable after World War II (and, to many, irrelevant in the nuclear era), there was an increased emphasis on technical, managerial, and bureaucratic concerns. Instead of being experts in the application of military force to achieve the political ends of the United States, we became neophyte political scientists and systems analysts and were outclassed by the civilian professionals who dominated national security policy under Secretary of Defense Robert S. McNamara after 1961. It is no wonder that the President turned to these civilian professionals rather than the military for strategic advice. Without a foundation in military art we could not compete with the rationalistic proposals of the defense analysts, and the effect was a failure in our responsibilities to present alternative strategies to our civilian leaders.[4]

The rationalistic economic approach dominated military strategy formulation throughout the Vietnam war. It is especially ironic that this so-called new approach to strategy was actually two centuries old. As Clausewitz had observed (and as Vietnam was to prove) the economic approach to military strategy "stood in about the same relationship to combat as the craft of the swordsmith to the art of fencing."[5] The problem was that Secretary McNamara's Planning, Programming, and Budgeting System (PPBS) approach was only half of the equation. To return again to Clausewitz:

> . . . We see clearly that the activities characteristic of war may be split into two main categories: those *that are merely preparation for war, and war proper*. The same distinction must be made in theory as well.

> The knowledge and skills involved in the preparation will be concerned with the creation, training and maintenance of the fighting forces. . . . The theory of war proper, on the other hand, is concerned with the use of these means, once they have been developed, for the purpose of the war.[6]

The rationalistic system introduced by Secretary McNamara—PPBS—did an excellent job in "getting control of the lines of supply." It was and is a useful system for "preparing for war." As former Under Secretary of the Navy, R. James Woolsey wrote in February 1980:

> . . . Systems analysis has come to be the conventional framework for decision-making in the Defense Department and in much of the rest of government as well. The catechism is familiar: objectives, criteria, options, costs, benefits, quantify as much as possible, focus on changes at the margin.

> It has made some contributions in Defense. In 1961, Robert McNamara had inherited a military establishment long on force structure and short on fighting capability—e.g. paper divisions with neither the material to sustain combat nor the airlift and sealift to get there. Systems analysis had laid bare and helped correct some of these problems over the years. Certain types of comparisons of competing weapons systems have also been usefully handled this way.[7]

But while it was efficient in structuring forces in preparation for war, it was neither designed for, nor was it capable of, fighting the war itself. As Woolsey said:

> . . . People who only ask how much is enough, or how few can we barely get by with, tend to develop an instinct for the capillaries.

> That is not the instinct it is wisest to cultivate if you want to win real —not bureaucratic—battles. There are more important questions: How can I destroy the enemy's strategy? . . . How can I keep him on the defensive? Analytical offices, staffed with economists and the like, are not especially good at answering, or asking, these sorts of questions . . .[8]

British defense analyst Gregory Palmer found that "the rationalistic approach is . . . characterized by the pretention to universality of its solutions, its intolerance of tradition and authority, quantification, simplification, and lack of flexibility. Its very efficiency prevents flexibility by eliminating what does not contribute to achieving the current objective so that alternative means are not available if the objective is changed." The effect was that "the pseudo-economic ideol ogy that dominated defense policy reduced the flexibility available to the President."[9] The fatal flaw was that *consistency* was a premise of rationalist policy, and the one thing that war is not is consistent. As Clausewitz wrote:

> . . . The conduct of war branches out in almost all directions and has no definite limits; while any system, any model, has the finite nature of a synthesis. An irreconcilable conflict exists between this type of theory and actual practice.[10]

But the systems analysts ignored this "irreconcilable conflict." They had an educated incapacity to see war in its true light. As Palmer observed:

> . . . By using the numerical techniques of economics . . . rationality could be assumed . . . In game theory, if all players make rational choices of strategy, they all do as well as possible given the total rewards available in the game, but if one player acts irrationally in terms of the game, he is sure to do worse. Therefore, when Hanoi appeared to be acting irrationally in not accepting American terms and yet did not appear to be near defeat, it could only be assumed that they were bluffing, and a little more pressure would force rationality upon them.[11]

Like McNamara and the systems analysts, Clausewitz too had compared warfare to economics. But Clausewitz saw that "the essential difference is that . . . in war, the will is directed at an animate object that *reacts*.[12] This was not news to the military professional who knew that the enemy could, and often did, frustrate even the most carefully drawn plans. As Lieutenant General James F. Hollingsworth used to observe, "Any damned fool can write a plan. It's the execution that gets you all screwed up." But these "traditional" views seemed old-fashioned and out-of-date. In what was to become the bible of the McNamara years *(How Much Is Enough: Shaping the Defense Program 1961–1969)* two of the leading systems analysts commented:

> What is commonly called "military science" is not scientific in the same sense as law or medicine or engineering. It encompasses no

agreed-upon body of knowledge, no prescribed curriculum, no universally recognized principles that one must master to qualify as a military professional. (The so-called "principles of war" are really a set of platitudes that can be twisted to suit almost any situation.) . . .

The point is that military professionalism is largely in the conduct of military operations, not in the analysis and design of broad strategies.[13]

Experience in military operations was not good enough, they believed. "Modern-day strategy and force planning has become largely an analytical process. . . . [and] civilians are often better trained in modern analytical techniques."[14]

From his perspective as National Security Advisor to President Nixon, Henry Kissinger commented on the impact of systems analysis on the military.

[In the 1960s] young systems analysts had been brought into the Pentagon to shake up the military establishment by questioning long-held assumptions. Intellectually the systems analysts were more often right than not; but they soon learned that the way a question is put can often predetermine an answer, and their efforts in the hallowed name of objectivity frequently wound up pushing personal preconceptions.

Misuse of systems analysis apart, there was a truth which senior military officers had learned in a lifetime of service that did not lend itself to formal articulation: that power has a psychological and not only a technical component. Men can be led by statistics only up to a certain point and then more fundamental values predominate. In the final analysis the military profession is the art of prevailing, and while in our time this required more careful calculations than in the past, it also depends on elemental psychological factors that are difficult to quantify. The military found themselves designing weapons on the basis of abstract criteria, carrying out strategies in which they did not really believe, and ultimately conducting a war that they did not understand. To be sure, the military brought on some of their own troubles. They permitted themselves to be co-opted too readily . . .

Throughout the 1960s the military were torn between the commitment to civilian supremacy inculcated through generations of service and their premonition of disaster, between trying to make the new system work and rebelling against it. They were demoralized by the order to procure weapons in which they did not believe and by the necessity of fighting a war whose purpose proved increasingly elusive. A new breed of military officer emerged: men who had learned the new jargon, who could present the systems analysis arguments so much in vogue, more articulate than the older generation and more skillful in bureaucratic maneuvering. On some levels it eased civilian-military relationships; on a deeper level it deprived the policy process of the simpler, cruder, but perhaps more relevant assessments which in the final analysis are needed when issues are reduced to a test of arms.[15]

The way the Department of Defense looked at military strategy was part of the problem, but the President himself also was a factor. In his 1970 book, *New York Times* military analyst Hanson W. Baldwin observed that:

President Johnson had relatively few military associations as Senator or Vice-President. As President, he had a mistrust of the military . . . There was no such closeness of contact between the Commander-in-Chief and his responsible advisers in uniform as existed between President Roosevelt, President Truman or President Eisenhower and their Chiefs of Staff.

. . . The Chairman of the Joint Chiefs of Staff was the only member of the Joint Chiefs who saw the President with any regularity in the crucial years 1965-1968 [but even he] rarely saw the President alone; only about once in every eight or nine White House visits. He was almost always accompanied either by the Secretary of Defense or his deputy, who never hesitated to "second-guess" the Chairman and to dilute and contradict his statements. The individual members of the Joint Chiefs—the responsible heads of the fighting services: Army, Navy, Air Force, Marines—seldom saw the President privately. In the crucial twelve months from June 1965 to June 1966, when large numbers of U.S. ground troops were committed to Vietnam . . . the Chief of Staff of the Army saw the President privately twice.[16]

This did not change when President Nixon took office. But the fault then was not so much with the President as with the military themselves. As then National Security Advisor Henry Kissinger wrote:

[Chairman of the Joint Chiefs of Staff, General] Earle Wheeler . . . believed, rightly, that military advice had not been taken seriously enough in the Pentagon of the Sixties, but when the time came to present an alternative, he offered no more than marginal adjustments of the status quo. He prized his direct access to the new President but rarely used it—partially because [Secretary of Defense] Laird discouraged meetings between the President and the Chairman in which he did not participate . . .

Wheeler's successor, Admiral Thomas Moorer, was . . . an uncanny bureaucratic infighter [but] by the time he took office Vietnam had become a rearguard action.[17]

And Congress offered no solution to the problem. They were following the Executive Branch's lead. As former Congressional staffer Richard Haass wrote:

. . . Since the creation of the Bureau of the Budget in 1921 [from 1974 known as the Office of Management and the Budget, or OMB], in the defense budgeting area the initiative has shifted to the executive . . . Congressional participation mainly takes the form of acting on proposals or choosing between alternatives presented by the executive branch. Several factors account for this development. First, there are the President's role of Commander-in-Chief, the large executive bureaucracy and close ties between the executive branch and the uniformed services. Second, Congress has lacked the staff and expertise to compete in this highly complex and important area, and could offer no alternative to the systems analysis capability developed in the early 1960s by the Department of Defense.[18]

In their testimony before Congress the military were in no position to present alternative strategies. As General Maxwell Taylor said in 1959, "Having made every effort to guide his civilian superiors in the direction which he believes right, the Chief of Staff must accept the decisions of the Secretary of his service, of the Secretary of Defense, and of the President as final and thereafter support them before Congress. The alternative is resignation."[19] If questioned directly during the course of their testimony, the military leaders had the Constitutional responsibility to answer openly and frankly regardless of whether it agreed with executive branch policy or not. But as former Chairman of the Joint Chiefs of Staff Admiral Thomas Moorer commented after his retirement, "The Congress most of the time does not ask the right questions."[20]

As we have seen, the PPBS approach to strategy came to dominate the Department of Defense, the White House, and the Congress. It provided the framework within which the questions were asked. This was crucial, for the power to frame the question is also the power to predetermine the answer. But after their "strategies" for the war in Vietnam began to come apart, Smith and Enthoven disingenuously commented that:

> PPBS was not involved in the really crucial issues of the Vietnam war. Should the United States have gone into Vietnam in the first place? Did we go in at the right time, in the right way, and on the right scale? What force level should we have had, and how should these troops have been used? What timetable should we have set up for withdrawals? How can we best achieve a speedy and just settlement?[21]

"These are the really crucial issues," they said. "While PPBS can help, it cannot by itself answer such questions. Nobody has ever claimed that it could." Commenting on this, Palmer said:

> If Enthoven's plea was to be accepted, it would itself question the validity of PPBS . . . A defense planning system can hardly be defended on the ground that it is only intended for managing a peacetime deterrent. The deterrent must consist of a credible fighting force and, according to the limited war theory, it is necessary that it fight limited wars.[22]

Palmer's comment illuminates the problem. While PPBS was effective in managing a peacetime deterrent, it was incapable of managing the war. Clausewitz explained why this was so. In words that could have been written about the PPBS approach to the Vietnam war, he said:

> They aim at fixed values; but in war everything is uncertain, and calculations have to be made with variable quantities.

They direct the inquiry exclusively toward physical quantities, whereas all military action is intertwined with psychological forces and effects.
They consider only the unilateral action, whereas war consists of a continuous interaction of opposites.[23]

In retrospect, the dilemma facing the defense establishment is apparent. We had to do two things simultaneously. One was the continued deterrence of the Soviet Union who alone among the nations of the world had the power to physically destroy us. For this task, defense economics were critical. The question posed by Enthoven and Smith: "How Much Is Enough?" was appropriate and PPBS a valid system for ascertaining the answer. But as Clausewitz had said, this was "merely preparation for war." The other horn of the dilemma was the actual war in Vietnam. In war the question "How Much Is Enough?" takes on a new dimension. As the official Army history of World War II states:

. . . The facts of war are often in total opposition to the facts of peace.
. . . The efficient commander does not seek to use just enough means, but an excess of means. A military force that is just strong enough to take a position will suffer heavy casualties in doing so; a force vastly superior to the enemy's will do the job without serious loss of men.[24]

NOTES

1. Henry Kissinger, *White House Years* (Boston: Little, Brown & Co., 1979), pp. 30–31.

2. Secretary of State John Foster Dulles, *Department of State Bulletin*, 12 January 1954, Vol. XXX, pp. 107–10.

3. Russell F. Weigley, *The American Way of War: A History of United States Military Strategy and Policy* (New York: MacMillan, 1973), p. 418.

4. Unfortunately this problem lingers on. See Edward N. Luttwak, "The Decline of American Military Leadership," *Parameters: Journal of the US Army War College*, Vol. X, No. 4, December 1980, pp. 82–88.

5. Clausewitz, *On War*, II:2, p. 133.

6. *Ibid*, II:·1, pp. 131–32.

7. R. James Woolsey, "Military Options: Backward March," *The Washington Post*, February 25, 1980, p. A22.

8. *Ibid.*

9. Gregory Palmer, *The McNamara Strategy And The Vietnam War: Program Budgeting In The Pentagon, 1960–1968* (Westport, Connecticut: Greenwood press, 1978), pp. 5, 131. For a more recent analysis see Eliot Cohen, "Systems Paralysis," *The American Spectator*, November 1980, pp. 23–27.

10. Clausewitz, *On War*, II:2, p. 134.

11. Palmer, *The McNamara Strategy*, pp. 139, 140.

12. Clausewitz, *On War*, II:3, p. 149.

13. Enthoven and Smith, *How Much Is Enough*, pp. 89–92.

14. *Ibid*, p. 106.

15. Kissinger, *White House Years*, pp. 34–35.

16. Hanson W. Baldwin, *Strategy For Tomorrow* (New York: Harper & Row, 1970), pp. 13–15.

17. Kissinger, *White House Years*, pp. 35–36.

18. Haass, *Congressional Power*, p. 16.

19. General Maxwell D. Taylor, *The Uncertain Trumpet* (New York: Harper & Row, 1959), p. 112.

20. John J. Kestor and Admiral James L. Holloway III, "The Joint Chiefs of Staff: A Better System?" *AEI Foreign Policy and Defense Review*, Vol. II, No. 1, p. 10n.

21. Enthoven and Smith, *How Much Is Enough*, p. 267.

22. Palmer, *The McNamara Strategy*, p. 115.

23. Clausewitz, *On War*, II:2, p. 136.

24. Mark S. Watson, *Chief of Staff: Pre-War Plans and Preparations (US Army in World War II)* (Washington, D.C.:USGPO, 1950), p. 12.

CHAPTER 5

FRICTION: THE DANGER

Danger is part of the friction of war. Without an accurate conception of danger we cannot understand war.

Clausewitz, *On War*[1]

SO FAR WE have discussed the frictions inherent in the relationship between the Army and the American people, their elected representatives in the Congress and the bureaucracy. There is another kind of friction that must be considered before one can discuss Army battlefield doctrine and the "theory of war proper." That friction is danger.

In his discussion of "the counterweights that weaken the elemental force of war, and particularly the attack" Clausewitz found that *fear* played an important part. Because one could not say that publicly a more plausible excuse had to be substituted. The effect was "constantly recurring shadowboxing in the dialectics of war" which led to misleading systems and theories. "Only a theory that will follow the simple thread of internal cohesion," he said, "can get back to the essence of things."[2] If we take Clausewitz's advice and trace "the simple thread of internal cohesion" of our Vietnam-era strategy back to its essence, we find a fundamental failing. We had failed to heed the advice of Stonewall Jackson a hundred years earlier, "Never take counsel of your fears."[3] It is important to understand the full import of General Jackson's remark. The key word is not "fears" since only a fool would

53

disregard the very real dangers of the battlefield. The key word is "counsel" because if fears dominate thinking the resulting paralysis will only increase the hazard.

As in General Jackson's day, the fears facing the United States were real. They began to develop during and after the Korean war when we found ourselves in a bipolar confrontation with what we believed to be monolithic world communism directed by the Soviet Union. Based on very real dangers, the first was fear of the nuclear destruction of the American homeland. The second was fear of becoming involved with Communist China in a land war in Asia.

At first these fears were downplayed. In the immediate post–World War II years, the Army, still confident of its essential role in national security, dismissed the importance of nuclear weapons. Without calling nuclear weapons by name, the 1949 *Field Service Regulations* was emphatic that "the fundamental principles of combat remain unchanged," and all that was required was dispersion, better signal communications, and improved transportation. "In the vast majority of instances," the manual stated, "a new development merely extends the capabilities of existing agencies without necessitating radical revision of existing doctrine."[4]

A month after this manual was published the Soviet Union exploded their first nuclear device, and the American monopoly was no more. In August 1953, the Soviets tested their first thermonuclear weapon and began to rapidly develop their delivery systems. But the Army still refused to be awed by nuclear weapons. As the 1954 edition of the *Field Service Regulations* stated, "Army forces, as land forces, are the decisive component of the military structure . . ." Atomic weapons were relegated to less than a page. While acknowledging that atomic weapons provide a commander with the most powerful destructive force yet known to influence operations," they were seen only as "additional fire-power of large magnitude." "But," the manual went on to state, "fire alone can rarely force a favorable decision. The effect of fire, including atomic fires, must be exploited by maneuver."[5]

But the Army was whistling in the wind. Beginning in

1953, when President Eisenhower took office, nuclear weapons began to dominate U.S. military policies. As we have seen, one of the reasons was defense economics. Other factors included "the domestic reaction to the Korean conflict, the continued faith in the efficacy of air power . . . and the American penchant for simple solutions."[6]

Under the leadership of then Chief of Staff General Matthew B. Ridgway, the Army fought what they believed to be a dangerous overreliance on nuclear weapons. But General Ridgway's beliefs eventually brought him into disfavor and led to his retirement in 1955. His successor as Chief of Staff, General Maxwell D. Taylor, also tried to stem the tide. He was ultimately no more successful in destroying the myth of what he called "the Great Fallacy that henceforth the use or the threatened use of atomic weapons . . . would be sufficient to assure the security of the United States."[7]

This "Great Fallacy" had a more fundamental effect than even General Taylor realized. Our reliance on nuclear weapons for "massive retaliation" not only had an effect on the Soviet Union, but also had an effect on ourselves. Our mirror image of the probable consequences of a nuclear attack changed the very nature of our strategy. Although Alexander Hamilton had warned that the United States might have to face "the vicissitudes that have been the common lot of nations," the day of reckoning had been a long time in coming. Shielded by our great ocean barriers we had not had to face the reality that most nations faced throughout their existence—that going to war meant risking the destruction of the homeland. Now, for the first time since the War of 1812, we were faced with an adversary who had the power to physically destroy us. The resulting "Better Red Than Dead" and "Ban The Bomb" movements indicated the vulnerability felt by a considerable portion of the American people. We began to take counsel of these fears and translate them, at least in part, into our strategic doctrine.

At the time many believed that nuclear weapons had changed the entire nature of war and that all past military theories were obsolete. But, as the late Bernard Brodie observed, "Clausewitz is probably as pertinent to our times as most of the literature specifically written about nuclear war [particularly] his tough-minded pursuit of the idea that war in all its phases must be rationally guided by meaningful political purposes."[8] Although atomic weapons were unknown in his day, Clausewitz did postulate what he called a theory for pure war—i.e., war waged to the extreme. Clausewitz did this for purposes of analysis, much as a physicist postulates absolute zero in order to study the effects of temperature. Clausewitz dismissed "pure war" as a play of the imagination, a way of "avoiding every difficulty with the stroke of a pen. . . . Move from the abstract to the real world [where wars are fought to secure political goals] and the whole thing looks quite different," he said.[9] With the advent of nuclear weapons Clausewitz's theoretical "pure concept of war" became a real possibility. As he had prophesized, many avoided all the difficulties of war with a stroke of the pen. War would always rise to the extreme (i.e., a "strategic" nuclear exchange) and would be over within a matter of minutes. With such a viewpoint armies were irrelevant.

As a consequence the Army suffered a serious blow to its prestige and its self-confidence from which it would not recover until after the Vietnam war. There were many who felt that the Army had lost its usefulness. In a newspaper article a quarter century later General Taylor recalled a proposal "that the Army be converted into essentially a home guard–civil defense force and that the major responsibility for limited wars be assigned to the Navy and the Marine Corps." General Taylor went on to say that the reaction to this proposal was so violent that all papers in the Pentagon bearing on the matter were ordered destroyed and the issue was officially closed. "But there was no such easy way," he said, "to terminate the . . . impaired reputation of the armed forces . . ."[10] There were still those who believed there was no role for the Army in the nuclear age.

But, as Clausewitz said, "Move from the abstract to the real world, and the whole thing looks quite different." The extreme (nuclear weapons) did not provide a *usable* form of military power. As General Taylor said, "Massive retaliation could offer our leaders only two choices, the initiation of general nuclear war or compromise and retreat."[11] Borrowing from the writings of the civilian strategists, General Taylor advocated the reappraisal of our military strategy and proposed what he called a strategy of flexible response which would give the U.S. "a capability to react across the entire spectrum of possible challenges."[12]

This strategy came into its own when President Kennedy took office in 1961. "Our defense posture," he said, "must be both flexible and determined. Any potential aggressor contemplating an attack on any part of the free world with any kind of weapons, conventional or nuclear, must know that our response will be suitable, selective, swift, and effective."[13] As we will see in the next chapter, this new strategy, although a vast improvement over "massive retaliation," was still haunted by the specter of a nuclear World War III and we were still more concerned with avoiding that eventuality than with the traditional task of defeating the enemy.

A nation that did not appear to be frightened by the specter of a nuclear World War III was Communist China. As early as 1946 Mao Tse-tung had said that the atomic bomb was only a paper tiger.[14] While this may have been only rhetoric cloaking the Chinese lack of a nuclear capability, it took on a new dimension after the Chinese exploded their first nuclear device on 16 October 1964, just as our involvement in Vietnam began to escalate. And it was not only the fear of a nuclear armed China but of China itself that influenced U.S. military strategy. In effect we still had not recovered from the blow struck on 25 November 1950 when Marshal Lin Piao's First Phase Offensive struck the "Manchu's" of the U.S. 9th Infantry Regiment on the Ch'ong ch'on River in North Korea.

The Chinese intervention changed the whole nature of the Korean war. It also changed the whole nature of U.S. military strategy. Until that time Army strategy was based on offensive action. The aim was destruction of the enemy's armed forces and his will to fight. While Clausewitz (and our own pre–World War II doctrine) had defined battlefield victory as a *means* to peace, during World War II battlefield victory (total destruction of the enemy) became an end in itself. It is not widely appreciated that we carried this same policy into the war in Korea. Testifying before the 1951 Joint Senate Armed Forces and Foreign Relations Committees, then Secretary of State Dean Acheson stated our interim war aims clearly. Our military mission was to crush the armed forces of North Korea. Our political objective was a unified, free, and democratic Korea. And, as Secretary Acheson said:

> In the period from shortly after the Inchon landings until the intervention of the Chinese Communists, it looked as though both of these objectives could be attained . . .
>
> After the Inchon landing, General MacArthur called on these North Koreans to turn in their arms and cease their efforts; that they refused to do, and they retired into the North, and what General MacArthur's military mission was was to pursue them and round them up, as he was trying to round up that part of their army which remained in the south; and, as I said many times, we had the highest hopes that when you did that the whole of Korea would be united. That did not come to pass, because the Chinese intervened.[15]

With the Chinese intervention we were caught on the horns of a dilemma. We could not defeat the Chinese armed forces without carrying the war to China itself. This ran the risk of not only a land war in Asia against a numerically superior force, but also ran the risk of bringing in China's then ally the Soviet Union and expanding the war into Europe. This was directly counter to U.S. interests, since we had entered the war in the first place to halt the spread of "monolithic communism" by force of arms. The political and military consequences of this dilemma were profound. As Henry Kissinger observed:

> . . . We had entered the Korean War because we were afraid that to fail to do so would produce a much graver danger to Europe in the near future. But then the very reluctance to face an all-out onslaught on Europe severely circumscribed the risks we were prepared to run to prevail in Korea. . . .

Ten years later we encountered the same dilemmas in Vietnam. Once more we became involved because we considered the warfare in Indochina the manifestation of a coordinated global Communist strategy. Again we sought to limit our risks because the very global challenge of which Indochina seemed to be a part also made Vietnam appear as an unprofitable place for a showdown . . .[16]

We solved this dilemma in Korea by consciously tailoring our political objectives to the military means we were prepared to use. Our original objective of a free and unified Korea was abandoned after the Chinese intervention and we substituted restoration of the status quo ante—a goal which was militarily attainable. In so doing we came to grips with the age-old problem of the military strategist—how to bring the political and military objectives into balance. Clausewitz stated the problem 150 years earlier:

Sometimes the political and military objective is the same—for example, the conquest of a province. In other cases the political object will not provide a suitable military objective. In that event, another military objective must be adopted that will serve the political purpose and symbolize it in the peace negotiations.[17]

Because we were suffering from a kind of hubris as a result of our overwhelming World War II victories, we saw our limited victory in Korea as a kind of defeat. In so doing we drew precisely the wrong lesson from that war. Instead of seeing that it *was* possible to fight and win a limited war in Asia regardless of Chinese intervention, we again (as we had done with nuclear war) took counsel of our fears and accepted as an article of faith the proposition that we should never again become involved in a land war in Asia. In so doing we allowed our fears to become a kind of self-imposed deterrent and surrendered the initiative to our enemies.

The failure to draw the proper lessons from our Korean war experience had serious consequences in Vietnam. One was that it allowed us to be bluffed by China throughout most of the war. As Professor Allen S. Whiting observed in his analysis of Chinese deterrence, China was not hesitant about using the Korean war example to warn the United States about the dangers of involvement in Vietnam.[18] Another consequence, an outgrowth of the first, was that as early as the Geneva Conference in 1954 we saw the North Vietnamese as military proxies for China and, as Australian diplomat Coral Bell observed, "by that very decision made them so, without any choice on their part."[19]

To return again to General Jackson's advice, our error was not that we were fearful of the dangers of nuclear war and of Chinese or Russian intervention in Vietnam. These were proper concerns of the military strategist. The error was that we took counsel of these fears and in so doing paralyzed our strategic thinking. Contributing to this paralysis was a distortion of the very real dangers we faced by what Professor John H. Kautsky has described as myth, self-fulfilling prophecy and symbolic reassurance. An example of *myth*, defined as "a complex of remote goals, tense moral moods and expectations of apocalyptic success," was our initial belief (what General Taylor called "the Great Fallacy") that nuclear arms represented the ultimate weapon. Our belief that North Vietnam was a Chinese proxy was a case of a *self-fulfilling prophecy*, defined as "a false definition of the situation evoking a new behavior which makes the originally false conception come true." To a degree so was the fear of Soviet or Chinese intervention in Vietnam.[20] Kautsky's final concept, *symbolic reassurance* defined as "emotional commitment to a symbol," was reflected in our tendency to judge the effects of our military actions against North Vietnam as a mirror image of the effects such actions would have had upon us.

These fears, distortions, and misperceptions were to have a profound effect on our battlefield doctrine. Their truth was to some degree immaterial. As Professor Kautsky explained:

. . . The point is that myths, no matter how untrue, do have very real consequences; that prophecies based on initially false perceptions can produce conditions which really exist (and thus fulfill the prophecy); that men react to symbols by real behavior, be it activity or quiescence. [As W. I. Thomas said] "If men define situations as real, they are real in their consequences."[21]

NOTES

1. Clausewitz, *On War*, I:4, p. 114.

2. *Ibid*, VI:8, p. 388.

3. Lieutenant General Thomas J. Jackson, CSA, 18 June 1862; quoted in Douglas Southall Freeman, *Lee's Lieutenants: A Study in Command*, Vol. 1 (New York: Scribners, 1942), p. 469.

4. Department of the Army Field Manual 100—5, *Field Service Regulations: Operations* (Washington, D.C.: USGPO, August 1949), pp. V, VI.

5. Department of the Army Field Manual 100-5, *Field Service Regulations: Operations* (Washington, D.C.: USGPO, September 1954), pp. 4, 40, 75.

6. Taylor, *The Uncertain Trumpet*, p. 17.

7. *Ibid*, p. 4.

8. Bernard Brodie, in Clausewitz, *On War*, p. 51.

9. *Ibid*, I:1, p. 78.

10. General Maxwell D. Taylor, ". . . But Not For A Pentagon Feud," *The Washington Post*, March 10, 1980, p. A27.

11. Taylor, *The Uncertain Trumpet*, p. 5.

12. *Ibid*, p. 6.

13. *Public Papers of the Presidents of the United States: John F. Kennedy* (Washington, D.C.: USGPO, 1962), p. 232.

14. John Gittings, *The Role of the Chinese Army* (New York: Oxford University Press, 1967), p. 16.

15. 82nd Congress, 1st Session, *Military Situation in the Far East*, Part 3, pp. 1734-35, 2257-58.

16. Kissinger, *White House Years*, p. 64.

17. Clausewitz, *On War*, I:1, p. 81.

18. See Chapter 6 "Indo-China and PRC Deterrence," Allen S. Whiting, *The Chinese Calculus of Deterrence: India and Indo-China* (Ann Arbor: University of Michigan Press, 1975), pp. 170-95.

19. Coral Bell, "The Asian Balance of Power: A Comparison with European Precedents," *Adelphi Papers No. 44* (London: The International Institute for Strategic Studies, February 1968), p. 7.

20. Whether the Soviets or the Chinese ever intended intervention is a matter of conjecture. According to Professor Chalmers Johnson, "the Soviets contend that Mao's refusal to agree to a joint action with them in support of Hanoi prolonged the war and, in fact, allowed the United States to intervene without risking thermonuclear war with Russia." (Johnson, *Autopsy on People's War*, p. 65.) On the other hand, Mao Tse-tung told Edgar Snow that he feared that Russia was trying to involve China in a war with

the United States over Vietnam, as the Soviet Union had done once before in Korea. (Edgar Snow, *The Long Revolution* (New York: Random House, 1972), pp. 19–20.

21. John H. Kautsky, "Myth, Self-fulfilling Prophecy, and Symbolic Reassurance in the East-West Conflict," *Journal of Conflict Resolution*, Vol. IX, No. 1, March 1965, pp. 1–2.

CHAPTER 6

FRICTION: THE DOCTRINE

The *conduct of war* is the art of employing the Armed Forces of a nation in combination with measures of economic and political constraint for the purpose of effecting a satisfactory peace . . . The ultimate objective of all military operation is the destruction of the enemy's armed forces in battle. Decisive defeat in battle breaks the enemy's will to war and forces him to sue for peace which is the national aim . . .

FM 100–5, 1 October 1939[1]

THE EFFECT THAT the fears, distortions, and misperceptions discussed in the previous chapter had on our doctrine was particularly damaging because, as Clausewitz made clear, "principles and rules are intended to provide a thinking man with a frame of reference."[2] As will be seen in Part II it was just such a faulty frame of reference that was responsible for many of our problems in Vietnam. It was not always so. As the above quotation illustrates, our pre–World War II *Field Service Regulations* provided a sound frame of reference for the conduct of war. As Clausewitz himself had said, "The original means of strategy is victory—that is tactical success—its ends, in the final analysis, are those objects which will lead directly to peace."[3] It is essential to note that although this 1939 definition carried us into total war in

World War II, it also accommodated the later requirements of limited war, since it did not necessarily require the total submission of the enemy. What was required was sufficient military force to cause the enemy to sue for peace. In World War II this linkage dropped out of our war theories,[4] for the national aim was no longer forcing the enemy "to sue for peace" but rather his unconditional surrender. The destruction of the enemy's armed forces were therefore no longer means to an end so much as an end in itself. Unlike the earlier definition, this World War II definition could not accommodate the problems we faced in Korea after the Chinese intervention.

Because of this doctrinal deficiency our war theories became cloudy and confused. The first point of confusion was over the meaning of "victory." With his frame of reference formed by his experiences in World Wars I and II, General MacArthur saw victory only in messianic terms—the *total* destruction of the enemy's armed forces and his unconditional surrender. In his testimony before the Senate during the "Great Debate" on the Korean war, General MacArthur called for just such a victory in Korea. General MacArthur said, "I believe if you do not [seek such a victory], if you hit soft, if you practice appeasement in the use of force, you are doomed to disaster."[5]

Rejecting such an apocalyptic view, Senator Brian McMahon of Connecticut questioned General of the Army Omar Bradley, then Chairman of the Joint Chiefs of Staff, on what constitutes "victory in war":

> General, in the course of our history I believe there have been a number of instances in which we accomplished our objectives without what might be called a final and complete defeat of the enemy, such as was visited on Germany. Certainly in the War of 1812 we fought the British on the sea and on our own mainland to maintain the security of our commerce and the safety of our nationals. We didn't insist on a military victory over England as essential, did we? . . . Now, in the Spanish-American War when we accomplished the liberation of Cuba, we didn't proceed to Madrid to capture Madrid, did we? . . . We negotiated a treaty after accomplishing our objectives. I am reminded of one war, and one perhaps less well known, in

1798 to 1800, when we fought a limited naval war against France to protect our commerce and our shipping. . . . Secretary of State, Timothy Pickering, who had insisted on an all-out war with France at that time, was retired as Secretary of State, and the President, Mr. John Adams, President Adams, accomplished a settlement of that thing through negotiation and by treaty.

The point that I want to make, General, to find out if you are in agreement with me, is that when you say that the object of the war is victory, you must have a definition of what constitutes victory, don't you?

To which General Bradley replied, "I think you must, and you vary from being willing to accept a rather small thing that you start out to correct up to an objective which we set in World War II of unconditional surrender. There are many variations in between the two."[6]

Elaborating on this theme, Senator William Knowland of California commented:

. . . The fact of the matter is, is it not, General, that we did not settle the controversy with the Spaniards being left in control of half of Cuba; we did not settle the Greek War with the Greek Communists being left in control of a substantial part of Greece; and we did not finish the War of 1812 with the British being left in control of New Orleans. While it is true that we did not carry the war into their home countries, nevertheless, we did clean up the particular situation in which we were involved.

Again General Bradley replied, "We restored it in some cases to the status quo when we started the war and won our point. That boils down then to the question of what our point is."[7]

Senator Bourke K. Hickenlooper of Iowa again raised the issue of "victory" with Secretary of State Acheson. "I understand that it is our policy to have a victory in Korea; it's our policy to have peace in Korea. [It is] what we expect to do to accomplish it that bewilders me." Secretary Acheson replied that U.S. strategy was to limit the geographic boundaries of the war "as the least dangerous and most effective way of coming to a situation where both the attack stops and the desire to renew it stops" and to wear down the enemy by attrition so that "they will suffer very disastrous losses to themselves, and a great many harmful results will happen to them in the way of the losses of their trained manpower and the absorption of the resources of China in a fight which is of no real profit to China."[8] Secretary Acheson went on to say that it was the U.S. intention to gain victory not on the battle- field but through discussion and agreement.

Another point of confusion was over the definition of limited war. General MacArthur complained that "my whole effort since Red China came in there has been to get some definition, military definition, of what I should do."[9] Com- menting on a statement by then Assistant Secretary of State Dean Rusk that "what we are trying to do is maintain peace and security without a general war . . ." MacArthur replied, "That policy seems to me to introduce a new concept into military operations . . . the concept that when you use force, you can *limit that force* . . . The very term of 'resisting aggression,' it seems to me that you destroy the potentialities of the aggressor to continually hit you. . . . When you say, merely, 'we are going to continue to fight aggression,' that is not what the enemy is fighting for. The enemy is fighting for a very definite purpose—to destroy our forces in Korea."[10] It is important to note that, General MacArthur's comments notwithstanding, the U.S. strategy in Korea after the Chinese intervention was not so much one of limiting the means as it was one of tailoring the political ends so that they could be accomplished within the military means that our political leaders were willing to expend. In the Korean war "limited war" was defined in terms of limited *objectives*. As our post- Korean *Field Service Regulations* stated, "The nature of the political situation at any time may require employment of armed forces in wars of limited objective. In such cases, the objective ordinarily will be the destruction of the aggressor forces and the restoration of the political and territorial integrity of the friendly nation."[11] As Senators McMahon and Knowland and Secretary of State Acheson had said, and as our 1954 doctrine acknowledged, in neither the past nor the present was "victory" defined only as total destruction of the enemy. Victory was the achievement of the political ends for which the war was being waged. As Clausewitz had written:

> ... In war many roads lead to success, and ... they do not all involve the opponent's outright defeat. They range from *the destruction of the enemy's forces, the conquest of his territory, to a temporary occupation or invasion, to projects with an immediate political purpose, and finally to passively awaiting the enemy's attacks.* ...

> Bear in mind how wide a range of political interests can lead to war, or ... think for a moment of the gulf that separates a war of annihilation, a struggle for political existence, from a war reluctantly declared in consequence of political pressure or of an alliance that no longer seems to reflect the state's true interests. Between these two extremes lie numerous gradations. If we reject a single one of them on theoretical grounds, we may as well reject all of them, and lose contact with the real world.[12]

In Korea the Army had learned the right lesson—that political considerations may require wars of limited objective —but it drew the wrong conclusions from that lesson. In what appears today to have been almost a fit of pique, the 1954 *Field Service Regulations*, while introducing the concept of "wars of limited objective," removed "victory" as an aim in war. As the manual said, "Victory alone as an aim of war cannot be justified, since in itself victory does not always assure the realization of national objectives."[13] Defining victory only in terms of total victory, rather than more accurately as the attainment of the objectives for which the war is waged, was a strategic mistake. It not only obscured the fact that we had won a victory in Korea (where the status quo ante was restored and has been maintained for almost 30 years), it also went a long way toward guaranteeing a lack of victory in Vietnam.

But even though we dropped victory as an aim in war, the overall doctrinal effects of our Korean war experience were beneficial. As a result of that war we shed our World War II delusions about total war. As Brigadier General Dave Palmer commented in his analysis of Vietnam, in historical terms it was limited war, not total war that was the norm. "Most wars, it can be argued, have been limited," he said. "One can dig way back in history to say that the final Punic War—when Rome defeated Carthage, slaughtered the population, razed the city, plowed under the ruins and sowed the furrows with salt—was not in any way limited. . . . But it is hard to find other examples; in some manner or other a limiting factor was always present."[14]

Unfortunately this was not to last. Another kind of total war—nuclear war—came to dominate our doctrine, and the fear of World War III soon distorted the lessons of Korea. Paradoxically these changes did not occur during the "massive retaliation" era but instead came into being after we had adopted the doctrine of flexible response. The 1962 *Field Service Regulations* (which governed our initial ground force involvement in Vietnam and remained in effect until 1968) introduced two major changes in our doctrine. First was the introduction of the concept of a "spectrum of war," and the second was the redefinition of limited war to limit the means rather than the objective.

From the point of view of the political scientists who formulated the limited war theories, the spectrum of war undoubtedly represented a truer picture of the world than the more simplistic concepts of war and peace. According to the 1962 manual, this spectrum ranged from cold war—"a power struggle between contending nations"—through limited war to general (nuclear) war. As the manual said, "The dividing line between cold war and limited war is neither distinct nor absolute."[15] But there was a major difference between cold war and limited war. Cold war was essentially a peacetime posture with a heightened state of tension; limited war was a wartime posture involving actual hostilities. Erasing the line between war and peace was to prove a serious flaw. It contributed to our failure to declare war over Vietnam, as well as to the credibility gap that developed between the government and the American people. The social critic and strategist Herman Kahn once remarked that academicians see the world in terms of shades of gray, while the average person sees things in black and white. But in so doing the academician can make a mistake that the average man can never make. He can confuse midnight and noon. While the new breed of strategists might have had difficulty with the distinction between peace and war, the American people were to prove they knew the difference full well.

This spectrum of war also led to the second doctrinal change. The 1962 manual dropped the concept of "wars of limited objective" which we had adopted after the Korean war and introduced the concept of limited means. According to the manual, "The essential objective of United States military forces will be to terminate the conflict rapidly and decisively in a manner best calculated to prevent its spread to general (nuclear) war."[16] On the face of it there is nothing intrinsically wrong in placing limits on military means, so long as your opponent follows suit and mutual deterrence is maintained. It is especially valid when applied against a nuclear-armed adversary when both sides have an interest in avoiding nuclear war. In such cases what Clausewitz called "polarity" exists. As he said, "The principle of polarity is valid only in relation to one and the same object, in which positive and negative interests exactly cancel one another out."[17] Our publicly expressed fears of the horrors of nuclear war lessened the polarity between us and the Soviet Union and cost us a major strategic advantage—what Professor Edward N. Luttwak called *escalation dominance*—the ability to pose a threat to the enemy to raise the level of warfare beyond his ability (or willingness) to respond.[18] In like manner the polarity with China was also weakened by our publicly expressed fears of becoming involved in a land war in Asia. This lack of polarity was to lead us into an untenable strategic position where the enemy's territory was inviolable while the territory of our ally was open to attack.

NOTES

1. FM 100–5, 1 October 1939, p. 27.
2. Clausewitz, *On War*, I:2, p. 141.

3. *Ibid*, II:2, p. 143.

4. War Department Field Manual 100-5, *Field Service Regulations: Operations* (Washington, D.C.: USGPO, 15 June 1944), p. 32.

5. 82nd Congress, 1st Session, *Military Situation in the Far East*, Part I, p. 40.

6. *Ibid*, pp. 960-61.

7. *Ibid*, p. 1083.

8. *Ibid*, p. 1800.

9. *Ibid*, pp. 30-31.

10. *Ibid*, pp. 39-40, 68. (Emphasis added)

11. Department of the Army Field Manual 100-5, *Field Service Regulations: Operations* (Washington, D.C.: USGPO, 27 September 1954), p. 6.

12. Clausewitz, *On War*, I:2, p. 94.

13. FM 100-5, September 1954, p. 7.

14. David Richard Palmer, *Summons of the Trumpet: U.S.–Vietnam in Perspective* (San Rafael, California: Presidio Press, 1978), p. xix.

15. Department of the Army Field Manual 100-5, *Field Service Regulations: Operations* (Washington, D.C.: USGPO, 19 February 1962), pp. 4-5.

16. FM 100-5, February 1962, p. 9.

17. Clausewitz, *On War*, I:1, p. 83.

18. Edward N. Luttwak, *The Grand Strategy of the Roman Empire: From the First Century* A.D. *to the Third* (Baltimore: The Johns Hopkins University Press, 1976), pp. 41-42. There were those who saw the danger in this kind of unilateral disarmament. In his 1958 U.S. Army War College student thesis, "The Mirage of Limited War," Colonel Francis X. Bradley pointed out this fault in our concepts of limited war. Comparing conflicts between nations "to a world-wide poker game without limits," he observed that if a nation doesn't "bet" it can't win, if it refuses to run risks it can easily be bluffed.

CHAPTER 7

FRICTION: THE DOGMA

The 1960s witnessed the high tide of both . . . people's wars and also of the Western reaction to them. No doubt the latter would not have existed without the former, but there can equally be no doubt that [as J. Bowyer Bell said in *The Myth of the Guerrilla* (New York: Knopf, 1971)] "the men of order by elaborating and extending their responses out of proportion to the reality of the threat" contributed greatly to the spread and the attractiveness of the original doctrine. This is not to imply that there should have been no response at all [but] a well-honed response required careful analysis . . . to ensure that American efforts were directed against the "export" of revolution, not the suppression of genuine revolution.

Professor Chalmers Johnson
Autopsy on People's War[1]

IT IS AXIOMATIC in military strategy that one can never factor out the enemy. When President Kennedy took office in 1961, it seemed at first that with his policy of "flexible response" the Army had come into its own and there was again a place for conventional strategy. But no sooner had we begun to adapt our doctrine to these new policies than our adversaries—the U.S.S.R. and China—changed the rules of the game. Suddenly the threat was not so much nuclear war or conventional war but "a whole new kind of warfare"— wars of national liberation and people's war. What was not apparent at the time was that their emphasis on guerrilla war had much to do with the same issue that had caused the Army so much grief—the issue of nuclear weapons.

71

Faced with U.S. nuclear superiority in the post–World War II period, both the Soviets and the Chinese began to develop and expand their own nuclear capabilities. This would eventually eliminate their vulnerability to U.S. intimidation, but it was a long-term effort that would take years to accomplish. In the meantime, a counter-strategy to U.S. nuclear superiority had to be devised. The Soviets found such a strategy in "Wars of National Liberation." Announced by Premier Nikita Khrushchev in January 1961 on the eve of President John Kennedy's inauguration, it was essentially a low cost effort using surrogate forces in order to avoid a direct confrontation with the United States.

This "new kind of warfare" had an immediate effect on U.S. strategic thinking, especially since it seemed to be reinforced by Mao's "people's war" successes in winning the Chinese mainland and Castro's activities in Latin America (activities made particularly galling by the U.S. humiliation at the Bay of Pigs). Returning from his meeting in Vienna with Khrushchev in 1961, President John F. Kennedy emphasized the need for a U.S. counterinsurgency capability. As he saw it:

> In the 1940s and early fifties, the great danger was from Communist armies marching across free borders, which we saw in Korea. . . . Now we face a new and different threat. We no longer have a nuclear monopoly. Their missiles, they believe, will hold off our missiles, and their troops can match our troops should we intervene in these so-called wars of liberation. Thus, the local conflict they support can turn in their favor through guerrillas or insurgents or subversion. . . . It is clear that this struggle in this area of the new and poorer nations will be a continuing crisis of this decade.[2]

Twenty years later, it is hard to envision the force with which the concept of counterinsurgency struck the Army. Its impact was particularly powerful, both because of the partial doctrinal vacuum that still existed as a result of the "massive retaliation" era, and because it was pushed by President Kennedy himself, who "took the lead in formulating the programs, pushing both his own staff and the government establishment to give the matter priority attention." Former Army

Chief of Staff General Maxwell Taylor was brought in as the President's special military representative and assigned the duties of monitoring counterinsurgency efforts, and the President himself sent a letter to the Army which indicated a need for new doctrine and tactics.[3]

Some appreciation of the effect can be gained from such publications as the March 1962 issue of *Army*, the influential publication of the Association of the U.S. Army, which was devoted to (in its own words) "spreading the gospel" of counterinsurgency. Reading it today sounds more like the description of a new liturgy rather than a discussion of strategic doctrine. Not all were taken in. The article reports that then Army Chief of Staff General George H. Decker "stoutly stood up to the President with the assurance that 'any good soldier can handle guerrillas.' " The President's response was "a brisk and spirited homily to the effect that guerrilla fighting was a special art,"[4] and six months later General Decker was out, replaced as Army Chief of Staff by General Earle G. Wheeler. The Army leadership got the message, especially since "[President] Kennedy dropped a broad hint that future promotions of high ranking officers would depend upon their demonstration of experience in the counter-guerrilla or sub-limited war field."[5] Counterinsurgency became not so much the Army's doctrine as the Army's dogma, and (as nuclear weapons had done earlier) stultified military strategic thinking for the next decade.

As had been the case with our fears of nuclear weapons and of China, "myths, self-fulfilling prophecies, and symbolic reassurance" also distorted our understanding of the guerrilla war challenge. There was the myth that such wars were something unique in the annals of warfare. Then there was President Kennedy's self-fulfilling prophecy that he would bet nine to one that they would be the most likely wars of the future,[6] and the symbolic reassurance that the American social structure could be exported to the rest of the world.

Although there were those who saw "revolutionary war" springing full-blown from the breast of Khrushchev or Mao Tse-tung in 1961, this type of warfare actually has a long history. Clausewitz himself devoted a chapter of *On War* to "The People in Arms." Long before either Khrushchev or Mao were born, external powers were seeking to profit from the internal instability of their neighbors. As Professor Geoffrey Blainey of the University of Melbourne found, from 1815 to 1939 "at least 31 wars had been immediately preceded by serious disturbances in one of the fighting nations."[7] He goes on to say that "civil strife was particularly dangerous when a group or interest in the disturbed nation had strong bonds with another nation . . . Of the civil disturbances which preceded international war in the period from 1815 to 1939, at least 26 of the 31 disturbances formed links with the outside nation which ultimately went to war."[8]

And the United States itself was no stranger to guerrilla war. Our own experience during the Indian Wars, the Philippine Insurrection, and the Mexican border skirmishes were reflected in our *Field Service Regulations*. The 1939 edition devoted four pages to this subject, including two and one-half pages on *combating* guerrilla warfare. Especially as a result of our World War II experiences with "partisan warfare," we saw guerrilla warfare as an adjunct to normal conventional operations, designed for ". . . harassing or delaying larger forces and causing losses through attrition . . . destroying signal communications, gaining military information, assisting regular forces to reconquer the country or make incursions on the enemy's lines of communications and supply."[9]

It was precisely in this light that we saw enemy guerrilla actions in Korea, and we devised tactics to deal with the guerrilla problem. It is interesting to note that during the "Great Debate" in 1951, Senator Richard Russell of Georgia asked General of the Army Omar Bradley, then Chairman of the Joint Chiefs of Staff, if we had learned anything in Korea. General Bradley replied:

> Yes, I think we have learned a few lessons. We certainly have been up against one type of warfare which we never had before, and that is the guerrilla type, in which you have infiltration of your lines by

large groups. . . . How helpful it will be in the future, no one knows, but certainly it is something that we should have experience in.[10]

The lesson we had learned in Korea was to orient U.S. forces on the external rather than the internal threat. Although from time to time the United States detached military units to assist in counter-guerrilla operations, such operations were the primary responsibility of the South Korean government. This military division of responsibility was a reflection of U.S. political policy toward Korea. As a sovereign nation the problem of *internal* security was the responsibility of the Government of the Republic of Korea, and the role of U.S. forces was (and is) limited to protecting South Korea from *external* attack. There were many reasons why we did not see the war in Korea as a model for the war in Vietnam. First, as we have seen, it was many years after the end of that war before we realized that we had actually won a victory there. Second was the continuing trauma of the intervention of Chinese troops. Perhaps more important, however, was the belief that the war in Vietnam was a whole new kind of war where the lessons of the past had no application.

The reason this was so can best be understood in terms of Kautsky's "symbolic reassurance." The Soviet Union and China used the symbol of revolutionary war to advance their own ends, and President Kennedy had reacted to that symbol with the doctrine of counterinsurgency. From our perspective it appeared that the strategies were in balance. But they could only remain in balance as long as our adversaries were in fact waging a "revolutionary war." For almost the entire Vietnam war we believed and acted on the enemy's people's war propaganda even in the face of considerable evidence to the contrary. As late as 1973, General William C. Westmoreland said, "An understanding of the American ground strategy in Vietnam begins with an understanding of the nature of the war the enemy waged, for that always affects the nature of the riposte. The Communists in Vietnam waged a classic revolutionary war."[11] One of the better known strategists in this "new kind of war," Sir Robert Thompson, explained how "classic revolutionary war" differed from conventional war:

> . . . Revolutionary war is most confused with guerrilla or partisan warfare. Here the main difference is that guerrilla warfare is designed merely to harass and distract the enemy so that the regular forces can reach a decision in conventional battles. . . . Revolutionary war on the other hand is designed to reach a decisive result on its own.[12]

General Westmoreland was exactly right that "an understanding of the nature of the war . . . always affects the nature of the riposte." But with hindsight it is clear that by Sir Robert Thompson's own definition, he was exactly wrong in seeing the war as "a classic revolutionary war." The guerrillas in Vietnam did *not* achieve decisive results on their own. Even at the very end there was no popular mass uprising to overthrow the Saigon government. Their actions fit precisely Sir Robert Thompson's definition of partisan warfare—they harassed and distracted both the United States and South Vietnam so that North Vietnamese regular forces could reach a decision in conventional battles.

It was only at the very end that this fact became apparent. In 1973–74, a colloquium was held at the Fletcher School of Law and Diplomacy. Thirty-one distinguished panelists (including General Westmoreland) critiqued the failures of our counterinsurgency strategy. Before their findings could be published, Saigon fell to the North Vietnamese and it became clear that their deliberations had obscured rather than illuminated the true nature of the war. As the organizers of the panel, Professor W. Scott Thompson and Colonel Donaldson D. Frizzell, concluded sadly in their Afterword:

> There is great irony in the fact that the North Vietnamese finally won by purely conventional means, using precisely the kind of warfare at which the American army was best equipped to fight. . . . In their lengthy battle accounts that followed Hanoi's great military victory, Generals Giap and Dung barely mentioned the contribution of local forces.[13]

Having said all this, however, is not to say there was no value in counterinsurgency doctrine. It has much to offer a nation faced with internal insurgency, but South Vietnam faced not only internal insurgency but also outside aggression and counterinsurgency doctrine could only be part of the answer. Second, to give credit to its originators, "President Kennedy and his advisors saw counterinsurgency as first and last a *political* task to be carried out under *civilian* management."[14] If it had remained at that level it could have been a valuable adjunct to U.S. military operations in Vietnam which should have been focused on protecting South Vietnam from outside aggression, leaving the internal problems to the South Vietnamese themselves.

But as we will see in Part II, we failed to distinguish between these two tasks. Counterinsurgency took on a life of its own. As Harvard researcher J. Bowyer Bell found, "Even before Vietnam justifiably absorbed the attention of America, guerrilla-revolution had become a fashionable challenge to be met in elegant and complex ways but ways which needed the talents, the scope, the capacities, and the experience of various available careerists."[15] It got so bad that, according to Professor Chalmers Johnson, "by 1967 the various counterinsurgency committees and task forces had proliferated to such a degree that a senior U.S. official [the State Department's Director of Intelligence and Research] warned against a possible "bureaucratic interest" in the existence of people's war."[16] There appeared to be something in it for everybody. As J. Bowyer Bell put it:

> . . . For the American intellectual theoreticians of order, the nature of the appropriate response—intricate and highly calculated reforms to transform Vietnamese society—fit the prejudices and aspirations of the moment . . . the guerrilla could be met by using the advanced tools of social science for the betterment of man . . . [Accordingly] the guerrilla threat was magnified because it was unconventional, requiring revolutionary reforms usually so difficult to force on static societies. . . .[17]

For the military, counterinsurgency appeared to give us a whole new mission—civil affairs activities, establishment of schools and public health systems, assistance to police, and other forms of "civic action." According to Blaufarb, "There was a brief period in the late 1960s when military intellectuals were advancing the notion that the U.S. Army was the arm of the government best equipped to carry out in the field the entire range of activities associated with 'nation-building.' "[18] This change in orientation was reflected in the 1968 successor to the *Field Service Regulations* which stated that "the fundamental purpose of the U.S. military forces is to preserve, restore, or create an environment of order or stability within which the instrumentalities of government can function effectively under a code of laws."[19] We had come a long way from the pre–Vietnam war doctrine that called for "the defeat of an enemy by application of military power directly or indirectly against the armed forces which support his political structure."[20]

By obscuring the true nature of military force, our own doctrine contributed to the subsequent failure of U.S. national policy in Vietnam. As Clausewitz had said, the primacy of policy in war rests on the assumption that "policy knows the instrument it means to use" and that *"only if statesmen look to certain military moves and actions to produce effects that are foreign to their nature do political decisions influence operations for the worse."*[21] The effect of this doctrinal confusion was emphasized by then Chief of Staff (and former MACV Commander) General Fred C. Weyand in 1976:

> . . . The major military error was a failure to communicate to the civilian decisionmakers the capabilities and limitations of American military power. There are certain tasks the American military can accomplish on behalf of another nation. They can defeat enemy forces on the battlefield. They can blockade the enemy's coast. They can cut lines of supply and communication. They can carry the war to the enemy on land, sea, and air. These tasks require political decisions before they can be implemented, but they are within the military's capabilities.
>
> But there are also fundamental limitations on American military power . . . the Congress and the American people will not permit

their military to take total control of another nation's political, economic, and social institutions in order to completely orchestrate the war. . . .

The failure to communicate these capabilities and limitations resulted in the military being called upon to perform political, economic, and social tasks beyond its capability while at the same time it was limited in its authority to accomplish those military tasks of which it was capable.[22]

NOTES

1. Johnson, *Autopsy on People's War*, p. 44.

2. President John F. Kennedy quoted in Johnson, *Autopsy on People's War*, p. 22.

3. Douglas S. Blaufarb, *The Counter-Insurgency Era: U.S. Doctrine and Performance 1950 to the Present* (New York: The Free Press, 1977), p. 52. See also Virgil Ney, "Evolution of the United States Army Field Manual: Valley Forge to Vietnam," *Combat Operations Research Group Memorandum 244*, January 1966, p. 104.

4. Lloyd Norman and John B. Spore, "Big Push In Guerrilla Warfare," *Army*, March 1962, p. 34.

5. *Ibid*, p. 33.

6. *Ibid*.

7. Geoffrey Blainey, *The Causes of War* (New York: The Free Press, 1973), p. 71.

8. *Ibid*, p. 83.

9. FM 100-5, August 1949, p. 231.

10. 82nd Congress, 1st Session, *Military Situation in the Far East*, Part 2, p. 1009.

11. W. Scott Thompson and Donaldson D. Frizzell (ed), *The Lessons of Vietnam* (New York: Crane, Russak & Co., 1977), p. 279.

12. Sir Robert Thompson, *Revolutionary War in World Strategy 1945–1969* (New York: Taplinger Publishing Co., 1970), pp. 16–17.

13. Thompson and Frizzell, *The Lessons of Vietnam*, p. 279.

14. Blaufarb, *The Counter-Insurgency Era*, p. 65. (Emphasis added)

15. J. Bowyer Bell, *The Myth of the Guerrilla: Revolutionary Theory and Malpractice* (New York: Alfred A. Knopf, 1971), pp. 257–58.

16. Johnson, *Autopsy on People's War*, pp. 29–30.

17. J. Bowyer Bell, *The Myth of the Guerrilla*, p. 257.

18. Blaufarb, *The Counter-Insurgency Era*, p. 287.

19. Department of the Army, Field Manual 100–5, *Operations of Army Forces in the Field* (Washington, D.C.: USGPO, September 1968), pp. 1–6.

20. FM 100–5, September 1954, p. 5.

21. Clausewitz, *On War*, VIII:6, pp. 607, 608. (Emphasis added)

22. Weyand, *CDRS CALL*, July-August 1976, pp. 5–6.

PART II

The Engagement

Theory will have fulfilled its main task when it is used to analyze the constituent elements of war, to distinguish precisely what at first sight seems fused, to explain in full the properties of the means employed and to show their probable effects, to define clearly the nature of the ends in view, and to illuminate all phases of warfare in a thorough critical inquiry. Theory then becomes a guide to anyone who wants to learn about war from books. . . .

Clausewitz, *On War*
(II:2, p. 141)

CHAPTER 8

TACTICS, GRAND TACTICS, AND STRATEGY

The first, the supreme, the most far-reaching act of judgement that the statesman and commander have to make is to establish . . . the kind of war on which they are embarking; neither mistaking it for, nor trying to turn it into, something that is alien to its nature. This is the first of all strategic questions and the most comprehensive.

Clausewitz, *On War*[1]

As MILITARY PROFESSIONALS, it was our job to judge the true nature of the Vietnam war, communicate those facts to our civilian decision-makers, and to recommend appropriate strategies. As Clausewitz said, that was the first strategic question and the most comprehensive. It is indicative of our strategic failure in Vietnam that almost a decade after our involvement the true nature of the Vietnam war is still in question. There are still those who would attempt to fit it into the revolutionary war mold and who blame our defeat on our failure to implement counterinsurgency doctrine.[2] This point of view requires an acceptance of the North Vietnamese contention that the war was a civil war, and that the North Vietnamese regular forces were an extension of the guerrilla effort, a point of view not borne out by the facts.

As Professor Raymond Aron recently pointed out, it is essential to distinguish the First Indo-China war between France and the Viet Minh from the Second Indo-China war between North Vietnam and South Vietnam.[3] The first was a revolutionary war. The second was not. The forces that besieged Dien Bien Phu grew out of the guerrilla movement; the forces that captured Saigon did not grow out of the Viet Cong but were the regular armed forces of North Vietnam. This critical difference validates the official U.S. government position that the Vietnam war was caused by aggression from the North.[4]

To have understood the true nature of the Vietnam war required not only a strict definition of the enemy, it also required a knowledge of the nature of war itself. As we saw in Part I, our understanding was clouded by confusion over preparation for war and the conduct of war, by fears of nuclear war, by fears of Chinese intervention, and by the misconception that we were being challenged by a whole new kind of "revolutionary" war that could only be countered by the "strategy" of counterinsurgency. Reviewing the literature on Vietnam in search of "lessons," Professor of History Joe Dunn concluded that while "George Santayana reminded us that 'those who cannot remember the past are condemned to repeat it,' some would argue that Gaddis Smith's rejoinder is more applicable: 'One of the most somber aspects of the study of history is that it suggests no obvious ways by which mankind could have avoided folly.' "[5]

There are many ways to look at the war in Vietnam. One way (Santayana's) suggests that by a proper understanding and application of military art we could have influenced the outcome. Another (Gaddis Smith's) would have it that we were caught up in a kind of Greek tragedy where the end was preordained and where there were "no obvious ways by which [we] could have avoided folly." There is an attraction —some would say a fatal attraction—in the Gaddis Smith approach. In the face of failure it is easy to salve your conscience with the notion that nothing you could have done would have made any difference, that fate rather than your action or inaction had predetermined the end. For example, there are those who would blame our failure in Vietnam on the forces of history or on the tide of human events. But, as we will see, it was four North Vietnamese Army corps, not "dialectical materialism," that ultimately conquered South Vietnam.

As Alexander Solzhenitsyn said, "We must not hide behind fate's petticoats." We must reject Gaddis Smith in favor of Santayana and believe that a thorough knowledge of the art of war through what Clausewitz called "critical analysis"—can influence the course of events. Critical analysis, according to Clausewitz, consists of three different intellectual activities—the discovery and interpretation of facts, the tracing of effects back to their cause, and the investigation and evaluation of the means employed. "Critical analysis is not just an evaluation of the means actually employed, but of *all possible means*," said Clausewitz. "One can, after all, not condemn a method without being able to suggest a better alternative."

Clausewitz further observed that "[we see] things in the light of their result, and to some extent come to know and appreciate them fully only because of it."[6] In retrospect, our entire approach to the war would have been different if at the beginning we could have foreseen the North Vietnamese tanks rumbling through the streets of Saigon on 1 May 1975. The North Korean conventional attack in June 1950—and the North Korean tanks rumbling through Seoul—left no doubt as to the nature of that war and the nature of the proper U.S. response. But the North Vietnamese, evidently learning from the Korean war that an overt attack could precipitate a massive U.S. military response, began the war on a different key. Unlike the North Koreans who had pulled their communist cadres out of South Korea in April 1948 and opted for a conventional attack, the North Vietnamese opened their campaign with a guerrilla attack. One reason undoubtedly was fear of the U.S. response to an open attack, but there were other reasons as well. Unlike Korea, where the South Korean leader Syngman Rhee personified Korean nationalism and the North Korean leader Kim Il-sung was seen as a Soviet puppet, in Vietnam the situation was reversed. Ho Chi Minh had captured the cloak of Vietnamese nationalism during the struggles with the French, while the South Vietnamese leader Ngo Dinh Diem (and his successors) were tainted with a civil service and army structure inherited from French colonialism. Another factor was that in Korea the Americans were seen as the liberators from Japanese colonialism, in Vietnam they were identified with the former French regime.[7]

All of these things combined tended to cloud our perception of how to counter North Vietnamese aggression. Judged by the results of the war, the basic mistake (as we will see) was that we saw their guerrilla operations as a strategy in itself. Because we saw it as a strategy, we attempted to understand it in terms of "people's war" theories of Mao Tse-tung, and devised elaborate theories of counterinsurgency. We attempted to counter it by using such models as the British model in Malaysia. These theories and models had some relevance for the government of South Vietnam which ultimately had to neutralize the internal threat to its existence, but they had only secondary relevance to the United States. Ironically, we had seen this clearly in Korea. While we could protect them from external attack, internal security was a problem only they could solve. We could aid them with political advice and economic and military assistance, but the task was primarily theirs. As we will see in a later chapter, it was not until the end that we rediscovered this fact in Vietnam.

Where did we go wrong? It can be argued that from the French withdrawal in 1954 until President Diem's assassination in 1963, the American response was essentially correct. The task at hand was one of assisting South Vietnam to become a viable nation state, and U.S. military advisors contributed to that end. In December 1963, the nature of the war began to change. The North Vietnamese made a decision to intervene directly both with military assistance and guerrilla cadres. In the late summer of 1964, the North Vietnamese again escalated the war by sending regular North Vietnamese Army forces south. In his analysis of the Vietnam war, Brigadier General Dave Palmer identifies this crucial turning point:

> By committing its regular forces to a cause which had previously been cloaked in the guise of an internal war, Hanoi dramatically altered the entire thrust and scope of the conflict. It was a key command decision. Indeed, it may well have been *the* key command decision of the war.[8]

Although it was not so dramatic, nor so obvious, as the North Korean invasion of South Korea in June 1950, the North Vietnamese had launched a strategic offensive to conquer South Vietnam. As in Korea, our initial response was defensive, relying primarily on South Vietnamese ground forces and limited U.S. air support. By mid-1965 it had become clear that this was not enough. U.S. combat troops were needed to stabilize the situation. In November 1965, the 32nd, 33rd and 66th regiments of the North Vietnamese Army clashed head-on with the U.S. 1st Cavalry Division in the Ia Drang Valley in central Vietnam. After ten days of heavy fighting the North Vietnamese were in full retreat. As General Palmer reports:

> On a strategic scale, a brilliant spoiling attack had completely derailed Hanoi's hopes of earning a decisive victory before full American might could be deployed to South Vietnam. Moreover, in a head-on clash between an American and a North Vietnamese division, on the enemy's chosen ground, the NVA unit had been sent reeling in retreat. For the moment, at least, an adverse tide had been reversed.[9]

Now was the time for the United States to take the offensive. Although in theory the best route to victory would have been a strategic offensive against North Vietnam, such action was not in line with U.S. strategic policy which called for the *containment* rather than the destruction of communist power. As we saw earlier this policy was based at least in part on our fears of sparking a nuclear war and our fears of Chinese intervention. As General Palmer reports:

> The Johnson administration had already barricaded the one sure route to victory—to take the strategic offensive against the source of the war. Memories of Mao Tse-tung's reaction when North Korea was overrun by United Nations troops in 1950 haunted the White House. America's fear of war with Red China protected North Vietnam from invasion more surely than any instrument of war Hanoi could have fielded.[10]

While a strategic offensive against North Vietnam may not have been politically feasible, we could have taken the tactical offensive to isolate the battlefield. But instead of orienting on North Vietnam—the source of war—we turned our attention to the symptom—the guerrilla war in the south. Our new "strategy" of counterinsurgency blinded us to the fact that the guerrilla war was tactical and not strategic. It was a kind of economy of force operation on the part of North Vietnam to buy time and to wear down superior U.S. military forces. As Norman Hannah, a career State Department Foreign Service Officer (FSO) with long experience in Southeast Asia wrote in 1975, "In South Vietnam we responded mainly to Hanoi's simulated insurgency rather than to its real but controlled aggression, as a bull charges the toreador's cape, not the toreador."[11]

We thought we were pursuing a new strategy called counterinsurgency, but actually we were pursuing a defensive strategy in pursuit of a negative aim—a strategy familiar to Clausewitz in the early nineteenth century. In his chapter on purpose and means in war Clausewitz discusses various methods of obtaining the object of the war. One way is what Clausewitz calls "the negative aim." It is, he said, "the natural formula for outlasting the enemy, for wearing him down."[12] In a later chapter, Clausewitz discusses the relationship between the negative aim and the strategic defensive. "The aim of the defense must embody the idea of waiting," he said. "The idea implies . . . that the situation . . . may improve . . . Gaining time is the only way [the defender] can achieve his aim."[13] Basic to the success of a strategic defensive in pursuit of the negative aim, therefore, is the assumption that time is on your side. But the longer the war progressed the more obvious it became that time was *not* on our side. It was American rather than North Vietnamese will that was being eroded. In his review of General Westmoreland's biography, Hannah writes:

> . . . [General] Westmoreland mentions several factors that prolonged the war, but . . . we are entitled to conclude that he did not regard these factors likely to be decisive. Indeed, he tells us he suffered these impediments because he believed that "success would eventually be ours." But it was not. Why not?

> General Westmoreland does not directly answer the question but the answer emerges without being stated. We ran out of time. This is the tragedy of Vietnam—we were fighting for time rather than space. And time ran out.[14]

In the introductory chapter to this book we posed the question—how could we have done so well in tactics but failed so miserably in strategy? The answer we postulated then—a failure in strategic military doctrine—manifested itself on the battlefield. Because it did not focus on the political aim to be achieved—containment of North Vietnamese expansion—our so-called strategy was never a strategy at all. At best it could be called a kind of grand tactics.

As a tactic it was extremely effective. As Professor Chalmers Johnson wrote in 1973, two years before the fall of Saigon:

> Both Lin Piao and Vo Nguyen Giap identified the Vietnam war as a test case for the efficacy of people's war. The United States too saw the war as a test of methods for resisting people's war. Therefore, any study of people's war is obliged to consider Vietnam and try to find out how the test came out. . . .

> None of the people's wars of the sixties did very well, including the one in Vietnam. Vo Nguyen Giap himself has admitted a loss of 600,000 men in fighting between 1965 and 1968. . . . Moreover, by about 1970 at least 80 percent of the day-to-day combat in South

Vietnam was being carried on by regular People's Army of Vietnam (PAVN) troops. . . . Genuine black-pyjama southern guerrillas . . . had been decimated and amounted to no more than 20 percent of the communist fighting force.[15]

But tactical success is not necessarily strategic success, and tactical failure is not necessarily strategic failure. As we saw earlier, Clausewitz had said 150 years ago that military victory is only an end when it leads directly to peace—i.e., the political object of the war. Ironically, our tactical successes did not prevent our strategic failure and North Vietnam's tactical failures did not prevent their strategic success, and in strategic terms, people's war *was* a success. It caused the United States to deploy against a secondary force and exhaust itself in the effort. It also caused the Army of South Vietnam to deploy in such a manner that it could not be massed to meet a conventional North Vietnamese cross-border conventional attack.

As was noted earlier, there are those who still question the true nature of the war, including many who actually fought there. Clausewitz warned of the "*vividness* of transient impressions,"[16] and most American military experience was during 1965–1970 when we were supposedly pursuing "counterinsurgency." Few experienced the North Vietnamese conventional attacks in 1972 and 1975. Most of the writings on the war also miss its true nature. Analysis after analysis condemns the United States for its overreliance on conventional methods. Yet these conventional tactics were militarily successful in destroying guerrilla forces. They were so successful that, according to press reports, the North Vietnamese imitated these same tactics to suppress the insurgent movement in Cambodia. From bitter experience they knew that such tactics worked. The reason for the confusion is that our announced strategy was counterinsurgency. The analysts, seeking the cause of our strategic failure, naturally focused on counterinsurgency. But since the insurgency itself was a tactical screen masking North Vietnam's real objectives (the conquest of South Vietnam), our counterinsurgency operations could only be tactical, no matter what we called them.

Our failure as military professionals to judge the true nature of the Vietnam war had a profound effect. It resulted in confusion throughout the national security establishment over tactics, grand tactics and strategy, a confusion that continues to this day. As author and strategist Herbert Y. Schandler commented, "The President had one view, the JCS another, and the field commander had another."[17]

In order to sort out this confusion the remaining chapters of this book will analyze our strategic defeat in terms of the classic principles of war. These principles can provide what Colonel Charles A. Hines describes as "military planning interrogatories"—i.e., an analytical framework to reduce general principles and theoretical postulations to pragmatic and operational situations.[18] Such an approach will present the Vietnam war in its true light—not as something new and unique with no lessons for the future, but as a war best understood in terms of war itself. In so doing it should illuminate the tasks that America may have to face on future battlefields. As Army Chief of Staff General Edward C. Meyer emphasized on 4 June 1980:

> The keystone of our contribution toward peace is total competence in waging war. That expertise can only come from an ardent study of tactics and strategy. It demands that we develop a full appreciation for applying the principles of war in our decision process . . .[19]

NOTES

1. Clausewitz, *On War*, I:1, pages 88–89.
2. Not only was it not the cause of our defeat, it had little to do with the North Vietnamese victory. As Lieutenant Colonel Stuart A. Herrington put it in a recent book (*Silence Was a Weapon*, Novato, California: Presidio Press, 1982): "Like us, Hanoi had failed to win the 'hearts and minds' of the South Vietnamese peasantry. Unlike us, Hanoi's leaders were able to compensate for this failure by playing their trump card—they overwhelmed South Vietnam with a twenty-two division force."

3. Raymond Aron, "On Dubious Battles," *Parameters: Journal of the US Army War College*, Vol. X, No. 4, December 1980, pp. 2–9.

4. President Lyndon B. Johnson, Press Conference, 28 July 1965, in *Why Vietnam* (Washington, D.C.: USGPO, 1965), p. 5.

5. Joe P. Dunn, "In Search of Lessons: The Development of a Vietnam Historiography," *Parameters: Journal of the US Army War College*, Vol. IX, No. 4, 1979, p. 37.

6. Clausewitz, *On War*, II:5, pp. 156, 161, 164–65.

7. See Selig S. Harrison, *The Widening Gulf: Asian Nationalism and American Policy* (New York: The Free Press, 1978), particularly pp. 100–1, 135, 138.

8. Palmer, *Summons of the Trumpet*, p. 62.

9. *Ibid*, p. 103.

10. *Ibid*, p. 110.

11. Norman B. Hannah, "Vietnam: Now We Know," Anthony T. Bouscaren (ed), *All Quiet on the Eastern Front* (New York: Devin-Adair, 1977), p. 149.

12. Clausewitz, *On War*, I:2, p. 94.

13. *Ibid*, VIII:8, pp. 613, 614.

14. Norman B. Hannah, *All Quiet on the Eastern Front*, p. 146.

15. Johnson, *Autopsy on People's War*, pp. 46–48.

16. Clausewitz, *On War*, I:3, p. 108.

17. Interview with Colonel (USA, Retired) Herbert Y. Schandler, 13 November 1980.

18. Interview with Colonel Charles A. Hines, U.S. Army; Strategic Analyst, USAWC, on 24 December 1980.

19. Letter, Office of the Chief of Staff U.S. Army, 4 June 1980.

CHAPTER 9

THE OBJECTIVE

Every military operation must be directed toward a clearly defined, decisive and attainable objective. The ultimate military objective of war is the destruction of the enemy's armed forces and his will to fight. The objective of each operation must contribute to this ultimate objective. Each intermediate objective must be such that its attainment will most directly, quickly, and economically contribute to the purpose of the operation. The selection of an objective is based upon consideration of the means available, the enemy, and the area of operations. Every commander must understand and clearly define his objective and consider each contemplated action in light thereof.

FM 100-5, 19 February 1962[1]

THE ORIGINAL INTENT was to begin each of the chapters in Part II with a discussion of the relevant principle of war extracted from our Vietnam-era *Field Service Regulations*, the 19 February 1962 edition of Field Manual 100-5. Theoretically, these principles form the basis for Army strategic and tactical doctrine and should therefore provide a framework for analysis of our Vietnam strategy. Since the principles of war are by definition of universal application, they should also provide a basis for the evaluation of North Vietnamese strategy. As the analysis began, however, it was found that the Vietnam-era manual discussed the principles of war only in terms of their *tactical* application. Significantly, their *strategic* application was missing. In order to discover this missing dimension, it was necessary to go back to the beginning.[2]

The first official American codification of the principles of war was in *War Department Training Regulations 10–5*, 23 December 1921. In its discussion of the principles of war this manual stated that "their application to the preparation for war and the direction of war is called strategy. Their application to specific battles and operations is called tactics." This distinction was especially evident in its discussion of *The Objective*, where both its strategic and tactical dimensions were emphasized. Strategically, "the selection of objectives depends on political, military, and economic conditions, which vary in force and effect. . . . The objective assigned military forces must be in consonance with the national objective." Its discussion of the tactical dimension did not vary appreciably from the 1962 definition quoted above.[3] By 1939, however, the strategic and tactical principles had begun to diverge. Although still side by side in the manual, the strategic principle of *The Objective* was discussed under "conduct of war," defined as "the art of employing the armed forces of a nation in combination with measures of economic and political constraint for the purpose of effecting a satisfactory peace." The tactical principle was discussed in the next paragraph as "the ultimate objective . . . the destruction of the enemy's armed forces in battle."[4] After World War II the strategic definition dropped out completely, only to be reintroduced in 1954 as a result of our Korean war experiences. "Since war is a political act," the introductory chapter to the manual stated, "Its broad and final objectives are political; therefore, its conduct must conform to policy and its outcome realize the objectives of policy."[5]

It is revealing that during the course of the Vietnam war there were changes in both the strategic and tactical definitions of *The Objective*. What had been a clear relationship between military strategy and political objectives was lost in an abstruse discussion of national objectives, rejection of aggression, deterrence and the whole concept of a spectrum of war.[6] The new definition obscured the Clausewitzian dictum that "the political object—the original motive for the war—will determine both the military objective to be reached and the amount of effort it requires."[7] In tactics, there was an even more startling change. While the 1962 edition still discussed *The Objective* as requiring "the destruction of the enemy's armed forces and his will to fight," the 1968 edition reduced this to "defeat of the enemy's armed forces."[8] We had eliminated the very factor that was to cause us the greatest difficulty—the psychological objective of destruction of the enemy's will to fight. This was especially paradoxical since this was ostensibly what we were trying to do in Vietnam, having been denied the objective of destruction of the enemy's armed forces.

Our loss of focus on *The Objective* was particularly damaging, since this is the driving principle of war. Clausewitz's clarification of the importance of the objective was one of his main contributions to understanding the nature of war. He emphasized that war was not waged for its own sake but was waged to obtain a particular aim—what Clausewitz called the political object of war. As he said, "the political object is a goal, war is the means of reaching it, and means can never be considered in isolation from their purpose."[9] This loss of focus also exacerbated a common American failing—the tendency to see war as something separate and apart from the political process. World Wars I and II had been not so much wars as crusades to punish evil. Even so astute a military professional as General of the Army Douglas MacArthur saw war in this light. As he told the Senate, "the general definition which for many decades has been acceptable was that war was an ultimate process of politics; that when all of the political means failed, we then go to force."[10] This statement reflected the rejection of the Clausewitzian belief that "it is clear that war should never be thought of as something *autonomous* but always as an *instrument of policy*."[11] The truth of this dictum was brought home with a vengeance during the Vietnam war and its aftermath.

With this framework for analysis we can now turn to an examination of how the principle of *The Objective* was applied during the Vietnam war. We will begin with an analysis of North Vietnamese actions using our own frame of reference. Not only are their doctrinal manuals not available, the material that is available primarily reflects North Vietnamese declaratory strategy which was designed to continue the smoke screen of revolutionary war to mask their own aggression. It was not until after their conquest of South Vietnam that they revealed (e.g., General Dung's "Great Spring Victory") the true nature of the war. Their smoke screen was so effective that we were blinded throughout the course of the war to the point that the majority of our analyses focused on revolutionary war and the Viet Cong. Volumes have been written on their organization, structure, doctrine and tactics. According to former CIA analyst, George Allen, one of the country's foremost experts on Vietnam, such analysis distorted the true nature of the war:

> The National Liberation Front was *not* . . . a viable, autonomous organization with a life of its own; it was a facade, a "front," by means of which the DLD (the Vietnamese Communist Party) sought to mobilize the people in the south to accomplish its ends, and to garner international sympathy and support.[12]

The guerrilla himself may well have believed in the revolutionary cause and have believed that he was fighting for a revolutionary government in Saigon under southern leadership. Such beliefs were essential if his morale and fighting spirit were to be sustained. But the Viet Cong were only a means to an end. As General Weyand said in his analysis of Tet-68:

> Applying the test of *cui bono* (for whose benefit) it can be seen that the real losers of Tet-68 were the South Vietnamese Communists (the Viet Cong or PRG) who surfaced, led the attacks, and were destroyed in the process. . . . Just as the Russians eliminated their Polish competitors [with] the Warsaw Uprising, the North Vietnamese eliminated their southern competitors with Tet-68. They thereby insured that the eventual outcome of the war would be a South Vietnam dominated and controlled, not by *South* Vietnamese Communists, but by the *North* Vietnamese.[13]

As we saw earlier, after Tet-68 the majority of the day-to-day combat in Vietnam was carried out by North Vietnamese troops, and the Viet Cong had been reduced to no more than 20 percent of the Communist fighting force.

Although most of the literature on North Vietnam and the Viet Cong is misleading, that is not to say that there were no analysts who were aware of the true nature of the war. The problem was that counterinsurgency dogma had so distorted our own frame of reference that such analyses did not fit the fashion of the time. For example, in 1963, a year before the Gulf of Tonkin incident, P. J. Honey, a lecturer in Vietnamese at the School of Oriental and African Studies of the University of London, wrote:

> The clearest statement of the long-term objectives of the Lao Dong Party which has yet come to light is to be found in a secret party document captured by the French Expeditionary Corps in North Vietnam during the spring of 1952. . . . The ultimate aim of the Vietnamese Communist leadership is to install Communist regimes in the whole of Vietnam, in Laos, and in Cambodia . . .[14]

The proof of Honey's analysis is in what Clausewitz called "judgements by results." A Vietnam under the domination of the North was achieved on 2 July 1976 when the Socialist Republic of Vietnam (SRV) with headquarters in Hanoi was proclaimed. Hegemony over Laos was achieved when the Pathet Lao seized control of Vientiane in August 1975. In Cambodia the attainment of the objective was delayed by the Khmer Rouge under Pol Pot, who seized control of Phnom Penh in April 1975. On Christmas Day 1978, Vietnam launched a multidivisional cross-border attack on Cambodia to overthrow the Pol Pot government. On 7 January 1979, they announced the foundation of the People's Republic of Kampuchea. Although sporadic fighting still continues, Indo-China is effectively under Vietnamese control.

In his 1973 analysis of North Vietnamese strategy John Collins, former director of Military Strategy Studies at the National War College and now a member of the Congressional Research Service, stated that "enemy strategy can be outlined quickly, since it was simple, concise, and consistent . . . the opposition knew what they wanted to do, they had the initiative, and they had the winning combination . . . Controlling and communizing all of Indochina have always been the foe's overriding objectives."[15]

In contrast with North Vietnam who could focus all of their attention on the conquest of South Vietnam, the formulation of U.S. objectives was much more complex. It is difficult to recall now that at the beginning Vietnam did not occupy center stage and was only subsidiary to a number of other issues facing the American President. Domestic issues, for example, were a major preoccupation. Even in the area of national security the primary concern was not Vietnam per se but the larger issue of the containment of Soviet and Chinese communism. The result was that American political objectives were never clear during the entire course of the war. University of Nebraska Professor Hugh M. Arnold examined the *official* justifications most often cited for America's involvement in Indochina from 1949 through 1967.[16] Compared to the *one* North Vietnamese objective, he found some *twenty-two* separate American rationales. They can be grouped into three major categories: from 1949 until about 1962, emphasis was on resisting Communist aggression; from 1962 until about 1968, the emphasis was on counterinsurgency; after 1968, preserving the integrity of American commitments was the main emphasis.

Only once during the early period from 1949 until 1962 did the United States seriously consider commitment of U.S. ground combat forces. This was in the spring of 1954 when the French garrison at Dien Bien Phu was under siege. Then Army Chief of Staff General Matthew B. Ridgway commented on his analysis of the situation, beginning with his view on the relationship between the Army leadership and its civilian decision-makers:

> The statesman, the senior civilian authority, says to the soldier (and by "soldier" I mean the professional military man—the Army, the Navy, and the Air Force as represented in the persons of the Chiefs of Staff): "This is our national policy. This is what we wish to accomplish, or would like to do. What military means are required to support it?"

The soldier studies this problem in detail. "Very well," he says to the statesman. "Here is what your policy will require in men and guns, in ships and planes." . . .

If civilian authority finds the cost to be greater than the country can bear, then either the objectives themselves should be modified, or the responsibility for the risks involved should be forthrightly accepted. Under no circumstances, regardless of pressures from whatever source or motive, should the professional military man yield, or compromise his judgment for other than convincing military reasons. To do otherwise would be to destroy his usefulness.[17]

He then went on to analyze the situation in Indochina. Some of the factors in this analysis were revealed by his Chief of Plans and Operations, Lieutenant General James M. Gavin. As we saw in an earlier chapter, fear of China was a major consideration. General Gavin wrote that "the more we studied the situation the more we realized that we were, in fact, considering going to war with China . . . If we would be, in fact, fighting China, then we were fighting her in the wrong place on terms entirely to her advantage. . . . It seemed to us military planners that if an effort were made by the United States to secure Vietnam from Chinese military exploitation, and that if force on the scale that we were talking about were to be employed, then the Chinese would very likely reopen the fighting in Korea."[18]

As a result of his analysis General Ridgway concluded that "we could have fought in Indo-China. We could have won, if we had been willing to pay the tremendous cost in men and money that such intervention would have required —a cost that in my opinion would have eventually been as great as, or greater than, that we paid in Korea." General Ridgway went on to say that:

As soon as the full report was in, I lost no time in having it passed on up the chain of command. It reached President Eisenhower. To a man of his military experience its implications were immediately clear. The idea of intervening was abandoned, and it is my belief that the analysis which the Army made and presented to higher authority played a considerable, perhaps a decisive part in persuading our government not to embark on that tragic adventure.[19]

President Eisenhower and General Ridgway were looking at the situation in Vietnam in the traditional military
frame of reference. Their concern was U.S. ability to "destroy
the enemy's armed forces and his will to fight." This frame of
reference was obvious in a later conversation between President Johnson and former President Eisenhower in February
1965. In his biography, President Johnson relates that:

> I asked him about the possibility of Chinese Communist or Soviet
> intervention in Vietnam, the two fears expressed to me so often by
> members of Congress. Eisenhower said that if they threatened to
> intervene we should pass the word to them, quietly but firmly, that
> they should take care "lest dire results occur." He recalled how the
> armistice had been achieved finally in Korea. Talks had been going
> on inconclusively for a long time. When he became President, he
> passed three messages through secret channels to the Koreans and
> the Chinese. The gist of the messages was that if a satisfactory armis-
> tice was not signed promptly, he was going to remove the "limits we
> were observing as to the area of combat and the weapons em-
> ployed." He thought we should do the same if there were a threat of
> Chinese Communist intervention in Vietnam.

> Eisenhower saw merit . . . putting an American division into Viet-
> nam just south of the demilitarized zone to help protect the South,
> but he did not favor any large deployment at that time. Later in our
> talk he said that we could not let the Indochina peninsula fall. He
> hoped that it would not be necessary to use the six or eight divisions
> mentioned in some speculation. But if it should prove necessary, he
> said, "so be it."[20]

This traditional frame of reference was also reflected by
Lieutenant General James M. Gavin in a February 1966
article in *Harper's*. Best remembered as advocating an
"enclave strategy," General Gavin also said that "if our
objective is to secure all of South Vietnam [a strategy which
General Gavin did not advocate] then forces should be
deployed on the 17th parallel and along the Cambodian
border adequate to do this. In view of the nature of the terrain, it might be necessary to extend our defenses on the 17th
parallel to the Mekong River, and across part of Thailand.
Such a course would take many times as much force as we
now have in Vietnam."[21]

But in the early 1960s, the traditional military frame of reference appeared to have no relevance. In 1962, we had adopted a whole new frame of reference—counterinsurgency. In his discussion of the Vietnam war, British researcher Gregory Palmer points out that:

> The official view supported by the advice of Diem's British advisor, Sir Robert Thompson, was that the appropriate strategy was counterinsurgency with emphasis on depriving the enemy of the support of the population by resettlement, pacification, good administration, and propaganda. This had two awkward consequences for American policy: it contradicted the reason given for breaking the Geneva declaration, that the war was really aggression from the North, and, by closely associating the American government with the policies of the government of South Vietnam, it made Diem's actions directly answerable to the American electorate.[22]

This contradiction is reflected in the mission statement for the Military Assistance Command, Vietnam (MACV). According to General Westmoreland, MACV's objective was:

> To assist the Government of Vietnam and its armed forces to defeat externally directed and supported communist subversion and aggression and attain an independent South Vietnam functioning in a secure environment.[23]

Even a cursory mission analysis reveals two divergent specified tasks. The first specified task—"To assist the Government of Vietnam and its armed forces to defeat externally directed and supported communist subversion and aggression"—is clearly a legitimate military objective, albeit one difficult to accomplish. The second specified task—to "attain an independent South Vietnam functioning in a secure environment"—is more a political than a military objective. The confusion over objectives inherent in the MACV mission statement was to plague our conduct of the war.

Even without this confusion the task was demanding enough. To veterans of the Korean war, the first objective—defeating externally directed and supported communist subversion and aggression—must have provoked a sense of *deja vu*. Given the political restrictions against carrying the

war to North Vietnam, the words of General MacArthur in
1951 seemed to apply:

> It seems to me the worst possible concept, militarily, that we would
> simply stay there, resisting aggression, so-called . . . it seems to me
> that [the way to "resist aggression" is to] destroy the potentialities of
> the aggressor to continually hit you . . . When you say, merely, ,'we
> are going to continue to fight aggression," that is not what the
> enemy is fighting for. The enemy is fighting for a very definite
> purpose—to destroy our forces . . .[24]

But in Vietnam the situation was even worse. In the Korean
war we had come to grips with General MacArthur's com-
plaint and reconciled our political and military objectives,
while keeping our focus and attention on the external aggressor—North Korea and the Chinese Communist forces. Such
an adjustment of objectives was not unusual in war. As
Clausewitz said, "The original political objects can greatly
alter during the course of the war and may finally change
entirely *since they are influenced by events and their probable consequences.*"[25]

In Vietnam such an adjustment was never made. Instead
of focusing our attention on the external enemy, North Vietnam—the source of the war—we turned our attention to the
symptom—the guerrilla war in the south—and limited our
attacks on the North to air and sea actions only. In other
words, we took the *political* task (nation building/counter-
insurgency) as our primary mission and relegated the *military* task (defeating external aggression) to a secondary consideration. As we will see in the next chapter, the effect was a
failure to isolate the battlefield, but because of the confusion
over objectives this fact was not readily apparent. Not only
was it not apparent to the American field commander in Saigon, it was also not apparent to the decision-makers in Washington, whose decision-making process was dominated by a
management approach heavily dependent on quantification
—the so-called Planning Programming and Budget System
(PPBS)—designed for "preparation for war" rather than for
the conduct of war proper.

It is instructive to note that the 1921 definition of strategy quoted earlier in this chapter listed "preparation for war" and "direction of war" as distinct elements of strategy. They are distinct elements because "preparation for war" is primarily concerned with military economics, while "direction of war" (or "war proper") is concerned with military strategy. Failure to understand this distinction led to the attempt to conduct "war proper" with decision-making apparatus designed for "preparation for war." According to Gregory Palmer, this led to the concept of "progressive escalating pressure which would at some point cause Hanoi to cease to support the Viet Cong." As he goes on to say:

> Such a limited and specific aim, instead of the traditional military objectives such as victory or unconditional surrender, constituted a measurable and clear programmed output satisfying the requirements of PPBS. The principle of selection [of options] was to provide "maximum pressure" with minimum risk," a military translation of the economists' ratio of benefits and cost.[26]

But, as events were to prove, "measurable and clear programmed outputs" were no substitute for a well-thought-out comprehensive plan of war. As Clausewitz said:

> War plans cover every aspect of a war, and weave them all into a single operation that must have a single, ultimate objective in which all particular aims are reconciled. No one starts a war—or rather, no one in his senses ought to do so—without first being clear in his mind what he intends to achieve by that war and how he intends to conduct it. The former is its political purpose; the latter is operational objective. This is the governing principle which will set its course, prescribe the scale of means and effort which is required, and make its influence felt throughout down to the smallest operational detail.[27]

One thing we did not "intend to achieve" was victory. As we have seen, our doctrine specifically excluded it as an aim in war. Testifying before the Senate in 1966, General Maxwell Taylor said that we were not trying to "defeat" North Vietnam, only "to cause them to mend their ways." General Taylor likened the concept of defeating the enemy to

"Appomattox or something of that sort."[28] Such a war aim lacked polarity with that of our enemy, who was fighting by the old rules and who kept victory as their ultimate objective throughout the war.

There was also another critical area where we lacked polarity. Concentrating our attention on South Vietnam's internal problems rather than on the external enemy led to defining the ground war in terms of South Vietnam alone, a geographic definition that lacked symmetry with that of our enemy who made no secret of the fact that he was fighting the *Indochina* war and who used Laos and Cambodia with impunity. Unlike the China sanctuary which at least made some strategic sense in avoiding a wider war against a major adversary, the sanctuaries in Laos and Cambodia were a self-inflicted wound. The myth of their neutrality gave North Vietnam an immense tactical and strategic advantage that plagued us throughout the war.[29]

When the Nixon administration came into office in January 1969, they were aware of the inadequacy of our objectives in Vietnam. Kissinger reports that Vietnam was discussed at the new administration's first meetings of the National Security Council. The military's lack of strategic thought is revealed in Kissinger's comment that their briefings "did not offer imaginative ideas to a new President eager for them." Kissinger goes on to say, "For years, the military had been complaining about being held on a leash by the civilian leadership. But when Nixon pressed them for new strategies, all they could think of was resuming the bombing of the North."[30] In June 1969, a new mission was given to MACV. As Kissinger reports:

> The new mission statement [which went into effect on August 15] focused on providing "maximum assistance" to the South Vietnamese to strengthen their forces, supporting pacification efforts, and reducing the flow of supplies to the enemy.[31]

This new mission statement formally announced our movement into the third category of political objectives—preserving the integrity of American commitments—which had been under way since Tet-68. Through Vietnamization, resisting aggression and nation building were to become a responsibility of the South Vietnamese government. Our military objective was now withdrawal, an objective accomplished in January 1973.

The confusion over objectives detailed above had a devastating effect on our ability to conduct the war. As Brigadier General Douglas Kinnard found in a 1974 survey of Army generals who had commanded in Vietnam, "almost 70 percent of the Army generals who managed the war were uncertain of its objectives." Kinnard goes on to say that this "mirrors a deep-seated strategic failure: the inability of policy-makers to frame tangible, obtainable goals."[32]

NOTES

1. FM 100–5, 19 February 1962, p. 46.

2. Partly as a result of this book, the principles of war have been revised to include both their strategic and tactical dimension and are contained in the 1981 editions of both Field Manual 100–1 *The Army*, and Field Manual 100–5 *Operations*. An extract of these new principles is contained in Appendix A.

3. Quoted in *Maneuver in War* by Lieutenant Colonel Charles Andrew Willoughby, USA (Harrisburg, Pennsylvania: Military Service Publishing Co., 1939), p. 27.

4. FM 100–5, 1 October 1939, p. 27.

5. FM 100–5, 27 September 1954, p. 7.

6. FM 100–5, 19 February 1962, p. 4, and FM 100–5, 6 September 1968, pp. 1–2.

7. Clausewitz, *On War*, I:1, p. 81.

8. FM 100–5, 6 September 1968, p. 5–1.

9. Clausewitz, *On War*, I:1, p. 87.

10. 82nd Congress, 1st Session, *Military Situation in the Far East*, Vol. 1, p. 45.

11. Clausewitz, *On War*, I:1, p. 88.

12. Interview at USAWC on 3 March 1980.

13. Weyand, *CDRS CALL*, July-August 1976, p. 5.

14. P. J. Honey, *Communism in North Vietnam: Its Role in the Sino-Soviet Dispute* (Cambridge, Massachusetts: The M.I.T. Press, 1963), pp. 168, 170.

15. John M. Collins, *Grand Strategy: Principles and Practices* (Annapolis, Maryland: Naval Institute Press, 1973), pp. 250–51.

16. Hugh M. Arnold, "Official Justifications for America's Role in Indochina, 1949–67," *Asian Affairs*, September/October 1975, p. 31.

17. General Matthew B. Ridgway, *Soldier: The Memoirs of Matthew B. Ridgway* (New York: Harper & Bros., 1956), pp. 271–72.

18. Lieutenant General James M. Gavin, "A Communication on Vietnam," *Harper's Magazine*, February 1966, p. 16. The Hanoi Delta planning force was "eight divisions plus 35 engineer battalions and other auxiliary units."

19. Ridgway, *Soldier*, p. 277. Eight Army divisions and one Marine division were committed in the Korean war, while seven Army divisions, a division equivalent, and two Marine divisions were ultimately committed to Vietnam.

20. Johnson, *The Vantage Point*, p. 131.

21. Gavin, "A Communication on Vietnam," p. 18.

22. Palmer, *The McNamara Strategy*, pp. 99, 100. According to a 17 April 1981 *National Review* article ("No More Vietnams," pp. 403–4), the roots of the decision to concentrate on the internal war (counterinsurgency) rather than the external North Vietnamese threat grew out of the Geneva Conference on Laos in the fall of 1961. Believing Soviet assurances of Laotian neutrality, President Kennedy approved only internal support to South Vietnam and delayed making a decision on a proposal to "man the northern borders." From this point on counterinsurgency tactics dominated strategy.

23. Westmoreland, *A Soldier Reports*, p. 57.

24. 82nd Congress, 1st Session, *Military Situation in the Far East*, Part I, pp. 39, 40, 68.

25. Clausewitz, *On War*, I:2, p. 92.

26. Palmer, *The McNamara Strategy*, p. 108.

27. Clausewitz, *On War*, VIII:2, p. 579.

28. 89th Congress, 2nd Session, Senate Committee on Foreign Relations, "To Amend Further the Foreign Assistance Act of 1961 as Amended," *Vietnam Hearings*, 1966, pp. 440, 460.

29. A myth still perpetuated today in such books as William Shawcross's *Side Show: Kissinger, Nixon and the Destruction of Cambodia* (New York: Simon & Schuster, 1979). This myth flies not only in the face of reason but also in the face of the Hague Convention of 1907 which states, "A neutral country has the obligation not to allow its territory to be used by a belliger-

ent. If the neutral country is unwilling or unable to prevent this, the other belligerent has the right to take appropriate counteraction." It is informative that, in his 4 August 1981 letter to the author, former Secretary of State Dean Rusk said that "the so-called neutrality of Laos would not, in my judgment, have been an obstacle [to sealing the DMZ]."

30. Kissinger, *White House Years*, p. 238.

31. *Ibid*, p. 276.

32. Douglas Kinnard, *The War Managers* (Hanover, New Hampshire, University Press of New England, 1977), p. 25.

CHAPTER 10

THE OFFENSIVE

Offensive action is necessary to achieve decisive results and to maintain freedom of action. It permits the commander to exercise initiative and impose his will upon the enemy; to set the pace and determine the course of battle; to exploit enemy weakness and rapidly changing situations, and to meet unexpected developments. The defensive may be forced on the commander, but it should be deliberately adopted only as a temporary expedient while awaiting an opportunity for offensive action or for the purpose of economizing forces on a front where a decision is not sought. Even on the defensive the commander seeks every opportunity to seize the initiative and achieve decisive results by offensive action.

FM 100–5, 19 February 1962[1]

THE KEY TO understanding the principle of *The Offensive* is contained in the first sentence of the definition: "Offensive action is necessary to achieve *decisive results* and to maintain *freedom of action.*" The task of achieving "decisive results" requires an appreciation of the difference between the *strategic* offensive and the *tactical* offensive. As Clausewitz explained:

The original means of strategy is victory–that is, tactical success; its ends, in the final analysis, are those objects which will lead directly to peace. . . . Insofar as [a tactical battlefield victory] is not the one that will lead directly to peace, it remains subsidiary and is also to be thought of as a means. . . .[2]

In other words, *The Offensive* is strategic when it leads directly to the political objective—the purpose for which the war is being waged. When it does not lead directly to the objective it is subsidiary and its value is tactical rather than strategic. One Clausewitz calls an end, the other a means. "All these ends and means must be examined by the theorist," he said, "in accordance with their effects and their relationship to one another."[3]

In his analysis of these ends and means, Clausewitz then goes on to discuss three broad military objectives—destruction of the enemy's armed forces, occupation of the enemy's country, and destruction of the enemy's will to resist. The quickest way to attain your ends is the destruction of the enemy's armed forces or the occupation of his territory. If that is not immediately possible then one should concentrate on what Clausewitz calls "wastage" of the enemy—making the war more costly to him through laying waste to the enemy's territory, increasing the enemy's suffering, and wearing the enemy down in order to bring about a gradual exhaustion of his physical and moral positions. Yet another way is to destroy his will by operations that have "direct political repercussions."[4]

The second task inherent in the principle of *The Offensive*—"maintaining freedom of action"—is obscured by the title of the principle itself. This principle in reality has to do with maintaining initiative through both *offensive* and *defensive* action. It was further obscured by our Vietnam-era manual which discussed the principles of war only at the tactical level. The result was that it was not apparent that both the strategic offensive and the strategic defensive each have tactical offensive and defensive dimensions. While the Vietnam-era manual would lead one to believe there are only two ways to wage war—through offense or defense—there are in fact *four* variants. To find how the strategic offensive and strategic defensive could be combined with the tactical offensive and tactical defensive it was necessary to go back before the turn of the century. They are found in Colmar, Baron von der Goltz's *The Conduct of War* which was translated and republished by faculty members at the U.S. Infantry and Cavalry School at Fort Leavenworth, the precursor of the present Command and General Staff College. Baron von der Goltz concisely portrayed the four variants in tabular form:[5]

	Strategical defensive & tactical defensive	Strategical defensive & tactical offensive	Strategical offensive & tactical defensive	Strategical offensive & tactical offensive
Results therefrom—	Complete absence of a decision.	Victory on the field of battle without general results for the campaign or war.	General situation favorable for a victory, which, however, is without results because the fighting power of the enemy is not impaired.	Destruction of the enemy, conquest of his territory.

TABLE I

Some of this thinking survived through World War II. The 1939, 1941, and 1944 editions of the *Field Service Regulations* mentioned the "strategically defensive mission" in their discussion of the principle of *The Offensive*. Emerging from World War II with overwhelming superiority, the need for the strategic defensive was evidently forgotten and all references to it dropped from our doctrine. This omission, together with the evolution of the principles of war from strategic to tactical, blurred the distinction between strategic and tactical operations. This was particularly damaging since the United States had deliberately opted for the strategic *defensive* (i.e., containment) in conflicts involving the Soviet Union, China, and their client states. As Norman Podhoretz pointed out in the March 1980 *Commentary:*

In refusing to do more in Korea than repel the North Korean invasion—in refusing, that is, to conquer North Korea as the commanding general, Douglas MacArthur, and his supporters on the

Right wanted to do—the United States under Truman served notice on the world that it had no intention of going beyond containment to rollback or liberation.

Any lingering doubt as to whether this was the policy of the United States rather than the policy of the Democratic party was removed when the Republicans came into office in 1952 under Eisenhower. Far from adopting a bolder or more aggressive strategy, the new President ended the Korean war on the basis of the status quo ante— in other words, precisely on the terms of containment. And when, three years later, he refrained from going into Hungary, he made it correlatively clear that while the United States would resist the expansion of Soviet power by any and every means up to and including war, it would do nothing—not even provide aid to colonies of the Soviet empire seeking national independence and wishing to throw in their political lot with the democratic world—to shrink the territorial dimensions of Soviet control. . . .

The decision [of the Kennedy Administration] to go into Vietnam . . . followed upon the precedent of Korea in the sense that Vietnam too was a country partitioned into Communist and non-Communist areas and where the Communists were trying to take over the non-Communists by force. The difference was that whereas in Korea the North had invaded the South with regular troops, in Vietnam the aggression was taking the form of an apparently internal rebellion by a Communist faction. Very few people in the United States believed that the war in Vietnam was a civil war, but even if they had, it would have made little difference. For whatever the legalistic definition of the case might be, there was no question that an effort was being mounted in Vietnam to extend Communist power beyond an already established line. As such, it represented no less clear a challenge to containment than Korea.[6]

In other words, in pursuit of its policy of containment the United States entered the Vietnam war on the strategic *defensive*. As we will see, our failure to appreciate what this strategic posture entailed contributed to our ultimate failure.

The North Vietnamese, on the other hand, had a clear appreciation of the relationship between the strategic and tactical dimensions of the offensive. Their overall posture throughout the course of the war was the *strategic offensive* with the conquest of South Vietnam as their objective. After their initial attempt to gain their objective with guerrilla forces alone they launched a *tactical offensive* in 1964 with the commitment of regular forces. Frustrated by the massive commitment of U.S. combat ground forces, and their defeat in the battle of the Ia Drang in November 1965, they reverted to the *tactical defensive*. As they had done earlier against the French, their objective was to wear us down. This time, however, they had an added advantage. Because of our public decision not to invade North Vietnam they were able to accomplish this with an economy of force effort—Viet Cong guerrillas supplied and augmented by selected North Vietnamese regular units—while preserving the bulk of their regular forces in their homeland sanctuary. As Clausewitz said, "Resistance is a form of action aimed at destroying enough of the enemy's power to force him to renounce his intentions,"[7] and while generally on the *tactical defensive*, the North Vietnamese assumed the *tactical offensive* when it suited their purpose.

The most striking examples were the Tet Offensive in 1968 and the Eastertide Offensive in 1972. During Tet 1968 both the North Vietnamese and the Viet Cong suffered heavy losses but, while it may have been a tactical failure, it was a strategic success since, by eroding our will, they were able eventually to capture the political initiative.

"Suppose a small power is at war with a greater one," Clausewitz said; "if the political initiative lies with the smaller power, it should take the military offensive."[8] The North Vietnamese evidently thought such a moment had arrived in the spring of 1972. American public opinion was decidedly against the war, the bulk of U.S. ground combat forces had been withdrawn, and the Army of South Vietnam was still building. Leaving only one division as a strategic reserve, in March 1972 they went on the *tactical offensive* with a 12-division invasion of South Vietnam. But they overplayed their hand. The Army of South Vietnam supported by massive U.S. air power held firm and beat back the North Vietnamese with terrible losses—one estimate runs as high as 100,000 casualties.[9] Not only was it a tactical defeat, it had the potential for being a strategic defeat as well, but unfortunately, neither the United States nor South Vietnam was able to take advantage of it. Again North Vietnam switched over to the *tactical defensive*. They reconstituted their forces, kept enough pressure on South Vietnam to keep its army disposed in a counter-guerrilla mode, and waited for political conditions to improve. In the spring of 1975, the time had arrived and North Vietnam again went on the *tactical offensive*, this time with a 17-division conventional attack with the object of total military victory and the conquest of South Vietnam. This time they were successful.

That the Vietnam war was in the final analysis a conventional war best understood in terms of conventional military strategy is attested by North Vietnamese Senior General Van Tien Dung's account of the final offensive to conquer South Vietnam.[10] As we have seen, prior to this offensive North Vietnam was on the tactical defensive. Having been burnt severely in 1972 when they prematurely went over to the tactical offensive, one of their principal concerns was the state of American resolve. In October 1974 the Political Bureau and Central Military Party Committee of North Vietnam held a conference to hear its General Staff present its strategic combat plan. According to General Dung, one of the first problems raised was the question "Would the United States be able to send its troops back to the south if we launched large-scale battles that would lead to the collapse of the puppet troops?" Their conclusion was that "the internal contradictions within the U.S. administration and among U.S. political parties had intensified:

The Watergate scandal had seriously affected the entire United States and precipitated the resignation of an extremely reactionary president—Nixon. The United States faced economic recession, mounting inflation, serious unemployment and an oil crisis. Also, US allies were not on good terms with the United States and countries who had to depend on the United States also sought to escape US control. US aid to the Saigon puppet administration was decreasing. Comrade Le Duan drew an important conclusion that became a resolution: "Having already withdrawn from the South, the United

States could hardly jump back in, and no matter how it might intervene, it would be unable to save the Saigon administration from collapse.[11]

Preparation to resume the tactical offensive had been under way for some time. The North Vietnamese Rear Service General Department had been busy. As General Dung reports:

> The strategic route east of the Truong Son Range [what we labeled the "Ho Chi Minh Trail"] was the result of the labor of more than 30,000 troops and shock youths. The length of this route, added to that of the other old and new strategic routes and routes used during various campaigns built during the last war, is more than 20,000 kms. The 8-meter wide route of more than 1,000 kms, which we could see now, is our pride. With 5,000 kms of pipeline laid through deep rivers and streams and on the mountains more than 1,000 meters high, we were capable of providing enough fuel for various battlefronts. More than 10,000 transportation vehicles were put on the road . . .[12]

They had also reorganized their combat forces. "To stage large scale annihilating battles," said General Dung, "it was no longer advisable to field only independent or combined divisions. Larger mobile armies composed of various armed branches were needed . . . In 1974, Army corps were gradually formed and deployed in strategic areas most vital to insure mobility."[13] The North Vietnamese War Council next turned to a discussion of strategic objectives. According to General Dung:

> While we discussed the 1975 strategic combat plan, another very important question was raised: Where to establish the main battlefield? On all the southern battlefields the enemy had deployed his forces in a strong and mobile position. Specifically, in the First Military Region adjoining the socialist north the enemy had five mainforce divisions, and in the Third Military Region, including the Saigon defense line, the enemy had three main-force divisions from the three divisions in the Fourth Military Region.

> As for the Second Military Region, including the Central Highlands, the two main-force divisions defending it were spread over many

areas. However, the Central Highlands was a very mobile battlefield and had much potential for developing southward along Route 14, or eastward along routes 19, 7, and 21. This is an area of highlands with only small variations in altitude. There, one can easily build roads, develop his technical and mobile capabilities and bring his strength into full play. In short, this was an extremely important area strategically. The conferees unanimously approved the General Staff's draft plan which chose the Central Highlands as a main battlefield in the large-scale, widespread 1975 offensive.[14]

At 0200 hours on 10 March 1975, the North Vietnamese began their offensive, striking first at Ban Me Thuot where they concentrated three divisions against one South Vietnamese regiment. Exploiting their tactical successes and taking advantage of the South Vietnamese government's decision to abandon the highlands, they moved rapidly to consolidate their gains. As we will see in subsequent chapters, by skillful application of the principles of mass and maneuver General Dung's 17-division offensive was able to defeat the Army of South Vietnam in detail. By 29 April, his four Army corps surrounded Saigon and on 30 April 1975, the South Vietnamese government capitulated. North Vietnam's final offensive met the criteria imposed by our own doctrine. It achieved decisive results; it maintained North Vietnamese freedom of action; it permitted Senior General Dung to exercise initiative and to impose his will upon the South Vietnamese; it set the pace and determined the course of battle; and it exploited South Vietnamese weaknesses, the rapidly changing situation and unexpected developments.

In comparing U.S. strategy with that of North Vietnam, it became apparent that our error was not so much that we were on the strategic defensive (since the strategic defensive was in consonance with our national policy), but that we confused that posture with the strategic offensive. Our allies could see the difference. As Colonel Hoang Ngoc Lung, Army of the Republic of Vietnam, observed in a recent monograph for the U.S. Army Center of Military History, "The Americans had designed a purely defensive strategy for Vietnam. It was a strategy that was based on the attrition of the enemy through a prolonged defense and made no allowance for decisive offensive action."[15]

The failure to distinguish between the strategic offensive and defensive can be seen in official statements on U.S. strategy. In his 1968 report on the war in Vietnam, Admiral U. S. G. Sharp, the Commander in Chief, Pacific Command (CINCPAC) and the strategic commander for the Vietnam war, stated that the U.S. military goal was to provide a secure environment in which the citizens could live and in which all levels of legal government could function without enemy exploitation, pressure, or violence. "Our strategy to achieve this goal," he said, "consisted of three interdependent elements—the ground and air campaign in South Vietnam, the nation building effort in South Vietnam, and our air and naval offensive against North Vietnam. . . . To this end," Admiral Sharp reported, "United States, South Vietnamese, and other Free World forces went into battle to defeat the Communists and the organizations in South Vietnam. . . . We took the war to the enemy [in North Vietnam] by a vigorous and unremitting—but highly selective—application of our air and naval power."[16] As we will see, our so-called *strategic* offensive in the South was never more than a *tactical* offensive, since we were unable to carry the war to the enemy's main force—the North Vietnamese Army—and instead expended our energies against a secondary force—North Vietnam's guerrilla screen. Admiral Sharp's second strategic element—the nation building effort in South Vietnam was a task that could only be accomplished by the South Vietnamese themselves. While U.S. forces could provide a shield against external aggression from North Vietnam behind which this activity could take place, "nation building" itself was clearly an inappropriate military task. As we will see in a subsequent chapter on Coalition Warfare, it was not until we "Vietnamized" this task after 1967 that nation building became a reality. His third strategic element—our air and naval offensive against North Vietnam—was faulted by Admiral Sharp himself. As he said:

From a military standpoint, both air and naval programs were inhibited by restrictions growing out of the limited nature of our conduct of the war . . .

The bombing of North Vietnam was unilaterally stopped by the United States a number of times, for varying periods of time, in the hope that the enemy would respond by stopping his aggressive activities and reducing the scope and level of conflict. In every case the Communists used the bombing pause to rush troops and supplies to reinforce their army in South Vietnam. Such unilateral truce efforts, while judged politically desirable, accrued some temporary military disadvantages to successful prosecution of the war.[17]

But these bombing halts were more than "temporary military disadvantages." They were fatal flaws. As Clausewitz had warned:

If the enemy is to be coerced you must put him in a situation that is even more unpleasant than the sacrifice you call on him to make. The hardships of the situation must not of course be merely transient —at least not in appearance. Otherwise the enemy would not give in but would wait for things to improve. . . .[18]

Ironically, the air offensive did have a strategic impact, but its impact was not on North Vietnam. The debate over the nature of our bombing campaign produced a strategic theory that was to have a devastating effect on American offensive operations—the theory of graduated response. In his analysis of the Vietnam war, Brigadier General Dave Palmer tells how this came about:

Within the larger framework of the debate over *whether* to bomb had raged an argument over *how* to go about it. . . . Civilian planners wanted to start out softly and gradually increase the pressure by precise increments which could be unmistakenly recognized in Hanoi. Ho Chi Minh would see the tightening pattern, the theory went, and would sensibly stop the war against South Vietnam in time to avoid devastation of his homeland. Assistant Secretary of Defense John T. McNaughton dubbed the strategy "slow squeeze" and explained it in musical terms—an orchestration of activities which would proceed in crescendo fashion toward a finale. "The scenario," he wrote, "would be designed to give the United States the option at any point to proceed or not, to escalate or not, and to quicken the pace or not."

The Joint Chiefs of Staff did not like McNaughton's tune. The generals argued that if force were to be used at all it should be applied hard and fast to obtain maximum impact with minimum loss. To start lightly and escalate slowly, they held, would be like pulling a tooth bit by bit rather than all at once and getting it over with. If the purpose were to affect Hanoi's will, the Joint Chiefs said, the United States would have to hit hard at vital points and demonstrate a willingness to apply unlimited force. . . .

The intelligence community—a panel comprising members of the C.I.A., the Defense Intelligence Agency, and State's Bureau of Intelligence—entered the debate strongly on the side of the military. . . .

President Johnson overrode the objections of his intelligence and military advisors. Indeed, it is not at all clear whether Secretary McNamara ever even bothered to convey their arguments to him. Ambassador Taylor, still addressed as "General," had given his blessings to their theory, approval which apparently cancelled the objections of the Joint Chiefs of Staff. *Thus was born the strategy of "graduated response."* [19]

This Defense Department strategic concept carried over into General Westmoreland's campaign plan for the conduct of the ground war in South Vietnam—a concept of operations to be executed in three general phases:

Phase One: Commit those American and Allied forces necessary "to halt the losing trend" by the end of 1965.

Phase Two: "During the first half of 1966," take the offensive with American and Allied forces in "high priority areas" to destroy enemy forces and reinstitute pacification programs.

Phase Three: If the enemy persisted, he might be defeated and his forces and base areas destroyed during a period of a year to a year and a half following Phase II. [20]

Evidently without realizing it, this campaign plan committed the U.S. Army in Vietnam to the *strategic defensive* in pursuit of the negative aim of wearing the enemy down. In retrospect it would appear that Phase One was strategically sound, since it was the essential foundation for all future tasks. The strategic error was in calling for the reinstitution of pacification programs in Phase Two. This task should have been the responsibility of Army of the Republic of Vietnam (ARVN) forces, while U.S. forces should have been committed to isolate the battlefield by sealing off South Vietnam from North Vietnam.

As we will see in a subsequent chapter on Coalition Warfare, such a strategy was proposed in 1965 by South Vietnamese General Cao Van Vien. His plan entailed fortifying a zone along the 17th parallel from the Dong Ha in Vietnam to Savannakhet on the Lao-Thai border. He further proposed to follow this up with a landing operation at Vinh or Ha Tinh in North Vietnam to "cut off the North's front from its rear."[21] The DMZ portion of General Vien's plan paralleled a concept proposed by the Joint Chiefs of Staff in August 1965. Their plan would deny North Vietnam "the physical capability to move men and supplies through the Lao corridor, down the coastline, across the DMZ, and through Cambodia . . . by land, naval and air actions." The plan was neither approved nor rejected by the Secretary of Defense or the President.[22] General Westmoreland also favored such an operation. In April 1967 he recommended a limited reserve call-up to President Johnson which he felt was justifiable particularly if he "could get authority for a drive into Laos and possibly Cambodia and for an amphibious hook north of the DMZ." According to General Westmoreland the plan ultimately foundered on President Johnson's unwillingness to mobilize the reserves, as did a subsequent plan in the spring of 1968.[23] Reserve mobilization therefore was a key strategic factor. According to Colonel Schandler's analysis, "When the President began to search for the elusive point at which the costs of Vietnam would become unacceptable to the American people, he always settled upon [Reserve] mobilization . . . This constraint, with all its political and social repercussions, not any argument about strategic concepts or the 'philosophy' of the war, dictated American war policy."[24] policy."[24]

Although our military instincts were correct, our military leaders evidently did not feel so strongly about their strategic concepts that they were willing to "fall on their swords" if they were not adopted. In his conclusions to the study of the causes of war, Australian Professor Geoffrey Blainey made the obvious point that in war, "defeat . . . is unintended."[25] Neither our civilian nor our military leaders dreamed that a tenth-rate undeveloped country like North Vietnam could possibly defeat the United States, the world's dominant military and industrial power. Our military leaders evidently assumed that although their strategies were preferable, the United States would prevail regardless of what strategy was adopted. General Westmoreland says as much in his autobiography, even going so far as quoting Napoleon's advice that:

> A commander-in-chief cannot take as an excuse for his mistakes in warfare an order given by his sovereign or his minister, when the person giving the order is absent from the field of operations and is imperfectly aware or wholly unaware of the latest state of affairs. It follows that any commander-in-chief who undertakes to carry out a plan which he considers defective is at fault; he must put forward his reasons, insist on the plan being changed, and finally tender his resignation rather than be the instrument of his army's downfall.

Westmoreland goes on to say that "I suffered my problems in Vietnam because I believed that success eventually would be ours despite them, that they were not to be, as Napoleon put it, instruments of my army's downfall.[26] In his analysis of decision-making at the national level, Colonel Schandler found that "it does not appear that the military leaders threatened or even contemplated resigning to dramatize their differences with the opposition to the limitations on the conduct of the war insisted upon by the president and his civilian advisors."[27]

Because they made the cardinal military error of underestimating the enemy, our military leaders failed in their role as "the principal military advisors to the President." There are some who have yielded to the temptation to blame everything on the Commander in Chief, President Johnson. But even his severest critics would have to admit that he certainly did not set out to put the nation in turmoil, ruin his political career, and lose the Vietnam war. It was the duty and responsibility of his military advisors to warn him of the likely consequences of his actions, to recommend alternatives, and, as Napoleon put it, to tender their resignations rather than be the instrument of their army's downfall. In failing to press their military advice they allowed the United States to pursue a strategic policy that was faulty from the start. Instead of deliberately adopting the *strategic defensive*, and tailoring our strategies and tactics to that posture, we slipped into it almost unaware and confused it with the *strategic offensive.* In so doing we lost sight of our strategic purpose and found the truth in the Clausewitzian observation: "Defense without an active purpose is self-contradictory both in strategy and in tactics."[28] By their own failure to understand what we were about, our military leaders were not able to warn our civilian decision-makers that the strategy we were pursuing could never lead to conclusive results.

Although from 1965 until 1975 (with the exception of Tet-68 and the ill-fated Eastertide Offensive of 1972) the North Vietnamese were also in a defensive posture, there was a critical difference. The North Vietnamese were on the tactical defensive as part of a strategic offensive to conquer South Vietnam. Our adoption of the strategic defensive was an end in itself and we had substituted the negative aim of counterinsurgency for the positive aim of isolation of the battlefield. This was a fatal flaw. As Clausewitz said, "A major victory can only be obtained by positive measures aimed at a *decision*, never by simply waiting on events. In short, even in the defense, a major stake alone can bring a major gain."[29] The North Vietnamese had a major stake— the conquest of Indochina. It was the United States that was "simply waiting on events."

As we saw in the previous chapter, Clausewitz defined critical analysis as "not just an evaluation of the means actually employed, but of *all possible means*. . . . One can, after all, not condemn a method without being able to suggest a better alternative."[30] From a "purely military" standpoint it might appear that the better alternative would have been a strategic offensive against North Vietnamese armed forces and their will to fight. But, as Clausewitz warned, there is no such thing as a "purely military" strategy. Military strategy exists to serve political ends, and, as we have seen, for a variety of very practical political reasons an invasion of North Vietnam was politically unacceptable.

We were faced with essentially the same dilemma we had faced in the Korean war. Our political policy was to contain the expansion of communist power, but we did not wish to risk a world war by using military means to destroy the source of that power. We solved that dilemma in Korea by limiting our political objectives to containing North Korean expansion and successfully applied our military means to achieve that end. In Vietnam we began with just such limited objectives. Our mistake was in failing to concentrate our military means on that task. It would appear that we sensed this deficiency, since the Korean war model was essentially the alternative that General Vien, General Westmoreland and the JCS recommended. It was not identified as such because it did not fit the frame of reference we had established for ourselves. For one thing, establishment of a Korean war-type objective in the mid-1960s would have branded Army leadership as hopelessly anachronistic. As we have seen, from the perspective of our total victory in World War II, Korea still looked like a defeat and it is only from the perspective of our actual defeat in Vietnam that we can see that Korea was actually a victory. Further, there was the tyranny of fashion. Counterinsurgency, not conventional tactics, appeared to be the wave of the future. Finally, their plans hinged on the mobilization of the Reserves, a political price President Johnson was not prepared to pay.

Time and bitter experience has removed these distortions from our frame of reference. In 1977, General Bruce Palmer, Jr. (USA, Retired), former commander of U.S. Army Vietnam and former Vice Chief of Staff, U.S. Army, saw clearly what should have been done. In a seminar at the U.S. Army War

College, he said that, together with an expanded Naval block-
ade, the Army should have taken the tactical offensive along
the DMZ across Laos to the Thai border in order to isolate
the battlefield and then *deliberately* assume the strategic and
tactical defensive. While this strategy might have entailed
some of the same long-term costs of our Korean strategy, it
would (like that strategy) have furthered our political objective of containing communist expansion. He said that in his
opinion this could have been accomplished *without reserve
mobilization*, without invading North Vietnam and running
the risk of Chinese intervention, and with substantially fewer
combat forces than were actually deployed to Vietnam.

In brief, General Palmer's strategic concept called for a
five-division force (two U.S., two ROK and one ARVN) along
the DMZ with three more U.S. divisions deployed to extend
the defensive line to the Lao-Thai border. An additional U.S.
division would have been used to stabilize the situation in the
central highlands and in the Saigon area. The Marine divisions would have been held in strategic reserve, to be available to reinforce the DMZ and to pose an amphibious threat,
thereby tying down North Vietnamese forces in coastal
defense.

General Palmer believed that the advantages of such a
strategy would have been enormous. It would have required
four fewer divisions than the ten and two-thirds divisions we
actually deployed. "Moreover," he said, "the bulk of these
forces would have fought on ground of their choosing which
the enemy would be forced to attack if he wanted to invade
South Vietnam. [This would have provided U.S. forces with a
clear and understandable objective—a peace-keeping operation to separate the belligerents.] In defending well-prepared
positions, U.S. casualties would have been much fewer . . .
The magnitude and likelihood and intensity of the so-called
'Big War,' involving heavy fire power, would have been lessened [one of the main causes of U.S. public disenchantment
with the war]." He went on to say that a much smaller U.S.
logistics effort would have been required and we would have
avoided much of the base development that was of no real

value to the South Vietnamese. "Cut off from substantial out-of-country support, the Viet Cong was bound to wither on the vine and gradually become easier for the South Vietnamese to defeat," he concluded.[31] This conclusion was recently reinforced by statements of former South Vietnamese leaders who believed that by providing a military shield behind which South Vietnam could work out its own political, economic, and social problems, the United States could have provided a reasonable chance for South Vietnamese freedom and independence.[32]

Writing after the U.S. withdrawal from Vietnam, Brigadier Shelford Bidwell, editor of RUSI, the distinguished British military journal of the Royal United Services Institute, commented on the view that the war in Vietnam was unwinnable. "This is rubbish," he said, blaming our failure on our election of a strategy which "not only conferred on the North Vietnamese the privilege of operating on safe exterior lines from secure bases but threw away the advantages of a tactical and strategic initiative." He went on to note that by "using firepower of crushing intensity" we succeeded in defeating both the insurgency and the 1972 North Vietnamese offensive but at the strategic price of "American society in turmoil. . . . All this . . . would have been avoided," he said, "by adopting the classical principles of war by cutting off the trouble at the root. . . . If this was not politically realistic, then the war should not have been fought at all."[33]

Just as the North Koreans and their Chinese allies were the "root of the trouble" in the Korean war, so the root in the Vietnam war was North Vietnam (*not* the Viet Cong). In Vietnam as in Korea our political objectives dictated a strategic defensive posture. While this prevented us from destroying the "root" at the source through the strategic offensive, Korea proved that it was possible to achieve a favorable decision with the strategic defensive. It restored the status quo ante, prevented the enemy from achieving his goals with military means, and provided the foundation for a negotiated settlement. All of this was within our means in Vietnam.

NOTES

1. FM 100–5, 19 February 1962, p. 46.

2. Clausewitz, *On War*, II:2, p. 143.

3. *Ibid.*

4. *Ibid*, I:2, pp. 92–93.

5. Colmar, Baron von der Goltz, *The Conduct of War: A Brief Study of its Most Important Principles and Forms*, translated by First Lieutenant Joseph T. Dickman, 3d Cavalry, Assistant Instructor in the Art of War, U.S. Infantry and Cavalry School (Kansas City, Missouri: The Franklin Hudson Publishing Co., 1896), p. 32.

6. Norman Podhoretz, "The Present Danger," *Commentary*, March 1980, pp. 3, 4.

7. Clausewitz, *On War*, I:2, p. 93.

8. *Ibid*, VIII:5, pp. 601–2.

9. Palmer, *Summons of the Trumpet*, p. 254.

10. Senior General Van Tien Dung, "Great Spring Victory," *Foreign Broadcast Information Service* (Vol. I, FBIS-APA-76-110, 7 June 1976; Vol. II, FBIS-APA-76-131, 7 July 1976). (Afterwards "Dung, *Great Spring Victory*")

11. *Ibid*, Vol. I, pp. 5–6. For a discussion why the United States failed to respond to the North Vietnamese violation of the Paris Accords and the open invasion of South Vietnam, see McGeorge Bundy, "Vietnam, Watergate and Presidential Powers," *Foreign Affairs*, Winter 1979/80, pp. 397–407.

12. *Ibid*, p. 15.

13. *Ibid*, p. 3.

14. *Ibid*, p. 6.

15. Colonel Hoang Ngoc Lung, *Strategy and Tactics* (Washington, D.C.; U.S. Army Center of Military History, 1980), p. 71.

16. Admiral U. S. G. Sharp, USN, "Report on Air and Naval Campaigns Against North Vietnam and Pacific Command-wide Support of the War, June 1964–July 1968," *Report on the War in Vietnam* (Washington, D.C.: USGPO, 1968), p. 6.

17. *Ibid*, p. 7.

18. Clausewitz, *On War*, I:1, p. 77. For a British diplomat's view of the initial effects of bombing on Hanoi in 1967, see John Colvin, "Hanoi in My Time," *The Washington Quarterly*, Spring 1981. He believes that by halting the bombing in the fall of 1967, "victory . . . was not so much thrown away as shunned with prim, averted eyes."

19. Palmer, *Summons of the Trumpet*, pp. 75–76. (Emphasis added.)

20. Westmoreland, *A Soldier Reports*, p. 142.

21. General Cao Van Vien, "The Strategy of Isolation," *Military Review*, April 1972, p. 26.

22. Schandler, *The Unmaking of a President*, pp. 34–35.

23. Westmoreland, *A Soldier Reports*, pp. 227, 239, 355.

24. Schandler, *The Unmaking of a President*, p. 56.

25. Blainey, *The Causes of War*, p. 249.

26. Westmoreland, *A Soldier Reports*, pp. 261–62.

27. Schandler, *The Unmaking of a President*, p. 59.

28. Clausewitz, *On War*, VIII:4, p. 600.

29. *Ibid*, VIII:8, p. 616.

30. *Ibid*, II:5, p. 161.

31. General Bruce Palmer, Jr. (USA Retired), "Remarks to USAWC Elective Course, The Vietnam War," 31 May 1977 (quoted by permission).

32. General Cao Van Vien and Lieutenant General Dong Van Khuyen, *Reflections on the Vietnam War* (Washington, D.C.: U.S. Army Center of Military History, 1980), p. 81.

33. Shelford Bidwell, *Modern Warfare: A Study of Men, Weapons, and Theories* (London: Allen Lane, 1973), p. 234.

CHAPTER 11

MASS, ECONOMY OF FORCE, AND MANEUVER

MASS

Superior combat power must be concentrated at the critical time and place for a decisive purpose. Superiority results from the proper combination of the elements of combat power. Proper application of the principle of mass, in conjunction with the other principles of war, may permit numerically inferior forces to achieve decisive combat superiority.

ECONOMY OF FORCE

Skillful and prudent use of combat power will enable the commander to accomplish the mission with minimum expenditure of resources. This principle is the corollary of the principle of mass. It does not imply husbanding but rather the measured allocation of available combat power to the primary task as well as secondary tasks such as limited attacks, the defense, deception or even retrograde action in order to insure sufficient combat power at the point of decision.

MANEUVER

Maneuver is an essential ingredient of combat power. It contributes materially in exploiting successes and in preserving freedom of action and reducing vulnerability. The object of maneuver is to dispose a force in such a manner as to place the enemy at a relative disadvantage and thus achieve results which would otherwise be more costly in men and materiel. Successful maneuver requires flexibility in organization, administrative support, and command and control. It is an antithesis of permanence of location and implies avoidance of stereotyped patterns of operation.

FM 100–5, 19 February 1962[1]

THE FIRST PRINCIPLE of war, *The Objective*, focuses our attention on *what* we are to accomplish. The second principle, *The Offensive*, tells us in general terms—i.e., the strategic offensive, the strategic defensive—*how* we are to go about attaining the objective. The next three principles— *Mass*, *Economy of Force*, and *Maneuver*—elaborate on the second principle by providing more details on *how* to conduct our operations.

Mass, *Economy of Force*, and *Maneuver* describe relational action and are best understood in concert. Viewed separately, they are often misinterpreted. Even in our own manuals, for example, the 1921 definition of *Mass* concentrated on "combat power":

> The term mass as used here means combat power. Numbers, weapons, tactical skill, fighting ability, resolution, discipline, morale, and leadership all contribute to this power. Success in war is attained by the employment of mass in a main effort.[2]

Economy of Force was defined in a sentence: "The time and place of the main effort having been determined, men and means are conserved by reducing their employment in other directions." Perhaps the most striking difference is in the definition of *Maneuver*, which the 1921 edition calls "Movement" and defines in tactical terms in relationship to the effective employment of fire.[3] Although these early definitions have been replaced in our manuals, there is still a tendency to view these three principles in isolation.

Our discussion will consider these three principles in tandem in their application against what Clausewitz called the enemy's *center of gravity*—"the hub of all power and movement on which everything depends. . . . The point against which all energies should be directed." He goes on to say that:

For Alexander, Gustavus Adolphus, Charles XII, and Frederick the Great, the center of gravity was *their army*. If the army had been destroyed, they would all have gone down in history as failures. In countries subject to domestic strife, the center of gravity is generally *the capital*. In small countries that rely on large ones, it is usually *the army of their protector*. Among alliances, it lies in the *community of interest*, and in popular uprisings it is the *personalities of the leaders and public opinion*. It is against these that our energies should be directed. . . . Not by taking things the easy way . . . but by constantly seeking out the center of his power, by daring all to win all, will one really defeat the enemy.[4]

As we saw in the previous chapter, we had adopted a strategy that focused on none of the possible North Vietnamese centers of gravity—their army, their capital, the army of their protector, the community of interest with their allies, or public opinion. The center of gravity could not be the North Vietnamese Army because we had made the conscious decision not to invade North Vietnam to seek out and destroy its armed forces. For the same reason it could not be Hanoi, the North Vietnamese capital. Our desire to limit the conflict and our fear of direct Soviet and Chinese involvement prevented us from destroying "the army of their protector" (more accurately, to block the influx of massive amounts of Soviet and Chinese military assistance). The same fears prevented us (until the Nixon-Kissinger initiatives of the early 1970s) from striking at the community of interest among North Vietnam, the Soviet Union, and China. Certainly "the personalities of the leaders and public opinion" were never targets the United States could exploit. Instead, by seeing the Viet Cong as a separate entity rather than as an instrument of North Vietnam, we chose a center of gravity which in fact did not exist. The proof that the Viet Cong guerrillas were not a center of gravity was demonstrated during Tet-68, when, even though they were virtually destroyed, the war continued unabated.

Not only was the selection of a center of gravity complicated at the strategic level in Vietnam, it was also complicated at the level of what might be called "grand strategy"— America's worldwide interests. As we discussed earlier, in both Korea and Vietnam the United States was caught up in a dilemma. We entered both wars to blunt what we saw as a coordinated global communist strategy. Yet the very global nature of the threat prevented us from applying our full power in either conflict. The question in both wars was where to mass and where to use an economy of force. As Major General (then Lieutenant Colonel) Charles Andrew Willoughby commented in his definitive 1939 analysis of maneuver in war, this question determines the very structure of maneuver.[5]

As we will see in a subsequent chapter, these issues were complicated by the lack of a *strategic* headquarters for Vietnam. The view from Honolulu or Washington could be quite different than the view from Saigon. As Air Force General William Momyer commented:

> . . . CINCPACAF, and the Air Staff had held the view that the main threat to US interests in the Far East was China and that PACAF's command structure should be designed to meet that threat. Consequently [they] believed that . . . The air forces assigned to South Vietnam should be limited to those absolutely needed to COMUSMACV to accomplish his mission.[6]

While to at least some in Honolulu the question of where to mass and where to use economy of force revolved around China, in Washington it revolved around America's worldwide interests. We have discussed earlier the fact that our decision-making mechanisms in the Department of Defense were more concerned with "preparation for war" rather than "war proper." This is reflected in Alain C. Enthoven and K. Wayne Smith's analysis of how the defense program was shaped from 1961 to 1969. In their more than 300 pages of analysis only about 50 pages were devoted to the war in Vietnam. The majority of the book dealt with NATO strategy, nuclear strategy and major defense programs such as the B-70 bomber, Skybolt, and the TFX (F-111).[7]

The same was true with the uniformed military as well. For example, in his detailed analysis of Washington decision-making after Tet-68, Colonel Herbert Y. Schandler found that the genesis of the controversial 200,000 man troop reinforcement for Vietnam supposedly requested by General Westmoreland was actually an attempt by the Joint Chiefs of Staff to precipitate a reserve call-up and to obtain additional manpower to meet worldwide contingencies. As Schandler writes:

> [Then Chairman of the Joint Chiefs of Staff] General Wheeler's major worry at this time, other than preventing a defeat in Vietnam, was the state of United States forces worldwide. Because there had been no reserve call-up, resources were being stretched too thin . . . The Army had skeletonized units throughout the world in order to provide the leadership and critical skills to meet the Vietnam build-up. . . .
>
> In the face of this American military inadequacy, the North Koreans were behaving in a warlike manner. There were indications of trouble in Berlin and the Middle East. General Wheeler felt quite correctly, that if a serious emergency arose that required the commitment of United States military force to an area other than Vietnam, the United States might not be able to act. . . .
>
> The troop request that Westmoreland and Wheeler came up with was designed to meet both global and local interests.[8]

But, according to Schandler, when General Wheeler presented his recommendations he said nothing "about contingencies . . . or about reconstituting the strategic reserve for possible use independent of Vietnam."[9] The Presidential decision not to approve the troop request turned on the question of reinforcements for Vietnam. Thus, the dilemma over whether to *Mass* for Vietnam at the expense of an *Economy of Force* elsewhere in the world precipitated a major turning point in the war.

This would have come as no surprise to the North Vietnamese. According to General Palmer, as early as December 1963 the North Vietnamese Politburo had reasoned that the chances of American intervention at all were "only remote possibilities because the U.S. cannot evaluate all the disastrous consequences she might bear if she wages the war on a larger scale. She realizes that if she is bogged down in a large-scale and protracted war, she will be thrown into a very passive position in the world."[10] While their analysis was faulty in the short-term, it ultimately proved to be all too correct. They were also correct in their selection of a strategic center of gravity. They knew, especially after their battlefield defeat in the Ia Drang, that it could not be the U.S. Army. Neither could it be the Army of the Republic of Vietnam (ARVN) as long as the United States was acting as its protector. They knew they did not have the military means to threaten our homeland or even to seize Saigon, the capital of South Vietnam. Based upon their successful experiences against the French, the center of gravity that they identified was the alliance between the United States and South Vietnam, and particularly the "community of interest . . . personalities of the leaders and public opinion." As Clausewitz said, "If you can vanquish all your enemies by defeating one of them, that defeat must be the main objective of the war. In this one enemy we strike at the center of gravity of the entire conflict."[11] It is in light of this center of gravity that North Vietnamese use of *Mass, Economy of Force*, and *Maneuver* must be evaluated.

Both prior to and after the American involvement the North Vietnamese were to make almost classic use of these principles. For example, in 1964 North Vietnam launched a tactical offensive and committed its regular army to combat in the South with the objective of conquering South Vietnam before the American buildup could be completed. According to General Palmer:

> General Giap intended to gain a spectacular victory—a Southern Dien Bien Phu with all the trimmings—by slicing South Vietnam in half on the line from Pleiku through An Khe to Qui Nhon. Between October 1965 and April of 1966 he planned to commit three full North Vietnamese divisions along that axis.
>
> . . . as Giap analyzed the situation, his three divisions, jumping off from secure bases in Cambodia and closely supported by Viet Cong units native to the area being invaded, would be superior to any countering force the Americans and South Vietnamese could employ. Strong holding attacks in the vicinity of Saigon and against

populated areas near the Demilitarized Zone would tie down
reserves, while the tough terrain itself would limit the employment
of such reaction forces as Saigon could muster.[12]

North Vietnam's strategy was thus to maneuver through
"neutral" Cambodia, mass in the highlands and use an economy of force around Saigon and on the DMZ. What they had
not counted on was that the U.S. ability to mass and maneuver far exceeded their own. Not only were we able to deploy
combat forces half way around the world, but we were able
to mass them to blunt and destroy the North Vietnamese
attack. The North Vietnamese tactical offensive ended in
November 1965 with its defeat by the 1st Cavalry Division in
the Ia Drang Valley.

With American military forces committed to combat in
South Vietnam, North Vietnam had to reassess its strategy. It
was caught in the same kind of dilemma that American
strategists had wrestled with earlier in attempting to devise
doctrine to deal with the nuclear battlefield. If decisive
results were to be achieved one had to mass, but in massing
one became vulnerable to devastating enemy fire. Conversely, if one stayed dispersed and avoided destruction by
enemy fire, decisive results could not be achieved. The United
States solved this dilemma by its own massive use of fire-
power and by developing the ability through mechanization
and air mobility to mass rapidly to achieve a decisive result
and then disperse to avoid vulnerability. The North Vietnamese did not have the technical means to use the American
approach to this problem. Instead they reverted to the tactical defensive in order to buy time and wait for the erosion of
U.S. public support for the war. As they watched American
public reaction against the war begin to build, they must
have felt that their strategy was correct. Evidently in order to
hurry things along and to take advantage of the American
Presidential election scheduled for that fall, they switched
over to the tactical offensive in the spring of 1968. Using their
regular troops on the periphery to distract and overextend
American forces (such as the Khe Sanh near the DMZ), they

committed their economy of force units—the Viet Cong guerrillas—to attack the population centers. The North Vietnamese offensive was a resounding tactical failure. They expended what one analyst described as about half their entire strength—over 100,000 fighting men—without any apparent gain.[13] The North Vietnamese had violated the principle of *Mass* and they paid a predictable price. As General Palmer summed it up, "Strategically, by attacking everywhere Giap had superior strength nowhere. Simply put, he failed to mass his forces, a strategic error which he committed knowingly, but an error nonetheless. Military victories are not won by violating military principles."[14]

But, as Clausewitz explains, tactical victories (and, by the same token, tactical defeats) are not ends but means to ends. With their disastrous tactical defeat North Vietnam struck what was to prove a fatal blow against our center of gravity—the alliance between the United States and South Vietnam. Now all they had to do was wait us out. Although they committed regular troops in the South to make up for the Viet Cong losses, they did not mass them but used them as an economy of force on the tactical defensive. As we saw in the previous chapter, the North Vietnamese evidently believed that by the spring of 1972 their strategy had succeeded. They believed the United States was no longer capable of supporting South Vietnam. They then selected a new center of gravity—the destruction of South Vietnamese Armed Forces —and once again massed their forces to assume the tactical offensive. On 29 March 1972 North Vietnam launched what was to become known as the Eastertide Offensive. It began with an armored attack across the DMZ. Leaving two divisions in Laos and one as a strategic reserve, North Vietnam committed some 12 divisions—a total of about 150,000 men —to the attack on South Vietnam. Supported by tanks, heavy artillery and mobile antiaircraft units, they had some initial success. But they had severely miscalculated both the fighting ability of the South Vietnamese Army and the ability of the United States to react. As President Nixon said, "The bastards have never been bombed like they're going to be bombed this time.''[15] By July 1972, the North Vietnamese had reverted to the tactical defensive. Their attempt to mass had proven disastrous—again over 100,000 battle deaths.[16]

Given the high price the North Vietnamese paid in 1965, 1968 and 1972 when they attempted to take the offensive, it is no wonder that they were extremely cautious in 1975. As we saw in the previous chapter, one of the first questions they asked was whether the center of gravity had really shifted from the U.S.-South Vietnamese alliance to a new center of gravity—the destruction of the South Vietnamese Armed Forces and the capture of Saigon. Only when they were convinced that that was so did they again mass their forces. Their spring offensive of 1975 made classic use of the principles of *Mass, Economy of Force*, and *Maneuver*. Their use of the so-called Ho Chi Minh Trail gave them the advantage of interior lines, since they could maneuver to any place in South Vietnam faster than the South Vietnamese could react. This was especially true since their economy of force guerrilla units (by now composed mostly of North Vietnamese regulars) kept the South Vietnamese Army deployed in a counter-guerrilla mode with little ability to mass. General Dung's estimate of the situation took all of this into account. As he said:

Though the enemy forces in the Central Highlands had to be stretched to defend numerous targets and though he had only a limited mobile force in the military region, the enemy could mobilize to resist us by bringing in troops from the First and Third Military Regions if we did not launch attacks in these regions in conjunction with attacks in the Central Highlands. . . .

It followed that tactics during the Central Highlands campaign should involve, on the one hand, using forces of division or regiment size to cut communication Routes . . . in order to divide the enemy forces strategically and cut off and isolate the Central Highlands from the coastal delta . . . [and] simultaneously and actively carrying out diversionary tactics to attract the enemy to the northwestern part of the Central Highlands in order to enable our side to maintain secrecy and surprise in the south until we opened fire on Ban Me Thuot.[17]

He made a detailed analysis of relative combat power:

> A comparison with the enemy over the entire area of the campaign showed that our infantry was not much superior to the enemy's. However, because we concentrated the majority of our forces in the main area of the campaign, we achieved superiority over the enemy in this area. As for infantry, the ratio was 5.5 of our troops for each enemy soldier. As for tanks and armored vehicles, the ratio was 1.2 to 1. In heavy artillery, the ratio was 2.1 to 1.[18]

On 10 March 1975, the North Vietnamese final offensive began. At Ban Me Thuot, according to General Dung, the North Vietnamese "had nearly 3 divisions against the enemy's [sic] one regular regiment of the 23rd division and 3 civil guard multibattalion units. Thus, the enemy was in a weak and isolated position."[19]

General Dung's account of the North Vietnamese final offensive read like a Leavenworth practical exercise on offensive operations. His selection of the "center of gravity" could have come directly from Clausewitz: "The basic law of the war," said General Dung, "was to destroy the enemy's armed forces, including manpower and war material. . . . the main target of our forces was the [South Vietnamese] regular army."[20] His discussion of mass and maneuver was also classic:

> The question was to determine the correct direction for developing the operations of the Central Highlands forces in the most continuous, rapid and effective manner in order to make full use of their might in the least possible time. Such a direction must be aimed at destroying as many vital forces of the enemy as possible and strategically dividing both militarily and administratively the territory under the Thieu administration's temporary control in the south in order to upset the arrangement of strategic positions and the strategic situation of the enemy . . .[21]

Again echoing Clausewitz, General Dung said, "Since war is by definition a deadly contest, the final and decisive strategic battle is always the ultimate test of strength between two sides and demands of both sides the utmost in leadership and practical action."[22]

Like the plaque at the entrance to our own Command and Staff College—*Audace, audace, toujours audace*—the North Vietnamese General Staff charged with planning the maneuver of Dung's four Army corps worked beside a large poster which read, "Lightning speed, more lightning speed; boldness, more boldness."[23] They put the motto into practice. For example, "the army II Corps, . . . covering a distance of 900 kms . . . had been ordered to report in Bien Hoa and Ba Ria in 18 days. . . . all 2,000 vehicles of the army corps [had] to cross six big rivers while having to fight the enemy en route."[24] In words that sounded like the accounts of Patton's Third Army in World War II, General Dung reported that "cadres of the front staff had to admit somewhat ruefully that they could not draw maps quickly enough to catch up with the advance of our forces."[25] The final attack on Saigon exemplified the use of the principle of *Mass* (and of *The Objective* and *Unity of Command*). According to General Dung, "Comrade Le Duc Tho told the corps commanders . . . The enemy has 5 divisions against our 15, excluding the strategic reserve forces. Thus, we cannot fail to win victory. This has been the view of the party Central Committee."[26] In his account of the battle itself, Dung reports that "the IV Corps, after capturing Xuan Loc, had closed in on [the east]. From the southeast, the II Corps had already closed in on Long Thanh, Vung Tau, Nuoc Trong and Ba Ria . . . The 5th and 8th divisions had taken up positions [in the southwest] close to My Tho . . . From the northwestern and northern directions, . . . the I and III Corps had already closed in on Dong Du, Cu Chi, Phu Loi, Binh Duong, Lai Khe and Ben Cat."[27] The result was inevitable. At 1130 hours, 30 April 1975, Saigon surrendered.

One of the great ironies of the Vietnam war was that our technical ability to use the principles of *Mass, Economy of Force*, and *Maneuver* far exceeded that of the North Vietnamese. We proved that at the Ia Drang Valley and in countless tactical operations. Our use of these principles enabled us to frustrate the North Vietnamese offensives of 1965, 1968, and 1972. As we have seen in earlier chapters, our strategic failure to apply the principles of *The Objective* and *The Offensive* caused us to fritter away our advantage in *Mass*, *Economy of Force*, and *Maneuver* in tactical operations rather than apply them to a strategic purpose.

The South Vietnamese on the other hand did not have our advantage. It can be argued that they were defeated because of their inability to use *Mass*, *Economy of Force*, and *Maneuver*. Contrary to the accepted wisdom, we did not create South Vietnamese regular units in our own image. With the exception of their marine and airborne units, the South Vietnamese Army was much like the American militia at the beginning of the Republic. Stationed in their home areas, with their families with them on their battle positions, they had great stability for counter-guerrilla operations (as our early militia did in protecting settlers from the Indians). The North Vietnamese economy of force guerrilla screen kept them deployed countrywide in this counter-guerrilla mode. This gave them great strength in the 1972 Eastertide Offensive when American military support allowed them to fight in place and destroy the North Vietnamese attack. But this defensive strength became a weakness in 1975. As we have seen, the North Vietnamese plan was to attack them in detail. Without American military support they were unable to hold. The presence of their families on their battle positions inhibited their ability to maneuver and it proved impossible to mass the South Vietnamese Army to meet the North Vietnamese attack. It was this faulty disposition rather than lack of fighting spirit that led to their defeat. This was proven at Xuan Loc, where the 18th ARVN division (whose families had moved to safety) fought heroically and virtually destroyed three North Vietnamese divisions.

During and after the war in Vietnam there have been arguments and counter-arguments over whether we should have trained the South Vietnamese for conventional operations or for counter-guerrilla operations. These arguments miss the central point. As Clausewitz had warned, "In war, the will is directed at an animate object that reacts."[28] The key word therefore is not "conventional" or "counter-guerrilla" but *flexibility*—the ability to react to rapidly changing circumstances. It was this lack of flexibility more than any material or moral factor that contributed most to the defeat of the South Vietnamese Army and the fall of South Vietnam. Of all the "lessons learned" from the Vietnam war the need for flexibility in both thought and action is perhaps the most critical.

NOTES

1. FM 100–5, 19 February 1962, pp. 46–47.

2. War Department Training Regulations 10-5, 23 December 1921, quoted in Willoughby, *Maneuver in War*, p. 27. While much has been written about the deterioration of the American Army in Vietnam, our discussion too will take "combat power" as a given. There is no convincing evidence that the "numbers, weapons, tactical skill, fighting ability, resolution, discipline, morale, [or] leadership" of the American Army in Vietnam had any significant *strategic* limiting effect. But to say that we will take "combat power" as a given is not to say that we did not have serious morale and disciplinary problems in Vietnam. Many of these problems were the direct effect of fighting the war in a "peacetime" mode—individual replacements, 12-month tours, battlefield "cost effectiveness," statistical measures of progress [body count]—all outgrowths of a top-level management structure concerned with "preparation for war" rather than "war proper."

3. *Ibid*, p. 27.

4. Clausewitz, *On War*, VIII:4, pp. 595–96. (Emphasis added.)

5. Willoughby, *Maneuver in War*, p. 44.

6. General William W. Momyer, USAF, Ret., *Air Power in Three Wars* (Washington, D.C.: USAF Office of History, 1978), p. 70.

7. Enthoven and Smith, *How Much Is Enough.*

8. Schandler, *The Unmaking of a President*, p. 109.

9. *Ibid*, p. 111.

10. Palmer, *Summons of the Trumpet*, p. 68.

11. Clausewitz, *On War*, VIII:4, pp. 596–97.

12. Palmer, *Summons of the Trumpet*, p. 92.

13. *Ibid*, pp. 171, 208.

14. *Ibid*, p. 199.

15. *Ibid*, p. 252.

16. *Ibid*, pp. 247–55.
17. Dung, *Great Spring Victory*, Vol. I, pp. 18–19.
18. *Ibid*, p. 18.
19. *Ibid*, p. 20.
20. Dung, *Great Spring Victory*, Vol. II, p. 52.
21. *Ibid*, p. 53.
22. *Ibid*, p. 62.
23. *Ibid*, p. 64.
24. *Ibid*, p. 66.
25. *Ibid*, p. 56.
26. *Ibid*, p. 76.
27. *Ibid*, p. 84.
28. Clausewitz, *On War*, II:3, p. 149.

CHAPTER 12

UNITY OF COMMAND

The decisive application of full combat power requires unity of command. Unity of command obtains unity of effort by the coordinated action of all forces toward a common goal. While coordination may be attained by cooperation, it is best achieved by vesting a single commander with the requisite authority.

FM 100–5, 19 February 1962[1]

To UNDERSTAND ITS full meaning, it is informative to trace the evolution of *Unity of Command.* In our earliest codified version this principle was entitled "cooperation."[2] By 1939 this principle had changed to "Unity of Effort."[3] While the words changed, one common thread runs through all of these definitions: the reason for this principle is to facilitate attainment of the objective. While at the tactical level this is best achieved by vesting authority in a single commander, at the strategic level it involves political and military coordination.

Clausewitz emphasizes that war cannot be divorced from political life. "Whenever this occurs in our thinking about war," he says, ". . . we are left with something pointless and devoid of sense."[4] "If war is to be fully consonant with political objectives, and policy suited to the means available for war," said Clausewitz, then either the political and the battlefield leader should be combined in one person (a rarity in modern warfare) or the military commander in chief should be made a member of the cabinet "so that the cabinet can share in the major aspects of his activities."[5]

141

It is instructive to note that North Vietnam followed Clausewitz's instructions almost to the letter. General Vo Nguyen Giap, the military commander in chief throughout most of the war, was a member of the ruling Politburo, a Deputy Premier of the North Vietnamese Government, the Minister of Defense and Commander in Chief of the People's Army of Vietnam.[6] The degree to which political and military leadership were combined is illustrated in General Van Tien Dung's account of the final North Vietnamese offensive in 1975. From the very first page he details how the Political Bureau and the Central Military Party Committee worked together to formulate the strategic combat plan and to direct the actual combat operations.[7] For example, in April 1975, Politburo member Le Duc Tho arrived at General Dung's headquarters in South Vietnam with Hanoi's detailed plan for the final assault on Saigon. Le Duc Tho told General Dung that prior to his departure "the Politburo and Uncle Ton [North Vietnamese President Ton Duc Thang] told him that he [Le Duc Tho] would not be allowed to return if he was not successful in his mission." This Politburo decision went so far as to establish the specific combat commands for the campaign and name the field commanders.[8] North Vietnamese *Unity of Command* gave them an enormous advantage. As former Under Secretary of the Air Force Townsend Hoopes wrote in 1969, "For the enemy the war remained fundamentally . . . a seamless web of political-military-psychological factors to be manipulated by a highly centralized command authority that never took its eye off the political goal of ultimate control in the South."[9]

Turning to the United States, it would appear at first glance that our *Unity of Command* at the national level was well established both in law and in fact. The Constitution establishes the President as Commander in Chief of our armed forces and, in principle, the responsibility for strategic coordination rests with him. Then Army Chief of Staff General Douglas MacArthur stressed this point in 1932:

The national strategy of any war, that is, the selection of national objectives and the determination of the general means and methods

to be applied in obtaining them, as well as development of the broad
policies applicable to the prosecution of the war, are decisions that
must be made by the head of state, acting in conformity with the
expressed will of the Government. . . .[10]*

In stressing that fixing the objective and determining the
means are the responsibility of "the head of state, acting in
conformity with the expressed will of the Government,"
General MacArthur was echoing Clausewitz. "Despite the
great variety and development of modern war," Clausewitz
said, "its major lines are still laid down by governments . . .
by a purely political and not a military body."[11] This point is
especially important, since much of the criticism of the Vietnam war has to do with "political interference" in military
operations. Such criticism is off the mark. Our problem was
not so much political interference as it was the lack of a
coherent military strategy—a lack for which our military
leaders share a large burden of responsibility. As Clausewitz
explains:

> When people talk, as they often do, about harmful political influence
> on the management of war, they are not really saying what they
> mean. Their quarrel should be with the policy itself, not with its
> influence. . . .[12]

Although our President is nominally the Commander in
Chief of our armed forces he does not actually command
troops in the field. This has been true since 1814 when President James Madison fought—and lost—the Battle of Bladens-
burg. But, as Clausewitz observed, "A certain grasp of military affairs is vital for those in charge of general policy."[13]
Unlike the system recommended by Clausewitz—and followed by the North Vietnamese—serving American military
officers were traditionally excluded from the President's

---

*In an evident attempt to hoist General MacArthur on his own petard, this
statement was read into the record during the 1951 Senate Hearings on
the MacArthur-Truman controversy. The bomb was defused by Mac-
Arthur's observation, "As I look back, Senator, upon my rather youthful
days then, I am surprised and amazed how wise I was."

cabinet and military counsel was provided through the Secretary of War and the Secretary of the Navy. In earlier years the primary task of the President was to coordinate Army and Navy efforts. In the 1932 statement quoted earlier General MacArthur went on to say: "The issues involved are so far-reaching in their effect and so vital in the life of the Nation that . . . coordinating Army and Navy efforts should not be delegated by the Commander in Chief to any subordinate authority. Any such attempt would not constitute delegation but rather abdication."[14]

But this simple approach to *Unity of Command* was not up to the complex demands of World War II. Beginning in 1942 with the Combined Chiefs of Staff—the British and American Service Chiefs—who were organized to formulate coalition strategy, the Joint Chiefs of Staff evolved as strategic advisors to the President. This informal arrangement was institutionalized in 1947 with the creation of what was to become the Department of Defense. The Secretary of Defense was named principal assistant to the President on military matters and a member of the National Security Council. The Joint Chiefs of Staff were to be the principal military advisors to the President, the National Security Council and the Secretary of Defense, and the Chairman of the Joint Chiefs of Staff a statutory advisor to the National Security Council.[15] Measured by the problem posed by General MacArthur—coordinating Army and Navy efforts—this new command structure was a success. Even MacArthur, in his 1951 testimony, praised the cooperation he received during the Korean war from the Joint Chiefs of Staff.[16] Likewise, in his autobiography, General Westmoreland stated that during the Vietnam war "no commander could ever hope for greater support than I received from . . . General Wheeler [then Chairman of the Joint Chiefs of Staff] and the other members of the Joint Chiefs."[17]

While the establishment of the Department of Defense had removed many of the problems of inter-Service coordination, the much larger problem of coordinating military efforts so that they would serve the political objectives of the

United States remained. As Clausewitz put it, and as Mac-Arthur was to learn:

> The only question . . . is whether . . . the political point of view should give way to the purely military (if a purely military point of view is conceivable at all). . . . Subordinating the political point of view to the military would be absurd, for it is policy that creates war. Policy is the guiding intelligence and war only the instrument, not vice versa. No other possibility exists, then, than to subordinate the military point of view to the political.[18]

The Korean war reinforced the primacy of the political point of view. As Secretary of Defense George C. Marshall told the Senate:

> From the very beginning of the Korean conflict, down to the present moment, there has been no disagreement between the President, the Secretary of Defense, and the Joint Chiefs of Staff that I am aware of.

> There have been, however, and continue to be basic differences of judgment between General MacArthur, on the one hand, and the President, the Secretary of Defense, and the Joint Chiefs of Staff, on the other hand. . . .

> It became apparent that General MacArthur had grown so far out of sympathy with the established policies of the United States that there was grave doubt as to whether he could any longer be permitted to exercise the authority in making decisions that normal command functions would assign to a theater commander. In this situation, there was no other recourse but to relieve him.[19]

In discussing why the system worked, former Under Secretary of the Air Force Townsend Hoopes highlighted several factors. One was the personalities involved—i.e., Secretary of State Dean Acheson, General of the Army George C. Marshall as Secretary of Defense, General of the Army Omar Bradley as Chairman of the Joint Chiefs of Staff. Another was the National Security Council (NSC) structure. The purpose of the NSC, according to Hoopes, was:

> To bring the separate organizations and traditions of the Military Services under sufficiently central authority to ensure an end to

multiple and conflicting strategies for defending the nation and its interests; and to bring the Military Establishment as a whole into close and continuous relations with the State Department, the intelligence agencies, and the economic counselors—for the purpose of planning foreign policy, weighing its military risks, judging the demands on national resources, and coordinating day-to-day operations. . . . The NSC was designed to ensure detailed coordination of all major factors that bear upon US foreign policy decisions.[20]

As we saw earlier, in the Vietnam war the problem was not so much coordination of effort toward a common objective as it was determining that objective in the first place. Contributing to this deficiency was the erosion of the NSC structure. According to Hoopes, "President Kennedy . . . scrapped the entire structure of the NSC." Instead he chose to rely on "irregular meetings at the White House attended by the President, [Secretary of State] Rusk, [Secretary of Defense] McNamara, and [National Security Advisor] Bundy, augmented from time to time by the Chairman of the Joint Chiefs of Staff, the Director of Central Intelligence, and others . . ." President Johnson inherited "this somewhat amorphous set of arrangements for foreign policy formulation, coordination, and control." Hoopes writes that:

I believe the decisions and actions that marked our large-scale military entry into the Vietnam War in early 1965 reflected the piecemeal consideration of interrelated issues, and that this was the natural consequence of a fragmented NSC and a general inattention to long-range policy planning.[21]

Another contributing factor was the military command structure itself. The Department of Defense/Joint Chiefs of Staff were modeled for the conduct of total war where all our energies were focused on a single objective. It was neither organized nor designed for the conduct of limited war where our focus was diffused. As Hoopes pointed out, this defect was hidden during the Korean war by the personalities involved and by the NSC structure which forced the system to work in spite of itself. We were able to reinforce NATO Europe to contain the Soviet threat and fight the war in

Korea simultaneously. In Vietnam we were not so successful. Again the Department of Defense was pulled in two directions. One focus was on the containment of the Soviet Union and the need for peacetime preparedness as a credible deterrent. The other focus was on the war in Vietnam itself. The contradiction between these two missions—what Clausewitz had called "preparation for war" and "war proper"—severely inhibited our conduct of the Vietnam war. Commenting on this from his perspective as the former chief of the Pacification Program, Ambassador Robert W. Komer criticized what he called the lack of unified conflict management in the Vietnam war. Noting that no Vietnam "high command" emerged to coordinate all aspects of Washington war management, he asked "Who was responsible for conflict management of the Vietnam war?" Answering his own question, he said, "The bureaucratic fact is that below Presidential level everybody and nobody was responsible . . ." With several minute exceptions "not a single senior level official above the rank of officer director or colonel in any U.S. agency dealt full-time with Vietnam before 1969." He went on to fault the use of "peacetime planning, programming, financial, resource allocation and distribution procedures" in the conduct of the war. Komer quotes approvingly Herman Kahn's observation that Vietnam reflected a "business as usual" approach with the bureaucracy locked into a peacetime management structure.[22]

Not only was *Unity of Command* lacking in Washington, it was also lacking in the theater of operations. During World War II the strategic headquarters for the conduct of the war in Europe was originally in London but displaced forward as the war progressed. The same was true in the Pacific where MacArthur's headquarters moved from Australia to New Guinea to the Philippines in order to direct the war. During the Korean war the strategic headquarters was close by in Japan. By comparison, during the Vietnam war the so-called strategic headquarters, Pacific Command, was located in Honolulu over 5,000 miles away. Commenting on command relationships, General Westmoreland noted that:

MACV functioned not directly under the Joint Chiefs of Staff in Washington but through CINCPAC. . . . The White House seldom dealt directly with me but through the Joint Chiefs. . . . What many failed to realize was that not I but [Admiral U. S. Grant Sharp, Commander in Chief Pacific Command] was the theater commander in the sense that General Eisenhower, for example, was the theater commander in World War II. My responsibilities and perogatives were basically confined within the borders of South Vietnam . . .[23]

In his criticism of the Vietnam war, Hoopes notes that the United States was actually fighting "three separate or only loosely related struggles. There was the large-scale, conventional war . . . there was the confused 'pacification' effort, based on political-sociological presumptions of astronomical proportions . . . and there was the curiously remote air war against North Vietnam."[24] In comparison with the Korean war (especially in the early period) where all of the strategic direction came from General MacArthur's GHQ Far East Command, there was no equivalent headquarters for the Vietnam war. General Westmoreland was only the tactical commander—the equivalent of the Eighth Army Commander in the Korean war. Part of the strategic direction (especially in air and naval matters) came from Honolulu, part came from Washington and there was no coordinated unity of effort.

In his autobiography General Westmoreland discussed the need for a strategic headquarters for the conduct of the Vietnam war. He visualized a "Southeast Asia Command" under his command with headquarters in Saigon.[25] In retrospect it would appear that such a headquarters would have greatly improved *Unity of Command.* But, rather than establish a strategic headquarters in-country as General Westmoreland envisioned, it should have been established outside of the immediate war zone. This would have avoided involvement in South Vietnamese internal affairs and would have facilitated perspective on the theater as a whole, which included operations not only in Vietnam but in Laos, Cambodia and Thailand as well. Such a location may well have been available in the Philippines. Agreement from the Philippine Government was likely since they allowed U.S. use of bases at Subic Bay and Clark Air Force Base to prosecute the war and later provided a civic action team for operations in Vietnam. This strategic headquarters would have reported directly to the Secretary of Defense through the Joint Chiefs of Staff. Within Vietnam itself a tactical field army headquarters should have been established and located well forward—perhaps initially at Da Nang. The responsibility for the military advisory effort should have been delegated to a subordinate commander as was the case during the Korean war. The problem of *Unity of Command* with the Armed Forces of the Republic of Vietnam (RVNAF) will be addressed in a subsequent chapter on Coalition Warfare. Suffice it to say here that it exacerbated the major problems that already existed.

Although we did not obtain *Unity of Command* in the Vietnam war, this failing was not the cause of our defeat but rather the symptom of a larger deficiency—failure to fix a militarily attainable political objective. Without such an objective we did not have unity of effort at the national level, which made it impossible at the theater level to obtain coordinated action among the ground war in the south, the pacification effort and the air war in the north. "Unity of command," our definition states, "obtains unity of effort by the coordinated action of all forces *toward a common goal.*" But the reverse is also true. Without a common goal it is impossible to have coordinated action or to obtain either unity of effort or unity of command. Our own definition predicted the outcome. Without *Unity of Command* we could never have "decisive application of full combat power."

NOTES

1. FM 100–5, 19 February 1962, p. 47.
2. Willoughby, *Maneuver In War*, p. 27.
3. FM 100–5, 1 October 1939, p. 28.

4. Clausewitz, *On War*, VIII:6B, p. 605.

5. *Ibid*, p. 608. The translators note that "by writing that the commander-in-chief must become a member of the cabinet so that the cabinet can share in the major aspects of his activities, Clausewitz emphasizes the cabinet's participation in military decisions, not the soldier's participation in political decisions."

6. Robert J. O'Neill, *General Giap: Politician and Strategist* (New York: Praeger, 1969), p. 179.

7. Dung, *Great Spring Victory*, Vol. I, pp. 1–8, and Vol. II, pp. 56–57.

8. *Ibid*. Vol. II, p. 73.

9. Townsend Hoopes, *The Limits of Intervention* (New York: David McKay Co., Inc., 1969), p. 61.

10. 82nd Congress, 1st Session, *Military Situation in the Far East*, p. 105.

11. Clausewitz, *On War*, VIII:6, p. 608.

12. *Ibid*.

13. *Ibid*.

14. 82nd Congress, 1st Session, *Military Situation in the Far East*, p. 105.

15. *United States Government Manual 1979–1980*, pp. 95, 174, 179, 180.

16. 82nd Congress, 1st Session, *Military Situation in the Far East*, Vol. 1, p. 13.

17. Westmoreland, *A Soldier Reports*, p. 261.

18. Clausewitz, *On War*, VIII:6, p. 607.

19. 82nd Congress, 1st Session, *Military Situation in the Far East*, Part I, pp. 323, 325.

20. Hoopes, *The Limits of Intervention*, p. 3.

21. *Ibid*, pp. 3, 4, 7.

22. R. W. Komer, *Bureaucracy Does Its Thing: Institutional Constraints on US-GVN Performance in Vietnam* (Santa Monica, California: Rand Corporation, August 1972), pp. ix, 75–84.

23. Westmoreland, *A Soldier Reports*, pp. 75–76.

24. Hoopes, *The Limits of Intervention*, pp. 61–62.

25. Westmoreland, *A Soldier Reports*, pp. 76–77.

CHAPTER 13

SECURITY
AND SURPRISE

SECURITY

Security is essential to the preservation of combat power. *Security is achieved by measures taken to prevent surprise*, preserve freedom of action, and deny the enemy information of friendly forces. Since risk is inherent in war, application of the principle of security does not imply undue caution and the avoidance of calculated risk. Security frequently is enhanced by bold seizure and retention of the initiative, which denies the enemy the opportunity to interfere.

SURPRISE

Surprise can decisively shift the balance of combat power. By surprise, success out of proportion to the effort expended may be obtained. Surprise results from striking an enemy at a time, place, and in a manner for which he is not prepared. It is not essential that the enemy be taken unaware but only that he becomes aware too late to react effectively. *Factors contributing to surprise include* speed, *deception*, application of unexpected combat power, effective intelligence *and counterintelligence, to include communication and electronic security*, and variations in tactics and methods of operation.

FM 100–5, 19 February 1962[1]

THE ITALICIZED PORTIONS of the Vietnam-era definitions of *Security* and *Surprise* quoted above highlight a point made more emphatically in earlier versions—that these two principles are reciprocal. Clausewitz, in fact, links them to-

151

gether and subsumes security as an element of surprise.[2] They are also intimately related to the other principles. For example, in their introduction to German General Waldemar Erfurth's 1938 treatise on *Surprise*, the translators comment that surprise is not luck. "At bottom," they state, "the strategy of surprise is nothing but an application of the principle of *Economy of Force.*"[3] General Erfurth himself ties it into *Mass* and *Maneuver.* "Absolute superiority *everywhere* is unattainable," he observes, "hence it must frequently be replaced by relative superiority *somewhere.* To achieve relative superiority somewhere is the main objective of almost all military movements and the essential purpose of generalship. Since relative superiority will hardly be accomplished if the enemy knows the plan of concentration before the hour of attack, the principle of surprise is of importance equal to that of the principle of concentration [what we call the principle of *Mass*]."[4] He also ties it into *Unity of Command.* "Frequently, surprise reduces the unity of the enemy forces and induces the commanders of the enemy army to issue conflicting orders. . . . Modern wars offer many examples of panic, which led to the frantic flight of whole armies."[5]

We have noted earlier that all the principles of war have both tactical and strategic application. Clausewitz notes that while *Surprise* as a key element of success in war is highly attractive in theory, it is difficult to achieve in practice. "Basically surprise is a tactical device," he says. "It is very rare . . . the one state surprises another, either by an attack or by preparations for war."[6] The reason why strategic surprise is a rarity, says Clausewitz, is that "preparation for war usually takes months. Concentrating troops at their main assembly points generally requires the installation of supply dumps and depots, as well as considerable troop movements, whose purpose can be guessed soon enough."[7] General Erfurth's analysis of modern warfare agrees with that assessment:

The history of modern war shows that the chances of strategic surprise are small indeed. The question might therefore be asked whether in a war which is fought by many millions of soldiers strategic surprises are still possible at all. . . .

In modern times, secrecy can be maintained only with great difficulties . . . As a remedy, every military plan should be executed with extreme speed. Unfortunately at present ideas can not be followed by action as quickly as in earlier wars. The movements of mass armies and the regrouping of large forces require much time. A great time-lag between the conception of a plan and its execution is unavoidable. This time-lag evidently must affect secrecy . . .

Strategic surprise, therefore, in the 20th century became the most difficult military undertaking. . . . When military preparations must be undertaken in vast areas and over many months, if not years, the maintenance of a military secret must be regarded as an extraordinary achievement.[8]

Both Clausewitz and Erfurth see the necessity for a prior materiel buildup as inhibiting strategic surprise. But there is another dimension to warfare. In his discussion on *Surprise* Clausewitz notes: "One more observation needs to be made, which goes to the very heart of the matter. Only the commander who imposes his will can take the enemy by surprise." He goes on to say that:

If general moral superiority enables one opponent to intimidate and out-distance the other, he can use surprise to greater effect, and may even reap the fruits of victory where ordinarily he might expect to fail.[9]

Given the fact that strategic surprise is a rarity, it is remarkable that the Vietnam war contained three instances of such surprise. One was directed against us—the Tet Offensive of 1968. Two were directed against the North Vietnamese—the U.S. decision to intervene with ground combat forces in 1965 and the "Christmas bombing" of Hanoi and Haiphong in 1972. None of these three strategic surprises involved materiel factors. In each instance the other side knew that their adversary possessed the necessary physical capabilities. What was achieved was psychological surprise

—the unexpected exercise of one commander's will on the other. As Clausewitz had predicted, these surprises had great effect.

Discussing the U.S. decision to intervene with ground forces in 1965, Brigadier General Dave Palmer commented on how badly the North Vietnamese misread American will:

> Policy makers in Hanoi were . . . dead wrong in believing Washington would neither carry the air war into North Vietnam nor inject ground forces into the South. At the time, though, these were not bad assumptions. . . . Americans, including military leaders had been for years proclaiming the folly of engaging in a land war on the Asian continent. Indeed, many Americans themselves had been convinced by political statements promising that the United States would not get enmeshed on the ground in Vietnam. That very August [1964], as a matter of fact, President Johnson had announced publicly that he would not consider bombing North Vietnam or "committing American boys to fighting a war that I think ought to be fought by the boys of Asia to help protect their own land."
>
> Just as the North Koreans, listening to American pronouncements in 1950, had become convinced that the United States would not make a stand for Korea, so was North Vietnam convinced fourteen years later that America would not fight for Vietnam.[10]

For one of the few times in the war the United States struck directly at the North Vietnamese center of gravity. To return again to Palmer's analysis:

> Having been at least partially convinced by the oft repeated American statement that the war in Vietnam must be waged by Vietnamese, the leaders in Hanoi were dumbstruck by Washington's reaction. Consternation and disbelief were their initial reactions. Aspirations for early victory dimmed as U.S. units streamed ashore.[11]
> ashore.[11]

Strategic surprise had been achieved and in the 1965 Battle of the Ia Drang the North Vietnamese invasion had been thrown off the track. Unfortunately, as we have seen, the United States did not exploit its advantage.

It was the North Vietnamese's turn for the next strategic surprise—the Tet Offensive of 1968. General Palmer quotes a 1969 West Point textbook which states that "Giap's Tet

Offensive . . . gained complete surprise." "But why should
the Allies have been surprised?" Palmer asks. "Why did commanders ignore the ample evidence available to them?"

> The answer is more psychological than military, more emotional
> than professional. They were victims of their own sturdy optimism
> and of General Giap's shrewd staging of his deception campaign.
>
> Ever since the turning point at the Battle of the Ia Drang, the fighting
> had been going well for the Allies. They had won every encounter.
> North Vietnamese and Viet Cong forces plainly were unable to over-
> come the firepower and mobility edge possessed by the Americans.
> By late 1967, Allied forces were near the peak of their strength while
> the communists were staggering noticeably, especially after their
> most recent maulings. It was inconceivable that the battered foe
> could bounce off the mat to deliver a punch capable of knocking out
> its opponent, incomprehensible that he should even want to try.
> Articulating the attitude of the vast majority of military men in
> Vietnam, a U.S. Army intelligence officer, who had seen and dis-
> counted all the evidence of an offensive against the cities, was quoted
> as admitting, "If we'd gotten the whole battle plan, it wouldn't have
> been credible to us." [12]

In earlier chapters we saw that as a tactical offensive, Tet 68
was a resounding failure for the North Vietnamese. But we
also saw that it was a strategic success against our center of
gravity—American public opinion and the American political leadership. Discussing the effects of the Tet Offensive,
W. Scott Thompson and Donaldson D. Frizzell commented
that:

> General Giap's offensive drove a wedge between optimistic public
> pronouncements and the realities as seen on American television. In
> spite of the generally good performance of the ARVN, the war began
> to look hopeless and irrational to the American people and to Ameri-
> can leaders. In Washington, the net effect of Tet was to convince our
> leaders that success in our goals in Vietnam could not be attained by
> military means.
>
> After Tet there was a golden opportunity to exploit the weakness of
> the enemy. Instead, Washington reacted with an investigation into
> charges that American forces had been taken by surprise in the
> coordinated attacks. There was an opportunity at this point in the

war to convert military success into meaningful political gain.
Instead, our resolve obviously wavered, we began to fold our hands
and started looking for a way out of the war.[13]

The final strategic surprise in Vietnam was the so-called
"Christmas bombing" of Hanoi and Haiphong in 1972.
Earlier, in May 1972, the United States had resumed bombing of the Hanoi area in order to "force North Vietnam to
realize the futility of trying to conquer South Vietnam by
force." This bombing was halted in October 1972 when the
North Vietnamese indicated their willingness to negotiate.
According to Air Force General William W. Momyer, then
commander of the Tactical Air Command, the North Vietnamese began stalling the negotiations as soon as the bombing
had ended. "As for the suspension of the bombing campaign," he said, "the North Vietnamese evidently interpreted
it (as they had interpreted earlier suspensions) to be an indi-
cation of weakness and lack of resolve."[14] The North Vietnamese had good reason for their interpretation. American
media reaction to the bombing had been one of outrage. Congressional criticism was virulent and there was heavy public
pressure on the President to stop the bombing. But what the
North Vietnamese could not anticipate was the will of the
American Commander in Chief. In a 9 May 1972 memorandum to his National Security Advisor, President Nixon said,
"We have the power to destroy [North Vietnamese] war-
making capacity. The only question is whether we have the
will to use that power. What distinguishes me from [Presi-
dent] Johnson is that I have the *will* in spades."[15] As Clausewitz had said, "Only the commander who imposes his will
can take the enemy by surprise." On 18 December 1972,
President Nixon directed an all-out air campaign against
North Vietnam's heartland to force a settlement of the war.
According to General Momyer:

> For the first time, B-52s were used in large numbers to bring the full
> weight of airpower to bear. What airmen had long advocated as the
> proper employment of airpower was now the President's strategy—
> concentrated use of all forms of airpower to strike at the vital power

centers, causing maximum disruption in the economic, military, and political life of the country. . . .

The 11-day campaign came to a close on the 29th of December 1972 when the North Vietnamese responded to the potential threat of continued air attacks to the economic, political, social, and military life of their country. It was apparent that airpower was the decisive factor leading to the peace agreement of 15 January 1973.[16]

Proof of the fact that the principles of war are guides to judgment and not ironclad rules is the paradox that the United States was able to achieve strategic surprise because of a *lack* of strategic security. In both instances the North Vietnamese were misled by the wealth of information they had available on American public and Congressional opinion.

NOTES

1. FM 100–5, 19 February 1962, pp. 47–48.

2. Clausewitz, *On War*, III:9, p. 198.

3. General Waldemar Erfurth, *Surprise*, translation of *Die Ueberraschung im Krieg* (Berlin, 1938), by Dr. Stefan T. Possony and Daniel Vilfroy (Harrisburg, Pennsylvania: Military Service Publishing Company, 1943), p. 5.

4. *Ibid*, p. 40. Note that Erfurth could have substituted "security" for "surprise" and not lost the meaning of his observation.

5. *Ibid*, p. 41.

6. Clausewitz, *On War*, III:9, pp. 198, 199.

7. *Ibid*, p. 198.

8. Erfurth, *Surprise*, pp. 31, 39–40.

9. Clausewitz, *On War*, III:9, pp. 200–1.

10. Palmer, *Summons of the Trumpet*, p. 69.

11. *Ibid*, p. 84.

12. *Ibid*, p. 180.

13. Thompson and Frizzell, *The Lessons of Vietnam*, p. 108.

14. Momyer, *Airpower in Three Wars*, p. 33.

15. Kissinger, *White House Years*, p. 1199.

16. Momyer, *Airpower in Three Wars*, pp. 33, 242–43. It must be noted that the "Christmas bombing" was to some degree a Pyrrhic victory since

American domestic criticism of this offensive led to restrictions that made the United States impotent in the face of the 1975 North Vietnamese invasion. For a recent analysis of press criticism of the "Christmas bombing" see Martin F. Herz's *The Prestige Press and the Christmas Bombing, 1972* (Washington, D.C.: Ethics and Public Policy Center, 1980).

CHAPTER 14

SIMPLICITY

> Simplicity contributes to successful operations. Direct, simple plans and clear, concise orders minimize misunderstanding and confusion. If other factors are equal, the simplest plan is preferred.
>
> FM 100–5, 19 February 1962[1]

To A LARGE degree this last principle of war is the sum of all the others. This can be seen in its evolution in our *Field Service Regulations*. The 1921 version stressed that *Unity of Command* was an important element. The 1939 version warned against complicated *Maneuver*. The 1949 version emphasized "simplicity of plans [because] even the most simple plan is difficult to execute," and the post-Korea 1954 version added a new twist when it stated: "Simplicity must be applied to organization, methods, and means in order to produce orderliness on the battlefield."

The need for *Simplicity* in war is deceptive. We saw in an earlier chapter that defense analysts Enthoven and Smith dismissed the principles of war as "a set of platitudes that can be twisted to suit almost any situation." They went on to say that "graduates of the military academies and war colleges cannot state with any precision what strategy and force posture may be needed to support certain foreign policy objectives, because there are no great immutable military laws to determine these requirements, and few military men would claim that there are."[2] Enthoven and Smith were echoing the modern prejudice where, as John Kenneth Galbraith once observed, "obscurity is next to divinity" and each profession—especially including defense systems analysis—has developed its own obscure and obtuse jargon. Unwittingly they were also echoing Clausewitz. In war, he said, "everything looks simple; the knowledge required does not look remarkable, the strategic options are so obvious that by comparison the simplest problem of higher mathematics has an impressive scientific dignity."[3] Clausewitz goes on to say that "the military machine—the army and everything related to it—is basically very simple and therefore seems easy to manage . . . In theory it sounds reasonable enough . . . In fact, it is different, and every fault and exaggeration of the theory is instantly exposed in war."[4]

The importance of the principle of *Simplicity* can be seen in the conduct of the Vietnam war. Using this principle alone the outcome is predictable. Applying it to the principle of *The Objective*, we saw earlier that North Vietnam concentrated on one objective—the conquest of South Vietnam. By comparison the United States was caught up in the conflicting and sometimes contradictory objectives of resisting aggression and counterinsurgency. In our chapter on *The Offensive* we saw how North Vietnam pursued the strategic offensive to conquer South Vietnam by switching from the tactical offensive to the tactical defensive and back again. The United States unwittingly confused the tactical offensive for the strategic offensive and conducted the war on the strategic defensive in pursuit of a negative aim—counterinsurgency—with results that should have been foreseen. Despite our enormous technological advantage the North Vietnamese were able to apply *Mass*, *Economy of Force* and *Maneuver* to greater strategic effect than we were, particularly in their use of the guerrilla screen as an economy of force effort that caused us to dissipate our efforts. The simplicity of North Vietnamese *Unity of Command* compared to the complex and convoluted system through which the United States prosecuted the war almost speaks for itself. At the national level their Politburo and Central Military Party Committee worked in close coordination to plan and direct the war. In Washington there was no such unity of effort. As we have seen, the inherent conflict between the peacetime task of war preparation necessary for the continued containment of the Soviet Union and the wartime task of prosecuting the war in Vietnam were never reconciled. Strategic direction was fragmented among Washington, Honolulu and Saigon. Within Vietnam itself the command structure was convoluted and confused with overlapping authority and responsibility diffused among Military Assistance Command Vietnam, the Army Republic of Vietnam Joint General Staff, United States Army Vietnam and the "Free World Military Forces." Although the application of the principle of *Surprise* may have been a draw, North Vietnamese *Security* was so pervasive that it even concealed the true nature of the war to the very end.

Not only did our failure to apply the principle of *Simplicity* confuse and complicate our conduct of the war, it also had a debilitating effect on the American people. Our inability to explain in clear and understandable language what we were about in Vietnam undercut American support for the war.

Besides simplicity of operations, there was another aspect that had an adverse effect on the conduct of the war. Although not normally considered as part of the principle of *Simplicity*, living conditions, and particularly the contrast in living conditions between the headquarters (particularly in Saigon but also at the elaborate base camps throughout the country) and soldiers in the field, were at least a partial cause of American public antipathy toward the war. This blatant disparity was the source of much of the critical reporting on Vietnam. Michael Herr, one of the more critical (but also one of the more observant) reporters on the Vietnam war, summed up the feelings of many when he wrote that "sitting in Saigon was like sitting inside the folded petals of a poisonous flower."[5] To some degree this was a function of geographic proximity. The sybaritic lifestyle of the headquarters always differed from the Spartan existence in the field. Troops on the beaches at Gallipoli in World War I cynically joked that their command ship offshore could never move because it had run aground on a reef of gin bottles. Certainly in World War II life in London or Melbourne was more luxurious than life in the Ardennes or the New Guinea jungles, and the contrast between Tokyo and the trenches in Korea was equally as stark. The difference in Vietnam was that these differences were only miles apart.

But the Army was also a victim of changing times. Some years ago the British social commentator C. Northcote Parkinson wrote a lengthy review of a book on Russell of *The Times*, the first British war correspondent. Parkinson noted that during the Crimean War British generals such as Lord Raglan and Lord Cardigan who lived in luxury while their troops died in the mud for lack of food, clothing, and shelter were no more uncaring or incompetent than their predecessors had been. The crucial difference was that for the first time their actions were being reported to the British people and headlined in the daily press. The ensuing uproar caused their disgrace and the reorganization of the British Army. The advent of the television camera had just such an effect in Vietnam. Part of the problem was the nature of the beast. As *Washington Post* columnist Henry Fairlie commented in July 1980, "It is in the nature of most important events to be dull, and by nature television cannot handle the dull. . . . It is monstrously untrue that the camera cannot lie. It is the most eager and pliant of liars. [The reason the motion camera lies is that] its nature is what its name says. Motion. It needs action, and of a particular kind. . . . It is adept at catching the moment of police brutality . . . But the long hours of provocation that yielded that brutality? The camera hasn't the eye for that."[6] As every combat veteran knows, war is primarily sheer boredom punctuated by moments of stark terror. The camera can record the terror, but the boredom is just not news. Adding to this fact of life were the reporters themselves. Quartered mostly in Saigon, they saw firsthand the contrast in lifestyles, and this experience made many of them cynical. Michael Herr commented on the contradiction between the "Dial Soapers in Saigon" and the "grungy men in the jungle."[7] This contradiction most certainly influenced their reporting. In American living rooms the television nightly news could and did portray the fleshpots of Saigon in juxta-position with the tattered infantry man in the jungle. The contrast was deadly.

A final impact of this violation of the principle of *Simplicity* may have even more serious long-term effects. The "business as usual" approach to the Vietnam war at the Washington level spilled over into our combat operations in Vietnam. Base camps were constructed that were even more elaborate than the training camps constructed in the United States during World War II and attempts were made to pro-vide all the amenities of home. The effect was an inordinate number of soldiers tied down in base camp operations and a reduction in our ability to rapidly redeploy our forces. We now have a generation of combat veterans raised with a "base camp mentality." Lieutenant General Joseph M. Heiser, former commander of the 1st Logistical Command, Vietnam, commented, "There is a need to establish standards of living for troops early in a campaign . . . In the absence of such criteria, every unit will establish its own standards, usually high; and constantly strive to upgrade them. This places excessive demands on an already busy logistic system."[8]

If we attempt to duplicate this effort in future wars not only will it overload our supply systems it will also hamper our operational flexibility. We need to use the simple litmus test for *Simplicity* in combat standards of living given by Clausewitz 150 years ago. Everything that fits this test is essential; everything that does not should be discarded:

> The whole of military activity must . . . relate directly or indirectly to [combat operations]. The end for which a soldier is recruited, clothed, armed, and trained, the whole object of his sleeping, eating, drinking, and marching *is simply that he should fight at the right place and the right time.*[9]

NOTES

1. FM 100–5, 19 February 1962, p. 48.
2. Enthoven and Smith, *How Much Is Enough*, p. 90.

3. Clausewitz, *On War*, I:7, p. 119.

4. *Ibid*.

5. Michael Herr, *Dispatches* (New York: Avon Books, 1978), p. 43.

6. Henry Fairlie, "TV's Conventions Will Be a Lie," *Washington Post*, 13 July 1980, pp. E-1, E-4.

7. Herr, *Dispatches*, p. 42. See also, Elegant, *op. cit.*

8. Lieutenant General Joseph M. Heiser, *Vietnam Studies: Logistic Support* (Washington, D.C.: USGPO, 1974), pp. 259–60.

9. Clausewitz, *On War*, I:2, p. 95.

CHAPTER 15

COALITION WARFARE

The concept of territorial protection and area defense became a strategic goal in the South's determination to withstand the North's aggressive military designs, to eliminate subversive activities within the South, and to build the republic. In other words, the objectives were survival and independence. In every political situation these remained the two most important objectives of the South.

Colonel Hoang Ngoc Lung[1]
Former J-2, JGS, RVNAF

THE ABOVE MISSION statement makes clear that the Republic of Vietnam (RVN) was pursuing two complementary tasks—resisting North Vietnamese aggression and building their republic in South Vietnam—that were parallel to the goals the United States had set for itself in Vietnam. Where then did the difficulty arise? The problem becomes apparent when we compare our actions in Vietnam to our experiences in Korea. Colonel Lung's mission statement could be transferred almost word for word to the mission of the Republic of Korea (ROK) in June 1950. It too was concerned with territorial protection, elimination of subversive activities, and building the republic. The difference was in the nature of the U.S. response. In Korea our military response was aimed at resisting and repelling outside aggression. The task of eliminating subversion and building the Korean republic was left to the Government of the Republic of Korea.

Although in Korea there was a facade of United Nations' participation (15 nations furnished some 39,000 troops), the war was actually fought by a U.S.–Republic of Korea (ROK) coalition. The United States had been in the ROK since the end of World War II, first as an occupation force to disarm the Japanese and later as advisors to the ROK military. When the war began a U.S. Korean Military Advisory Group (KMAG) organization was located in the country. Instead of building on the existing KMAG structure when U.S. combat forces entered the war we instead immediately established our own headquarters. When the U.S. 24th Infantry Division —the initial combat elements—landed in Korea, the commander established a U.S. Army Forces in Korea (USAFIK) headquarters and assumed operational control of KMAG. Ten days later the Eighth Army Headquarters closed in Korea and took operational control of KMAG, which shared headquarters with the Korean Army. A proposal to make KMAG part of the Eighth Army general staff was defeated and KMAG was left a separate entity throughout the war.[2] The attention of Eighth Army was thus kept focused on the external enemy and did not become involved in the internal affairs of the Republic of Korea Government. This concentration of attention was assisted by Korean President Syngman Rhee's decision on 14 July 1950 to place his armed forces under the United Nations' command. Under authority of this command the Eighth Army commander directed the Korean Army through its own Chief of Staff. Later when ROK units were attached to U.S. units and when Korean soldiers were integrated into U.S. units (the so-called KATUSA—Korean Augmentation To The U.S. Army—program) command was exercised directly by the United States. As the official history states, "From a military point of view there was no conflict on this score."[3] Throughout the war the ROK retained its political autonomy. Although there was some divergence, especially in the latter stages, between the U.S. and ROK war aims, the U.S. position prevailed.[4]

We rejected the Korean model in Vietnam, even though there were obvious similarities. As in Korea, the commitment of American ground combat troops was preceded by a military advisory mission designed to equip South Vietnam to counter North Vietnamese aggression. Also, as in Korea, the commitment of American troops was preceded by an invasion from the north, albeit on a much smaller scale. Seeing the war from a different perspective, Australian diplomat Coral Bell commented on what she saw as "President Johnson's decision on 'Koreanization' of the war in February 1965."[5] Unfortunately the analogy was not apt. As General Maxwell Taylor stated:

> Many leading American officials, including some senior military officers, had thought from the beginning of the US troop build-up that General Westmoreland should receive operational control over the South Vietnamese forces, as the American Eighth Army commander had controlled the Korean forces from 1950 to 1953. However, in Korea the American commander was a representative of the United Nations, and he exercised operational control of all U.N. forces in that capacity. In South Vietnam, no such U.N. authority existed and a demand for operational control by the Americans would be likely to raise serious resistance among the Vietnamese whose nationalist pride was as intense as their repugnance to the charge of being American puppets. Westmoreland was firmly against such an action and strongly recommended that command relationships be regulated by the principle of cooperation and mutual support, a view which eventually prevailed.[6]

While General Taylor's analysis of South Vietnam's sensitivities was probably true before late 1964, changing circumstances—the intervention by North Vietnamese regular units and the virtual collapse of the Republic of Vietnam—caused Vietnam to more closely resemble Korea. It must be recalled that when we intervened in Korea in July 1950 the Korean Army had collapsed and President Syngman Rhee knew that his only chance for survival—and for rejuvenation of his armed forces—was to ally the ROK as closely as possible with the United States. As U.S.–ROK relations in the subsequent 30 years have demonstrated, it was the alliance with the United States that counted; the UN label was a convenient facade. Not only was the Republic of Vietnam also on the verge of collapse in the spring of 1965, the parallel with Korea was strengthened by the commitment of U.S. ground combat forces and by the 60,000 "Free World Military Forces" sent to Vietnam by other nations (a number far surpassing the 39,000 UN soldiers sent by nations other than the United States to fight in Korea). As former RVN Minister of Defense Tran Van Don wrote in 1978: [The U.S. and RVN] were fighting two separate wars against a common enemy, one of the reasons for our common military defeat. We should have had a single allied command charged with detailed coordination of all forces, as in the Korean war.[7]

While the analogy with Korea is apparent in retrospect, it was not obvious in 1965 when General Westmoreland categorically rejected the idea of a combined command:

> I consistently resisted suggestions that a single, combined command could more efficiently prosecute the war. I believed that subordinating the Vietnamese forces to U.S. control would stifle the growth of leadership and acceptance of responsibility essential to the development of Vietnamese Armed Forces capable eventually of defending their country. Moreover, such a step would be counter to our basic objective of assisting Vietnam in a time of emergency and of leaving a strong, independent country at the time of our withdrawal.[8]

General Westmoreland was technically correct and there was no single U.S.-RVN combined command. But the war was dominated by the United States and not only did we not promote "the growth of leadership and acceptance of responsibility" we also failed to "leave a strong independent country at the time of our withdrawal." In 1969, General Cao Van Vien, then Chairman of the South Vietnamese Joint General Staff (JGS), told a delegation of South Vietnamese congressmen: "We Vietnamese have no military doctrine because the command of all operations in Vietnam is in the hands, is the responsibility, of the American side. We followed the American military doctrine."[9] After the war, in a series of interviews with some 27 former high ranking South Vietnamese military and civilian leaders, the question of strategic planning was addressed. The respondents made it clear that:

> There was little strategic planning; that, in fact, Saigon, which had no strategy of its own when the Americans were in the country, also failed to develop a real strategy after they had left . . . These respondents pointed to their weak and ineffective General Staff, their poor and unimaginative leadership, or the unfortunate conditioning of their leaders by the Americans.[10]

Colonel Hoang Ngoc Lung, former JGS J-2, in a separate analysis of Vietnam strategy and tactics, emphasized that "the Americans . . . dictated the grand strategy of the conflict. With their monopoly over weaponry and equipment, they also shaped how that strategy would be executed, what tactics and techniques would be employed."[11] We had deliberately opted for cooperation to coordinate our actions in Vietnam. In so doing we violated our own principle of *Unity of Command*. As it states, "While coordination may be attained by cooperation, it is best achieved by vesting a single commander with the requisite authority."[12]

Not only did we not follow the Korean model on *Unity of Command*, we also did not follow it on the principle of *The Offensive*. In Korea we saw clearly that the primary military task was repelling external aggression and (after the Chinese intervention) had deliberately adopted the Strategic defensive to accomplish that end. The South Vietnamese had also seen the importance of this task. According to Colonel Lung:

> In 1965, when US forces started pouring into the South, the Minister of Defense, General Cao Van Vien, wrote a paper entitled "The Strategy of Isolation" in which he likened the task of stopping infiltration to that of turning off the faucet of a water tank. General Vien advocated turning off the faucet through the isolation of North Vietnam. He would fortify a zone along the 17th parallel from Dong Ha to Savannakhet and follow this with a landing operation at Vinh or Ha Tinh, just north of the 18th parallel, cutting off the North's front from its rear. In 1972 General Vien published the original paper with the following added conclusions: "In her alliance with the United States, Vietnam was hamstrung in her action, causing her strategy to be confined to the defensive."[13]

Ironically, although we did not realize we were on the strategic defensive in Vietnam, this fact was apparent to our enemies. Colonel Lung writes that "Vo Nguyen Giap observed that the reason the U.S. imposed restrictions on targets in the North was to prevent the Vietnam war from adversely affecting political, economic, social, and diplomatic objectives of the United States. . . . In other words," Lung continues, "the American strategy, according to Giap, was designed to accomplish American objectives." Given that U.S. support and intervention was at that time critical to the survival of South Vietnam, "the leaders of the South had no rational alternative but to accept American leadership in strategy."[14]

As we have seen, that strategy did not focus on the primary threat. In a 1976 interview, former South Vietnamese Secretary of Defense Tran Van Don stated his belief that no strategy could have been successful unless it effectively stopped the infiltration from the North, a task General Don thought could have been done. Elaborating on this, former I Corps commander Lieutenant General Ngo Quang Truong said that in hindsight halting infiltration was the most critical requirement. He believed that South Vietnam could have solved its internal problems if the infiltration could have been brought under control. Once that had been stopped, everything else would have been "easy."[15] General Truong's comment is telling. As he said, "South Vietnam could have solved its internal problem if the infiltration could have been brought under control." Conversely, the opposite was also true—if the infiltration could not be brought under control South Vietnam could never solve its internal problems. And his comment is telling in another sense. The United States could (as it had done in Korea) bring the infiltration from the North under control. What the United States could never do was "solve the internal problems" of South Vietnam. Only the Vietnamese themselves could accomplish that task.

A clue to why coalition warfare failed in Vietnam was given by a North Vietnamese Army (NVA) major in Hanoi a week before Saigon's fall. "You should not feel badly," he said. "You have done more than enough . . . more than enough."[16] Even worse than the mortification of being in the enemy's capital while he is celebrating your defeat is the humiliation of his trying to lessen your discomfort with reassuring words. Yet the NVA major was more correct than he knew. We failed in Vietnam because we attempted to do too much. Instead of concentrating our efforts on repelling external aggression as we had done in Korea we also took upon ourselves the task of nation building. This was an error we never made in Korea. Although the situation in South Korea was far worse in June 1950, with their government in disorderly retreat, their economy destroyed and their social fabric torn to shreds, we did not intervene but left the resolution of their internal problems to the ROK government.

Why didn't we do the same thing in South Vietnam? There are several reasons for our overinvolvement. One has to do with the climate of the times. Observers have faulted our intervention in Vietnam as evidence of American arrogance of power—attempts by the United States to be the World's Policeman. But there is another dimension to American arrogance, the international version of our domestic Great Society programs where we presumed that we knew what was best for the world in terms of social, political, and economic development and saw it as our duty to force the world into the American mold—to act not so much the World's Policeman as the World's Nanny. It is difficult today to recall the depth of our arrogance. In March 1962, discussing the degree to which American military advisors become political—"directing, influencing, or even managing the local government's policies and operations"—the editors of *Army* wrote: "Although the official U.S. policy is to refrain from injecting Americans into foreign governments *under our tutelage and support*, the pragmatic approach is to guide the *inexperienced and shaky* governments of the emerging nations by *persuasion and coaxing* if possible, and by *hard-selling and pressure* if the soft methods don't work."[17] In his examination of the roots of our Vietnam involvement Norman Podhoretz noted the fact that the Kennedy administration "was, if anything, more zealous in its commitment to containment than the Eisenhower administration had been." In fact, "the new strategic doctrine of the Kennedy administration had been conceived precisely for the purpose of [not only containment in the conventional sense but] meeting . . . indirect non-overt aggression, intimidation and subversion, and internal revolution." The only dissent within the Kennedy administration to intervention in Vietnam "came from those who argued that military measures would fail unless we also forced the South Vietnamese government to undertake programs of liberal reform." But as Podhoretz points out, "this argument implicitly called for a greater degree of American intervention than the dispatch of troops alone (and led eventually to the assassination of Diem and the assumption of complete American responsibility for the war)."[18]

Earlier this overinvolvement had been minimal, since the concentration was on conventional containment of potential North Vietnamese aggression rather than counterinsurgency. According to Ambassador Komer, from 1954 to 1959 "MAAG concentrated . . . on preparing ARVN for a conventional, delaying action against what it regarded as the most serious threat: a conventional, Korea-style NVA attack across the DMZ."[19] "In sum," continued Komer, "little was done during 1954–1960 to develop an effective counterinsurgency capability . . ."[20] As Clausewitz had warned, "In war, the will is directed at an animate object that *reacts*"[21] and the North Vietnamese reacted to ARVN's growing conventional capability by stepping up the guerrilla war. From one extreme we swung to the other. Where earlier we had emphasized conventional forces, after 1960 the emphasis was on counterinsurgency. From only 335 U.S. military advisors in 1954, advisor strength grew to about 3,150 by April 1962. This was half again as large as the 2,000 U.S. advisors with KMAG at the height of the Korean war.

In 1964, MACV adopted a series of terms to describe the basic missions performed by the *Vietnamese* military forces in support of the counterinsurgency effort. These ranged in intensity from "search and destroy" operations designed to find, fix, fight, and destroy enemy forces to "clearing operations" to drive large enemy forces out of populated areas to "securing operations" to protect pacification teams.[22] But again the North Vietnamese reacted by committing conventional forces to the war in the south. ARVN collapsed under this increased pressure and the decision was made to commit U.S. ground combat forces to the war.

It was here that the basic error was made in the conduct of the war. Instead of leaving ARVN to pursue the counterinsurgency mission, assisted at least initially by U.S. combat forces, and concentrating U.S. efforts on repelling North Vietnamese aggression, the U.S. instead committed the United States forces in support of counterinsurgency. There were several reasons why this error was committed. First, as we saw earlier, was our misapprehension that North Vietnam was a Chinese proxy and our fear that any effort against the North Vietnamese would bring China into the war. Allied with this was the mythology surrounding Laotian and Cambodian neutrality which prevented us from sealing off the infiltration routes. Second was the gradual nature of the Vietnam war which promoted inertia. In Korea there was a clear break between the advisory phase of our involvement and the war-fighting phase. As we saw earlier, the KMAG commander did not become the field army commander, but instead was relegated to a subordinate position once American troops were committed. The KMAG headquarters did not become the field army headquarters, but was left co-located with the headquarters of the Korean Army. The Eighth Army headquarters established itself in the field in close proximity to its combat elements.

In Vietnam this clear break did not occur. General Westmoreland and his Military Assistance Command Vietnam were already located in Saigon in close proximity to the South Vietnamese government and to the headquarters of the South Vietnamese military. The tendency was therefore to build on the existing structure and to continue the emphasis on South Vietnamese internal security rather than reorienting the effort to confront North Vietnam. Finally there was the nature of our counterinsurgency doctrine itself. Our doctrine failed to clearly differentiate between what a beleaguered nation could and should do for itself and the limits of assistance an outside power could provide. Failure to understand and apply these differences led the United States to involve itself in nation building tasks that only the South Vietnamese could ultimately accomplish and diverted our attention from the tasks that were within our capability.

When American combat units arrived in country in 1965, General Westmoreland positioned them to support the counterinsurgency effort he had begun earlier as military advisor to the South Vietnamese. U.S. Army combat divisions were scattered throughout the country. Against the North Vietnamese along the DMZ he placed the units least organized and equipped for sustained defensive operations—the 1st and 3rd U.S. Marine Divisions.[23] This initial deployment may have been justified to blunt the ongoing North Vietnamese offensive and allow ARVN to regain its balance. But even after the situation had been stabilized U.S. Army units continued to be committed to "search and destroy" operations in support of counterinsurgency, and the Marines with their Combined Action Platoons pursued counterinsurgency with a vengeance. As we have seen, they enjoyed great tactical success. But it was at a fatal strategic price. Almost all of the criticism of the U.S. actions in Vietnam have to do with "search and destroy" operations—Ben Suc and My Lai being but two examples. In a postwar reassessment General Westmoreland himself acknowledged the adverse effect of U.S. public opinion:

> The term "search and destroy" fed a general American abhorrence for the destruction that warfare inevitably produces. A few graphic newspaper photographs and TV shots of American troops setting fire to thatched-roof huts were enough to convince many that "search and destroy" operations were laying waste to civilian property and the land. Yet, in reality, the operations were directed primarily against military installations—bunkers, tunnels, rice and ammunition caches, and training camps. . . .[24]

"There was no alternative to 'search and destroy' type operations, except, of course, a different name for them," General
Westmoreland said. "One can point to few cases, if any, in
military history where victory was achieved by passive
defense."[25] General Westmoreland was more correct than he
knew. Our *tactical offensives* in "search and destroy" operations in South Vietnam masked the fact that in reality we
had committed ourselves and our South Vietnamese allies to
just such a *passive strategic defense.* As we have seen, the
alternative was an *active* strategic defense to deny North
Vietnamese infiltration and isolate the battlefield.

It was not until after the war had already been lost on the
American homefront that we put counterinsurgency in
proper perspective as a valuable adjunct to our military
operations against North Vietnam. According to Ambassador
Komer (who admittedly is not an unbiased source), it was
only after the creation of CORDS (Civil Operations and
Revolutionary Development Support) in May 1967 that
genuine progress was made toward countering the insurgency. Although CORDS was ostensibly under the military
this organization resulted in greater U.S. civilian influence
than had ever existed before.[26]

General Creighton Abrams, then MACV Commander,
told Ambassador Komer that "the in-depth U.S. advisory
network became the 'glue' that held the situation together in
many respects at the critical local level." "If Pacification
1967–1971 can be adjudged at least a partial success," said
Komer, "it was largely due to the expanded CORDS advisory
effort . . . At its peak strength, around the end of 1969,
CORDS had about 6,500 military and 1,100 civilians
assigned to it. . . . They were advising over 900,000 Vietnamese in every district and province of Vietnam—over
500,000 RF/PF, 50,000 RD cadre, 80,000 police, and on the
order of 300,000 civil servants—on a wide variety of civil
and military matters. Their cumulative impact has been
incalculable."[27] But while the CORDS effort may have been
a short-term success it had serious long-term disadvantages.
After the fall of Saigon an unnamed high-ranking ARVN

staff officer was asked, "What mistakes do you think the Americans made in preparing South Vietnamese to fight this war?" "Two things," he replied. "First, when American troops came to Vietnam, they try to do everything. And make the Vietnamese lose the initiative . . . So the Vietnamese don't rely on themselves. They rely on the Americans."[28]

In his mission analysis of the RVN, Colonel Lung stated that "the South's national goals and strategy were based on the assumption that full American support would be available until proven unnecessary. This assistance was perceived as being part of the U.S. strategy which followed the end of World War II with respect to the containment of Communism in Asia as well as in Europe."[29] This was to prove a faulty assumption. For one thing, the North Vietnamese had been successful in following Clausewitz's advice that one way to win a war is "to disrupt the opposing alliance, or to paralyze it."[30] Our successes with CORDS were paralleled by a decline in American public support for the Vietnam war after Tet-68. U.S. domestic public pressure was pushing for an end to U.S. involvement and for a withdrawal of U.S. forces. Soon after President Nixon took office in 1969 the policy of "Vietnamization" was born. According to Colonel Lung the objectives of this program were to turn over military responsibility to the South by giving it sufficient strength to withstand invasion, to reduce American losses, and to maintain U.S. obligations and interests in Asia while heading toward peace. The trouble was, said Colonel Lung, that the Vietnamese had "missed the vital point: a new *strategy* had been announced by the Americans." He went on to say that:

> Vietnamization was more than modernization and expansion of the RVNAF; it was essentially a strategy that would require the Vietnamese to survive with greatly reduced American participation. Had President Thieu and the Joint General Staff fully realized this fact, perhaps they would have begun then to build a strategy to cope with it. Instead, the RVNAF made no adjustments in doctrine, organization or training to compensate for the departure of American troops and firepower.[31]

Another reason it was a faulty assumption was that there had been a fundamental change in U.S. strategy. The strategy of containment of communism in Asia lost its focus with the 1971 presidential visit to China. Not only that, as Norman Podhoretz argues, Vietnamization was actually "the model or paradigm of a new strategy of retreat." Vietnam was to be "the paradigmatic testing-ground of [that] new strategy . . . of containment through surrogate power." But, "in the case of Vietnam, not only was the surrogate power unable to hold the line on its own, but in the event, the United States refused even to provide it with the promised aid to defend itself against a military invasion encouraged and supplied with massive quantities of Soviet arms."[32] In the end the exercise of coalition warfare by the U.S. and RVN came to a close on a note sounded by Clausewitz a century and a half earlier:

> One country may support another's cause, but will never take it so seriously as it takes its own. A moderately-sized force will be sent to its help; but if things go wrong the operation is pretty well written off, and one tries to withdraw at the smallest possible cost.[33]

There are several ironic postscripts to this analysis of coalition warfare. On 25 July 1969, President Nixon had announced a new approach to U.S. security assistance based at least in part on our experiences in Vietnam. In what came to be known as the "Nixon doctrine" he said that while we would keep our treaty commitments, would provide a nuclear shield, and would continue to provide military and economic assistance as appropriate, "we shall look to the nation directly threatened to assume the primary responsibility of providing the manpower for its defense."[34] The irony was that the "Nixon doctrine" described almost exactly what the Soviet Union and the People's Republic of China had been doing since the start of the war. They had provided a nuclear shield that had been an effective deterrent against a U.S. invasion of North Vietnam. They had provided massive amounts of military equipment to North Vietnam. But they had not intervened with their own ground combat troops and had left the actual conduct of the war to the North Vietnamese. This gave the North Vietnamese an advantage. According to Bui Diem, former RVN Ambassador to Washington:

> American support, even when it was militarily effective, was not an unmixed blessing . . . The enemy, of course, even though he was maneuvering between Moscow and Peking and therefore may have seemed to possess a modicum of independence, was solidly dependent on foreign support, too. However, he had the advantage of having no foreign troops in his ranks, and his allies . . . disguised their influence quite effectively, whereas the United States did not . . .[35]

Another irony is in the results of the war. One of the primary reasons we got involved in the first place was to check Chinese communist expansion. According to Hugh Arnold's analysis of the official justifications for U.S. involvement in Vietnam, "The general threat of communism is the rationale most often given for U.S. actions in Indo-China . . . fifty-seven percent of all the material analyzed contained a reference with some variety of communism. The Chinese threat was cited [five times] more frequently than the Russian."[36] Australian diplomat Coral Bell cites as the root of this justification "Secretary of State John Foster Dulles's assumption, after the Geneva Conference in 1954, that any extension of the area of Ho Chi Minh's control in Vietnam . . . would mean a dangerous enlargement of the area of China's effective power."[37] This attitude undoubtedly grew out of our experience in Korea, where the United States and China engaged in a bitter war. But in Korea both nations emerged "winners." Thirty years later China still has a buffer state on its northeastern frontier and South Korea is still an independent nation. In Vietnam, on the other hand, the Chinese succeeded in deterring a ground attack on North Vietnam and the United States succeeded in avoiding a war with China. But the strategic result of these successes was that we both lost. China now has a hostile state allied with its most dangerous enemy (the Soviet Union) on its southern border and the independent nation of the Republic of Vietnam in the south has ceased to exist.

But, as Clausewitz said, "In war the result is never final." The outcome is "merely a transitory evil, for which a remedy may still be found in political conditions at some later date."[38] The degree to which political conditions have changed since the Vietnam war was revealed in a 4 June 1980 address by Assistant Secretary of State for East Asian and Pacific Affairs Richard Holbrooke. "On the Southeast Asian mainland, the focus of bitter mutual hostility less than a decade ago," he said, "we now share many objectives in common with China . . ."[39]

NOTES

1. Lung, *Strategy and Tactics*, p. 6.

2. Major Robert K. Sawyer, *Military Advisors in Korea: KMAG In Peace and War* (Washington, D.C.: USGPO, 1962), pp. 135, 155–56.

3. Roy H. Appleman, *U.S. Army in the Korean War: South to Naktong, North to the Yalu* (Washington, D.C.: USGPO, 1960), pp. 112, 385–89.

4. The divergence was on the question of the unification of Korea. See Harrison, *The Widening Gulf*, p. 242.

5. Coral Bell, *The Asian Balance of Power*, p. 7.

6. Taylor, *Swords and Plowshares*, p. 350.

7. Tran Van Don, *Our Endless War*, Presidio Press, San Rafael, CA, 1978, p. 156.

8. Westmoreland, *Report on the War in Vietnam*, p. 104.

9. Stephen T. Hosmer, et al, *The Fall of South Vietnam: Statements by Vietnamese Military and Civilian Leaders* (Santa Monica, California: Rand, December 1978), p. 46.

10. *Ibid*, p. 47.

11. Lung, *Strategy and Tactics*, p. 73.

12. FM 100–5, 19 February 1962, p. 47.

13. Lung, *Strategy and Tactics*, p. 72. General Vien's article was published in *Military Review* in April 1972.

14. *Ibid*.

15. Hosmer, *The Fall of South Vietnam*, p. 45.

16. Conversation on 25 April 1975 in Hanoi between Colonel Harry G. Summers, Jr. and Major Huyen, North Vietnamese Army.

17. Norman and Spore, *Big Push in Guerrilla War*, p. 34. (Emphasis added.)

18. Podhoretz, "The Present Danger," p. 4.

19. Komer, *Bureaucracy Does Its Thing*, p. 41.

20. *Ibid*, p. 130.

21. Clausewitz, *On War*, III:3, p. 149.

22. Westmoreland, *Report on the War in Vietnam*, p. 91.

23. Westmoreland, *A Soldier Reports*, pp. 162–64, 168.

24. Thompson and Frizzell, *The Lessons of Vietnam*, p. 64.

25. *Ibid*.

26. Komer, *Bureaucracy Does Its Thing*, pp. 114–18.

27. *Ibid*, p. 123.

28. Hosmer, *The Fall of South Vietnam*, p. 37.

29. Lung, *Strategy and Tactics*, pp. 6–7.

30. Clausewitz, *On War*, I:2, p. 92.

31. Lung, *Strategy and Tactics*, pp. 49, 56.

32. Podhoretz, "The Present Danger," p. 6.

33. Clausewitz, *On War*, VIII:6, p. 603.

34. Kissinger, *White House Years*, pp. 222–25.

35. Hosmer, *The Fall of South Vietnam*, p. 38.

36. Arnold, *Official Justifications*, pp. 35–36.

37. Coral Bell, *The Asian Balance of Power*, p. 8.

38. Clausewitz, *On War*, I:1, p. 80.

39. Richard Holbrooke, "China and the U.S.: Into the 1980s, *Current Policy No. 187* (Washington, D.C.: Department of State, June 1980), p. 2.

TO PROVIDE FOR
THE COMMON DEFENSE

It was significant . . . that [the] metaphoric use of "picture" [as in "The Big Picture"] had come into vogue at the time when all the painters of the world had finally abandoned lucidity.

Evelyn Waugh
Officers and Gentlemen (1955)[1]

WAUGH'S OBSERVATION, BASED on his World War II experience, gives us an insight into an understanding of the Vietnam war. Vietnam was not a canvas by Daumier or even by Degas. It was more an abstract by Dali or De Kooning. Yet, as art critics would tell us, even these abstracts follow certain truths of color and composition. The same is true in war. "Critical analysis," said Clausewitz, "is the application of theoretical truths to actual events."[2] The preceding analysis has applied the theoretical truths of the principles of war to the actual events of the Vietnam war to produce an explanation for our failure there.

If we are to profit by our mistakes, we must understand that it was a violation of these truths, not evil or wicked leaders, that was the cause of our undoing. As David Halberstam pointed out in *The Best and the Brightest*,[3] one of the saddest aspects of the war is that it was waged by well-meaning and intelligent men doing what they thought best.

The tendency to find devils, however, is still with us. A recent CBS television special[4] would have us believe that it was General Westmoreland's deliberate underestimation of enemy strength that did us in. But as General Eisenhower found out at the Battle of the Bulge, estimation of enemy strength is always obscured by the fog of war. In fact, the usual tendency is to overestimate. For example, during the Civil War, President Lincoln sarcastically told a visitor that the rebels had "1,200,000 troops in the field according to the best authority. You see," he went on, "all of my generals, when they get whipped, say the enemy outnumbers them from three to five to one and I must believe them. We have 400,000 men in the field, and three times four makes twelve. Do you see it?"[5] But as Clausewitz warned, "A critic should . . . not check a great commander's solution to a problem as if it were a sum in arithmetic. To judge . . . it is necessary for a critic to take a more comprehensive point of view."

> If a critic points out that a Frederick or a Bonaparte made mistakes, it does not mean that he would not have made them too. He may even admit that in the general's place he might have made far greater errors. What it does mean is that he can recognize these mistakes . . . based on the pattern of events and therefore also *on their outcome.*[6]

"Based on the pattern of events and . . . their outcome" makes it obvious that the problem in Vietnam, as in the early days of the Civil War, was not evil leaders or faulty arithmetic as much as it was a lack of strategic thinking. As George Allen, one of the CIA's primary Vietnam analysts put it, it wasn't so much the numbers, "it was a fundamental question of the soundness of our policy, of our whole approach to the war."[7]

This lack of understanding of the "Big Picture" was not peculiar to Vietnam. It is a common failing. Writing about 14th century warfare, Barbara Tuchman observed that "what moved knights to war was desire to do deeds of valor . . . not the gaining of a political end by force of arms. They were concerned with action, not the goal—which was why the goal was so rarely attained."[8] Fifty years before Clausewitz, Marshal Maurice de Saxe observed that "very few men occupy themselves with the higher problems of war. They pass their lives drilling troops [an essential skill, by the way, for 18th century *tactical* success] and believe that this is the only branch of the military art. When they arrive at the command of armies they are totally ignorant, and in default of knowing what should be done, they do what they know."[9]

In Vietnam we also did what we knew. As was said in the introduction to this book, in "logistics and in tactics . . . we succeeded in everything we set out to do."[10] But, as we have seen, our failure in strategy made these skills irrelevant. This is the lesson we must keep in mind as we look to the future. While we will still need "deeds of valor" and proficiency in logistics and tactics, we must insure that these skills are applied in pursuit of a sound strategy.

As we devise a strategy for the future, we must begin with a mission analysis of the tasks assigned us by the American people by their elected representatives in the Congress. The National Security Act of 1947, as amended, specifies three primary missions: defend the American homeland from external attack; safeguard our internal security; and uphold and advance the national policies and interests of the United States, including insuring the security of areas vital to those interests.

Although our military policies are often justified in terms of the first mission—protection of the homeland—it is the third mission—protection of American worldwide interests—that has most often led to the commitment of American armed forces. It was easier to say "fight them in Vietnam or fight them in the streets of San Francisco" than it was to attempt to explain the complex network of interests behind our Vietnam policy, and "protection" is much less open to argument than "interests" over which one may or may not agree. But as Vietnam illustrated, this divergence between what we were doing and what we said we were doing led to such serious problems as the "credibility gap" and the loss of public support. As Senator Jacob Javits observed, "We have failed to perceive that people will probably respond to arguments made on the basis of enlightened self-interest. . . . The apocalyptic language of the past has tended to deceive those who used it as well as those who got the message."[11] In the future we must take care to avoid jeopardizing American public support for their military with misstatements—either intentional or unintentional—of what we are about.

Another fact we must remember is that we are not very good at predicting future events. For example, as we emerged from World War II the locality of our next conflict—Korea—could not even be found on world maps. It was still labeled by its Japanese name, Chosen. By the same token, as we emerged from the Korean war the maps of the world did not show Vietnam. It was still part of French Indochina. It is as true now as it was then that we cannot know the future. While scenarios of likely conflict areas are of some utility in contingency planning, we must not become so fixated by such scenarios that we lose our flexibility to cope with real conflicts.

We must also understand the nature of military forces themselves. They are designed, equipped and trained for a specific task: to fight and win on the battlefield. They are, in effect, a battle-ax. In the past we have tried to use them to accomplish tasks for which they were not designed—nation building in Vietnam being the most recent case in point. Perhaps the most dangerous misuse of military force is the attempt to bluff a potential adversary when they do not have the necessary combat power (the combination of both materiel and moral strength) to carry out the threat if the bluff is called. If we are to use our armed forces to deter a potential adversary, we must remember Clausewitz's warning:

> Combat is the only effective force in war; its aim is to destroy the enemy's forces as a means to a further end. *That holds good even if no actual fighting occurs, because the outcome rests on the assumption that if it came to fighting, the enemy would be destroyed.*[12]

With this background we can now examine the tools with which to apply our military judgment to national security issues. Among these "tools" are the principles of war. As Professor Peter Paret pointed out in his new translation of Carl von Clausewitz's *On War*, such theories are not designed to serve as immutable rules but instead give "points of reference and standards of evaluation . . . with the ultimate purpose not of telling [us] how to act but of developing [our] judgment."[13] In other words, as Colonel Charles Hines put it, they provide "military planning interrogatories," a series of questions that provide a framework for analysis. The first question, "What are we trying to accomplish with the use of military force?", is contained in the principle of *The Objective*. The second principle, *The Offensive*, helps us with the next question, "How are we going to do it?" The principles of *Mass, Maneuver, Economy of Force, Security* and *Surprise* refine the question of the means to be applied. "Who is going to control it?" is covered by *Unity of Command*. Finally, the principle of *Simplicity* serves as a check on the clarity of our thinking.

The first principle of war is the principle of *The Objective*. It is the first principle because all else flows from it. It is the strategic equivalent of the mission statement in tactics and we must subject it to the same rigorous analysis as we do the tactical mission. How to determine military objectives that will achieve or assist in achieving the political objectives of the United States is the primary task of the military strategist, thus the relationship between military and political objectives is critical. Prior to any future commitment of U.S. military forces, our military leaders must insist that the civilian leadership provide tangible, obtainable political goals. The political objective cannot be merely a platitude, but must be stated in concrete terms. While such objectives may very well change during the course of the war, it is essential that we begin with an understanding of where we intend to go. As Clausewitz said, we should not "take the first step without considering the last."[14]

For example, it is not good enough to say that our armed forces are to protect access to vital raw materials. General Sir John Hackett pointed out in a recent article on the military requirements for protecting oil supplies how complex the application of the principle of *The Objective* can become. First, he said, we have to determine our objective *area:*

> In choosing an area of operations it would first be necessary very clearly to specify the requirement. This can be identified in four degrees:
> - to supply U.S. needs alone;
> - to supply U.S. needs plus those of Japan;
> - to supply U.S. needs plus those of NATO allies;
> - to supply U.S. needs plus those of NATO allies *and* Japan.

Once the objective *area* has been determined, we must then decide the actual objective of the operation. Hackett goes on to say:

> Such operations could only be said to have succeeded if they satisfied five requirements.
> - to seize the vital oil installations virtually intact;
> - to secure them for weeks, months and even years;
> - to restore wrecked resources rapidly;
> - to operate installations with little or no cooperation from the owners;
> - to guarantee the safe passage of petroleum products from the area and supplies to it.

As Hackett concludes, "It would be idle to pretend that there are not truly formidable difficulties to be faced here."[15]

It can be seen that the selection of objectives is not an easy task. Even the seemingly simple matter of "protecting access to vital raw materials" becomes complicated when applied to a specific situation. Yet, if we don't have the firm objectives, if we don't know where we are going, it is impossible to determine when we get there. That was one of the major problems of Vietnam and it will continue to be a problem in the future if we do not determine precisely what we are attempting to achieve with the use of military force. In other words, we (and perhaps what is more important, the American people) need to have a definition of "victory." This victory need not be a total destruction of the enemy or the complete conquest of his territory. It need only be the attainment of a political goal that prompted our involvement, such as the restoration of the status quo in the Korean war. It also should be recognized that in obtaining a decision on the precise definition of the objective, there is an inherent contradiction between the military and its civilian leaders. For both domestic and international political purposes the civilian leaders want maximum flexibility and maneuverability and are hesitant to fix on firm objectives. The military, on the other hand, need just such a firm objective as early as possible in order to plan and conduct military operations.

What we are faced with is the obverse of the problem President Kennedy faced when he issued an order in 1961 directing the Joint Chiefs of Staff to be "more than military men."[16] Just as the military need to be aware of political, economic and social issues, so our civilian leadership must be aware of the imperatives of military operations. They need to understand that national policy affects not only selection of the military objective but also the very way that war is conducted. As Clausewitz put it, the primacy of policy in war rests on the assumption that "policy knows the instrument it means to use. . . . A certain grasp of military affairs is vital for those in charge of general policy."[17]

Carrying the war to the enemy and the destruction of his armed forces and his will to fight through the strategic offensive is the classic way wars are fought and won, hence the second principle of war is labeled *The Offensive*. For the past generation, however, U.S. national policy vis-à-vis our major adversary has rejected the strategic offensive (roll-back or liberation) in favor of the strategic defensive (containment). While it might appear on the surface that *The Offensive* is no longer valid, the essence of this principle is primarily concerned with maintaining initiative and freedom of action in the face of the enemy. Maintaining initiative and freedom of action is easiest on the strategic offensive, but it can also be done on the strategic defensive. It is instructive to remember that Waterloo, one of the most decisive battles in history, was won on the strategic defensive. Recently some critics of our NATO strategy have argued for a declaratory posture of the strategic offensive rather than the strategic defensive in the event of war in Europe. They need to understand, however, that such a change requires not only a change in military strategy but, more importantly, a change in national policy, for army strategies must, at all times, be in consonance with national policy, as must the doctrines and tactics that flow from these strategies.

Redefining this principle in terms of *initiative* rather than purely in terms of offensive action also highlights another dimension. In order to maintain initiative, commanders at all levels, both strategic and tactical, must be allowed maximum freedom of action. Such freedom of action at the strategic level appears to have suffered a lasting blow during the Truman-MacArthur controversy, when General MacArthur's actions (in then Secretary of Defense George Marshall's words) raised "grave doubt as to whether he could any longer be permitted to exercise the authority in making decisions that normal command functions would assign to a theater commander."[18] If we are to operate at full efficiency, the military must regain the trust of its civilian leaders for, even with instantaneous modern communications, only the commander on the ground can react to the rapidly changing situations of the modern battlefield. One of the beneficial contributions of such critics as John Boyd and Edward Luttwak has been the public resurfacing of the military importance of delegation of authority and mutual trust as a means of promoting initiative and freedom of action. Growing out of the reforms of the German Army of the 19th century by Field Marshal von Moltke and others, it is exemplified by what the German Army calls *Auftragstaktic*, i.e., the promotion of harmonious thinking at all echelons of command which enables subordinates to both understand and carry out the mission concept of their superiors. Such initiative thus promotes the use at every echelon of the best means available to accomplish the mission.

These "means" are described by the principles of *Mass, Maneuver,* and *Economy of Force.* Grouped together in the single principle of *Concentration* until the 1949 version of the *Field Service Regulations*, these principles have to do with relational action against the enemy's center of gravity. As Clausewitz puts it, "out of [the enemy's dominant] characteristics a certain center of gravity develops, the hub of all power and movement, on which everything depends. That is the point against which all our energies should be directed."[19] Although he goes on to say that "the defeat and destruction of [the enemy's] fighting force remains the best way," our Vietnam war experience has proved the truth of his observation that there are other equally valid centers of gravity, including the Army of the protector of a small country, the community of interests among alliances, and the personality of the leaders and public opinion."[20]

Keeping their relational aspects in mind, we can now examine these three principles in more detail. *Mass* and *Economy of Force* (considered in tandem since they are often the reciprocal of each other) are critical principles for the United States. As we look at the world it is likely that we will face two intertwined phenomena: a continued bipolar confrontation with the Soviet Union, the only other worldwide military power and the only nation capable of destroying us; and at the same time threats to our interests from heavily armed Soviet surrogates and independent, militarily sophisticated Third World nations. This dichotomy has caused us serious difficulty in the past. In both Korea and Vietnam we became involved to blunt what we saw as an attempt by the Soviet Union and China to expand communism by force of arms. But the fear of becoming involved in a war with the Soviet Union and China inhibited our efforts. Former Secretary of State Henry Kissinger put the problem succinctly, "Our perception of the global challenge at the same time tempted us to distant enterprises and prevented us from meeting them conclusively."[21] We were constantly plagued during the Vietnam war with the dilemma over whether to mass to fight the war in Vietnam and employ an economy of force in Europe or whether to attempt to mass in both places simultaneously. This problem has not gone away. As Army Chief of Staff General Edward C. Meyer said in his *White Paper 1980:*

The most demanding challenge confronting the U.S. military in the decade of the 1980s is to develop and demonstrate the capability to successfully meet threats to vital U.S. interests outside of Europe, without compromising the decisive theater in Central Europe.[22]

Maneuver is another strategic and complicating factor for the American military. Although the MacKinder Theory of the heartland is supposedly out of date, the facts of geography remain. Our major adversary, the Soviet Union, is a continental power. The USSR can influence events in Western Europe, the Middle East, and North East Asia merely by massing troops within her own borders. The United States by comparison is an insular power. In order to influence events we must deploy troops overseas. This places a premium on strategic sealift and airlift, as well as on base rights in strategic areas of the world. Although lift is a priority item for the Army, since it must be moved to the point of decision, it is of lesser importance to the Navy and Air Force whose first priority is sea and air control. In a time of constrained budgets they can be expected to emphasize their higher priorities. One of the ways that we have attempted to alleviate this problem is through POMCUS—positioning of military equipment in strategic overseas locations, primarily in NATO. But this has been at the price of our worldwide flexibility and of the readiness of our forces here at home, since prepositioned equipment is not available for training. As the Army *White Paper 1980* puts it:

Our capabilities to project combat power worldwide must be improved. We are approaching the upper limits of feasibility in the POMCUS programmed for Europe. Further improvements must come from improved strategic mobility (particularly fast sealift), force structure changes, Host Nation Support, and, where possible, lighter more capable forces.[23]

Turning from the problem of *how* we are to wage war, we must also address the issue of *who* will insure the unity of our efforts. *Unity of Command* has plagued the American military for many years. As described in an earlier chapter, the Department of Defense is charged with two distinct tasks.

One is the normal peacetime task of preparation for war. The other is the task of conducting war itself. These divergent tasks would be automatically reconciled in the event of total war, but, as the Vietnam war made obvious, they work against each other during limited war. It would appear that this deficiency could be eliminated through minor modifications to the existing command structure. In future contingency operations the Secretary of Defense could designate a specific element to deal with the task of maintaining our deterrence through preparation for war and another separate element to conduct the actual war itself.

With the next two principles, *Security* and *Surprise*, we run into a fundamental problem in the conduct of U.S. military strategy options. That is the inherent conflict between a free and democratic American society and the need for security in the conduct of U.S. military operations. Short of total war it is unlikely that the United States would impose total censorship over military operations. Our experiences in Vietnam demonstrate what a serious problem this can become. Although there was no instance where the news media jeopardized *tactical* security and surprise, the very nature of their craft makes it almost impossible for them to preserve *strategic* security and surprise. The American people rightly demand to know what their government is doing and it is the responsibility of the news media to supply that information. In so doing, however, they also supply such information to our enemies. North Vietnamese accounts of the war showed how closely they monitored the American media. There is no doubt that this inability of the United States to preserve strategic security causes us great problems. But the alternatives are even worse. As we saw in our discussion of the nature of the U.S. military, it is a military that belongs to the American people who take a proprietary interest in its commitment. Imposition of total censorship would not only jeopardize the very basis of American society but would also sever the link between the American people and their military. The ultimate price could well be higher than any advantages that might accrue through improved U.S. strategic security. It is also important to recall the paradox of the Vietnam war where we were able to achieve strategic surprise with our initial ground force intervention and again with the 1972 "Christmas bombing" because the free and open American media acted as a kind of deception device.

This paradox illustrates another aspect of Security and Surprise that is an important part of American strategic decision-making. During a briefing by the Army's Strategic Assessment Group in 1974, then Deputy Director of the CIA, Lieutenant General Vernon Walters, commented that if on 26 June 1950 a Russian spy was able to break into the Pentagon and the State Department and steal our most sensitive and Top Secret plans on Korea, he would have found that we had no strategic interest whatsoever in that country. "But," General Walters went on, "the one place he couldn't break into was the mind of President Truman, and on 27 June 1950 we went to war over Korea."[24] American vital interests are determined in large measure by the President alone, when he makes the decision to commit American forces to their defense. The resulting volatility and unpredictability of American action promotes both strategic surprise and strategic security and in so doing gives us a major advantage. At the same time it imposes an enormous burden on the armed forces who must maintain the flexibility to be able to respond immediately to such decisions.

Such high-level strategic decision-making also has another impact. Especially in recent years, the prevalence of "leaks" within the Federal Government has made decision-makers reluctant to commit sensitive planning and operational details to paper, and to provide those in the planning and operational chain with all the relevant data. This can have disastrous results. In the introduction to his 1943 translation of German General Waldemar Erfurth's *Surprise*, Dr. Stefan T. Possony quotes the Austrian World War I General Alfred Krauss. "Secrecy," General Krauss points out, "cannot be maintained by hiding one's intentions from subordinates. One should not believe that secrecy can be maintained if only a handful of superior officers know of the battle plan. Such secrecy is not desirable, because any operation must be thoroughly trained and rehearsed if it is to be successful."[25] The solution to the problem of intra-government security is beyond the purview of the Army but it is a problem that must be taken into account in future crises.

The last principle of war, *Simplicity*, has application both in generating public support and in the conduct of war itself. On the one hand the American people must understand what we are about and why their sacrifices are necessary. On the other hand we ourselves must understand what we are trying to achieve with the use of military force. Overly complex and convoluted plans and operations should in themselves be a danger signal. As the 1949 version of the *Field Service Regulations* warned, "Simplicity of plans must be emphasized, for in operations even the most simple plan is usually difficult to execute. The final test of a plan is its execution; this must be borne constantly in mind during planning."[26]

Siegfried Sassoon, wounded in action and decorated for bravery as a British infantry lieutenant in the trenches in Flanders, put the awesome responsibility of the military planner succinctly in his 1917 poem, *The General:*

> "Good morning; good morning!" the General said
> When we met him last week on our way to the Line.
> Now the soldiers he smiled at are most of 'em dead.
> And we're cursing his staff for incompetent swine.
>
> "He's a cheery old card," grunted Harry to Jack
> As they slogged up to Arras with rifle and pack.
> But he did for them both with his plan of attack.[27]

How to avoid doing our country and our soldiers in with the "plan of attack" has been the prime concern of military tacticians and strategists long before Vietnam. In 1935, also drawing from his World War I experiences, then Army Chief of Staff General Douglas MacArthur discussed how this could be done:

> The military student does not seek to learn from history the minutiae of method and technique. In every age these are decisively influenced by the characteristics of weapons currently available and by means at hand for maneuvering, supplying and controlling combat

forces. But research does bring to light those fundamental principles, and their combinations and applications, which, in the past, have been productive of success. These principles know no limitation of time. Consequently, the army extends its analytical interest to the dust-buried accounts of wars long past as well as to those still reeking with the scent of battle.[28]

It is one of the anomalies of Vietnam that accounts of our experience there are more "dust-buried" than "reeking with the scent of battle." Yet, as the preceding analysis has shown, research on that war has "brought to light those fundamental principles, and the combinations and applications which . . . have been productive of success." That it was not *our* success makes it even more imperative that we learn from that experience. The quintessential "strategic lesson learned" from the Vietnam war is that we must once again become masters of the profession of arms. The American people deserve, demand and expect nothing less of their Army.

NOTES

1. Evelyn Waugh, *Officers and Gentlemen* (Boston, Massachusetts: Little, Brown and Company, 1955), pp. 184–85.

2. Clausewitz, *On War*, III:5, p. 156.

3. David Halberstam, *The Best and the Brightest* (New York: Random House, 1972).

4. CBS Reports, *The Uncounted Enemy: A Vietnam Deception*, 23 January 1982.

5. President Abraham Lincoln, quoted in Carl Sandburg, *Abraham Lincoln: The War Years*, Vol. I (New York: Harcourt, Brace & Company, 1939), p. 594.

6. Clausewitz, *On War*, II:5, pp. 165–66. (Emphasis added.)

7. "Replaying an Old War Game," *Newsweek*, 8 February 1982, p. 95.

8. Barbara Tuchman, *A Distant Mirror: The Calamitous 14th Century* (New York: Knopf, 1978), p. 502.

9. Marshal Maurice de Saxe, "My Reveries Upon the Art of War" (1757), in Major Thomas R. Phillips' *Roots of Strategy* (Harrisburg, Pennsylvania: Military Service Publishing Company, 1940), pp. 296–97.

10. *Op cit.*, p. 1.

11. Senator Jacob Javits (with Don Kellermann), *Who Makes War: The*

President versus Congress (New York: William Morrow & Company, Inc., 1973), p. 265.

12. Clausewitz, *On War*, I:2, p. 97. (Emphasis added.)

13. *Ibid.*, p. 15.

14. *Ibid.*, VIII:3, p. 584.

15. Sir John Hackett, "Protecting Oil Supplies: The Military Requirements," *Adelphi Papers #166, Third World Conflict and International Security, Part I* (London: The International Institute of Strategic Studies, 1981), pp. 42–43.

16. National Security Action Memorandum No. 55, "Relations of the Joint Chiefs of Staff to the President in Cold War Operations," June 28, 1961; quoted in Kester and Holloway, *The Joint Chiefs of Staff: A Better System?*, pp. 3–4.

17. Clausewitz, *On War*, VIII:6, pp. 607–8.

18. 82nd Congress, 1st Session, *Military Situation in the Far East, Part I*, pp. 323, 325.

19. Clausewitz, *On War*, VIII:4, pp. 595–96.

20. *Ibid.*

21. Kissinger, *White House Years*, p. 64.

22. Chief of Staff, U.S. Army, *White Paper 1980*, p. 1.

23. *Ibid.*, p. 3.

24. Author's personal notes.

25. Erfurth, *Surprise*, p. 6.

26. FM 100–5, 15 August 1949, p. 21.

27. Siegfried Sassoon, "The General (1917)" in Field Marshal Viscount A. P. Wavell's *Other Men's Flowers* (New York: G. P. Putnam's Sons, 1945), p. 110.

28. "Annual Report of the Chief of Staff for the Fiscal Year Ending June 30, 1935" (Washington, D.C.: USGPO, 1935).

THE PRINCIPLES OF WAR AND THE OPERATIONAL DIMENSION*

INTRODUCTION

MODERN WARFARE REQUIRES the application of both the science and the art of war. The science of war is in a constant state of change, driven by new technological developments which can radically change the nature of the battlefield. The art of war, on the other hand, involves the critical historical analysis of warfare. The military professional derives from this analysis the fundamental principles—their combinations and applications—which have produced success on the battlefields of history. The principles of war, thus derived, are therefore a part of the art rather than the science of war. They are neither immutable nor causal, and they do not provide a precise mathematical formula for success in battle. Their value lies in their utility as a frame of reference for analysis of strategic and tactical issues. For the strategist,

*Chapter 3, Field Manual 100–1, *The Army*, 14 August 1981 (Washington, D.C.: USGPO, 1981).

the principles of war provide a set of military planning inter-rogatives—a set of questions that should be considered if military strategy is to best serve the national interest. For the tactician, these principles provide an operational framework for the military actions he has been trained to carry out. They are neither intended nor designed to be prescriptive; the principles of war, if understood and applied properly, should stimulate thought and enhance flexibility of action.

THE PRINCIPLES OF WAR

The United States Army published its first set of principles of war in a 1921 Army training regulation. These principles were in large measure drawn from the work of British Major General J. F. C. Fuller, who developed a set of principles of war during World War I to serve as guides for his own Army. In the ensuing years, these original principles of war adopted by our Army have undergone minor revisions and changes, but have essentially stood the test of analysis, experimentation, and practice. For the United States Army today, the Principles of War are:

> **Objective**
> **Offensive**
> **Mass**
> **Economy of Force**
> **Maneuver**
> **Unity of Command**
> **Security**
> **Surprise**
> **Simplicity**

1. **Objective.** *Every military operation should be directed towards a clearly defined, decisive, and attainable objective.*

As a derivative of the political aim, the *strategic military objective* of a nation at war must be to apply whatever degree of force is necessary to allow attainment of the political purpose or aim for which the war is being fought. When the political end desired is the total defeat of the adversary, then the strategic military objective will most likely be the defeat of the enemy's armed forces and the destruction of his will to resist. It is essential, however, that the political purpose be clearly defined *and* attainable by the considered application of the various elements of the nation's power. Not until the political purpose has been determined and defined by the President and the Congress can strategic and tactical objectives be clearly identified and developed. Once developed, the strategic objectives must constantly be subjected to rigorous analysis and review to insure that they continue to reflect accurately not only the ultimate political end desired, but also any political constraints imposed on the application of military force.

Just as the strategic military objective focuses on the political ends, so must tactical military operations be directed toward clearly defined, decisive, and attainable *tactical objectives* that ultimately assist in achieving the strategic aims. Similarly, intermediate tactical objectives must quickly and economically contribute, directly or indirectly, to the purpose of the ultimate objective. The selection of objectives is based on consideration of the overall mission of the command, the commander's assigned mission, the means available, and the military characteristics of the operational area. Every commander must clearly understand the overall mission of the higher command, his own mission, and the tasks he must perform and the reasons therefore; he must consider each contemplated action in light of his mission, and he must communicate clearly to his subordinate commanders the intent of the operation upon which the command as a whole is about to embark.

2. **Offensive.** *Seize, retain, and exploit the initiative.*

While the principle of the objective requires that all efforts be directed toward a clearly defined "common goal," the principle of offensive suggests that offensive action, or maintenance of the initiative, is the most effective and decisive way to pursue and attain that "common goal." This is fundamentally true in both the *strategic and tactical sense.* While it may sometimes be necessary to adopt a defensive posture, this should be only a temporary condition until the necessary means are available to resume offensive operations. An offensive spirit must be inherent in the conduct of all defensive operations—it must be an *active* defense, not a *passive* one. This is so because offensive action, whatever form it takes, is the means by which the nation or a military force captures and holds the initiative, achieves results, and maintains freedom of action. It permits the political leader or the military commander to capitalize on the initiative, impose his will on the enemy, set the terms and select the place of confrontation or battle, exploit weaknesses and react to rapidly changing situations and unexpected developments. No matter what the level, strategic or tactical, the side that retains the initiative through offensive action forces the foe to *react* rather than *act.*

3. **Mass.** *Concentrate combat power at the decisive place and time.*

In the *strategic context*, this principle suggests that the nation should commit, or be prepared to commit, a predominance of national power to those regions or areas of the world where the threat to vital security interests is greatest. For nations such as the United States, which have global security interests in terms of politico-military alliances and commitments and resource dependencies, the accurate and timely determination of where the threat to vital national interests is greatest is becoming increasingly more difficult. In today's volatile world, the nature and source of threat often change in dramatic fashion. It is therefore incumbent upon military strategists to anticipate the most likely areas of concern and develop suitable contingency plans. Since every possible contingency or trouble spot cannot be anticipated, much less planned for, it is absolutely essential for Army planners and Army forces to retain flexibility of thought and action.

In the *tactical dimension*, this principle suggests that superior combat power must be concentrated at the decisive place and time in order to achieve decisive results. This superiority results from the proper combination of the elements of combat power at a place and time, and in a manner of the commander's choosing, in order to retain the initiative. The massing of forces, together with the proper application of other principles of war, may enable numerically inferior forces to achieve decisive battle outcomes.

4. **Economy of Force.** *Allocate minimum essential combat power to secondary efforts.*

As a reciprocal of the principle of mass, economy of force in the *strategic dimension* suggests that, in the absence of unlimited resources, a nation may have to accept some risk in areas where vital national interests are not immediately at stake. This means that if the nation must focus predominant power toward a clearly defined primary threat, it cannot allow attainment of that objective to be compromised by unnecessary diversions to areas of lower priority. This involves risk, requires astute strategic planning and judgment by political and military leaders, and again places a premium on the need for flexibility of thought and action.

At the *tactical level*, the principle of economy of force requires that minimum means be employed in areas other than where the main effort is intended to be employed. It requires, as at the strategic level, the acceptance of prudent risks in selected areas in order to achieve superiority in the area where decision is sought. Economy of force missions may require the forces employed to attack, defend, delay, or conduct deception operations.

5. **Maneuver.** *Place the enemy in a position of disadvantage through the flexible application of combat power.*

In the *strategic sense*, this principle has three interrelated dimensions: flexibility, mobility, and maneuverability. The first of these involves the need for flexibility in thought, plans, and operations. Such flexibility enhances the ability to rapidly react to unforeseen circumstances. Given the global nature of U.S. interests and the dynamic character of the international scene, such flexibility is crucial. The second dimension involves strategic mobility, which is especially critical for an insular power such as the United States. In order to react promptly and concentrate and project power on the primary objective, strategic airlift and sealift are essential. The final strategy dimension involves maneuverability within the theater of operations so as to focus maximum strength against the enemy's weakest point and thereby gain the strategic advantage.

In the *tactical sense*, maneuver is an essential element of combat power. It contributes significantly to sustaining the initiative, to exploiting success, to preserving freedom of action, and to reducing vulnerability. The object of maneuver is to concentrate or disperse forces in a manner designed to place the enemy at a disadvantage, thus achieving results that would otherwise be most costly in men and materiel. At all levels, successful application of this principle requires not only fire and movement, but also flexibility of thought, plans, and operations, and the considered application of the principles of mass and economy of force.

6. Unity of Command. *For every objective, there should be unity of effort under one responsible commander.*

This principle insures that all efforts are focused on a common goal. At the *strategic level*, this common goal equates to the political purpose of the United States, and the broad strategic objectives which flow therefrom. It is the common goal which, at the national level, determines the military forces necessary for its achievement. The coordination of these forces requires unity of effort. At the national level, the Constitution provides for unity of command by appointing the President as the Commander in Chief of the Armed forces. The President is assisted in this role by the national security organization, which includes the Secretary of Defense and the Joint Chiefs of Staff at the highest level, and the unified and specified commands and joint task forces at the operational levels.

In the *tactical dimension*, it is axiomatic that the employment of military forces in a manner that develops their full combat power requires unity of command. Unity of command means directing and coordinating the action of all forces toward a common goal or objective. Coordination may be achieved by cooperation; it is, however, best achieved by vesting a single tactical commander with the requisite authority to direct and coordinate all forces employed in pursuit of a common goal.

7. **Security**. *Never permit the enemy to acquire an unexpected advantage.*

Security enhances freedom of action by reducing friendly vulnerability to hostile acts, influence, or surprise. At the *strategic level*, security requires that active and passive measures be taken to protect the United States and its Armed Forces against espionage, subversion, and strategic intelligence collection. However, implementation of such security measures must be balanced against the need to prevent them from severing the link between the American public and its Army. In addition, they should not be allowed to interfere with flexibility of thought and action, since rigidity and dogmatism increase vulnerability to enemy surprise. In this regard, thorough knowledge and understanding of enemy strategy, tactics, and doctrine, and detailed strategic staff planning can improve security and reduce vulnerability to surprise.

At the *tactical level*, security is essential to the protection and husbanding of combat power. Security results from the measures taken by a command to protect itself from surprise, observation, detection, interference, espionage, sabotage, or annoyance. Security may be achieved through the establishment and maintenance of protective measures against hostile acts or influence; or it may be assured by deception operations designed to confuse and dissipate enemy attempts to interfere with the force being secured. Risk is an inherent condition in war; application of the principle of security does not suggest overcautiousness or the avoidance of calculated risk.

8. **Surprise.** *Strike the enemy at a time and/or place and in a manner for which he is unprepared.*

To a large degree, the principle of surprise is the reciprocal of the principle of security. Concealing one's own capabilities and intentions creates the opportunity to strike the enemy unaware or unprepared. However, *strategic surprise* is difficult to achieve. Rapid advances in strategic surveillance technology make it increasingly more difficult to mask or cloak the large scale marshaling or movement of manpower and equipment. This problem is compounded in an open society such as the United States, where freedom of press and information are highly valued. However, the United States can achieve a degree of psychological surprise due to its strategic deployment capability. The rapid deployment of U.S. combat forces into a crisis area can forestall, or upset, the plans and preparations of an enemy. This capability can give the United States the advantage in both a physical and psychological sense by denying the enemy the initiative.

Surprise is important in the *tactical dimension* for it can decisively affect the outcome of battle. With surprise, success out of proportion to the effort expended may be obtained. Surprise results from going against an enemy at a time and/or place, or in a manner, for which he is unprepared. It is not essential that the enemy be taken unaware, but only that he become aware too late to react effectively. Factors contributing to surprise include speed and alacrity, employment of unexpected forces, effective intelligence, deception operations of all kinds, variations of tactics and methods of operation, and operations security.

9. **Simplicity.** *Prepare clear, uncomplicated plans and clear, concise orders to insure thorough understanding.*

In both the *strategic and tactical dimension*, guidance, plans, and orders should be as simple and direct as the attainment of the objective will allow. The *strategic importance* of the principle of simplicity goes well beyond its more traditional tactical application: it is an important element in the development and enhancement of public support. If the American people are to commit their lives and resources to a military operation, they must understand the purpose which is to be achieved. Political and military objectives and operations must therefore be presented in clear, concise, understandable terms: simple and direct plans and orders cannot compensate for ambiguous and cloudy objectives. In its military application, this principle promotes strategic flexibility by encouraging broad strategic guidance rather than detailed and involved instruction.

At the *tactical level*, simplicity of plans and instructions contributes to successful operations. Direct, simple plans, and clear, concise orders are essential to reduce the chances for misunderstanding and confusion. Other factors being equal, the simplest plan executed promptly is to be preferred over the complex plan executed later.

APPLICATION

While any set of principles of war adopted by a nation has application across the entire spectrum of warfare, it must be understood that these principles are interdependent and interrelated. No single principle can be blindly adhered to, or observed, to the exclusion of the others; none can assure victory in battle without reinforcement from one or more of the others. Indeed, the military forces of each nation conduct operations on the basis of operational concepts which are derived from combinations of principles. For example, an operational concept deriving from a combination of offense, mass, surprise, and maneuver might suggest a large military force, using masses of swiftly moving armored forces, whose dominant mode of operation is to overwhelm, disrupt, and destroy, using surprise and maneuver to assist in the execution.

Although the most common application of the principles of war is in the form of operational concepts on the field of battle, the principles can also be useful integrated into the *military estimate and decision process* as an aid to judgment and analysis. The principles of objective and unity of command, for example, can assist in mission analysis both at the strategic and tactical level. They are also valuable aids in determining the purpose and direction of effort. In a like manner, the principle of simplicity can serve as a measure for the formulation of tasks. The principles of offense, mass, economy of force, maneuver, security, and surprise can assist in the analysis of the situation as well as in the formulation of courses of action. Again, simplicity can serve as the measure against which the courses of action can be compared.

Planning. *Planning* is essential to the operation of the Army both in preparing for war and in the conduct of war itself. Planning is both an art and a science. As a science it deals with the specifics of manpower, arms, equipment, and monies, both actual and projected. However, since the future cannot be accurately predicted nor the rate of change held constant, planning is also an art. As such, it deals in intangibles; as a distillation of military art, the principles of war are particularly valuable as an aid to planning.

Force Planning, as part of the planning, programing, and budgeting system, is an integral part of preparation for war. Such planning deals primarily with fixed values, physical quantities, and unilateral action; with the mechanics of force structuring and force manning; and with the research, development, and acquisition of arms and equipment. While thus primarily concerned with the science of war, force planning also involves an appreciation of the art of war. Using the principles of war as a frame of reference, the force planner can better appreciate the potential utility of the designed force on the field of battle.

Contingency planning is the closest approximation among all planning forms to the conduct of actual war. It deals primarily with variable quantities, intangible forces and effects, and a continual interaction of opposites. While also concerned with the science of war, primarily the characteristics of weapons and the means for maneuvering, supplying, and controlling military forces, contingency planning draws more closely on the art of war. Like the principles of war, contingency plans are not absolutes, but are designed to identify the right things to do and assist in doing things right. Application of the principles of war to the contingency planning process insures practicality and simplicity and provides a direct link to actual execution on the battlefield.

Selected Bibliography

Appleman, Roy H. *U.S. Army in the Korean War: South to the Naktong, North to the Yalu.* Washington, D.C.: USGPO, 1960. Official U.S. Army history of the Korean war from the beginning to the Chinese intervention in November 1950. (Note that the volume covering this intervention *[Ebb and Flow]* still has not been published 30 years later.)

Arnold, Hugh M. "Official Justifications for America's Role in Indochina, 1949–67." *Asian Affairs*, September/October 1975. A useful compendium of official U.S. justifications of the Vietnam war.

Baldwin, Hanson W. *Strategy for Tomorrow.* New York: Harper & Row, 1970. Somewhat dated but the first chapters provide insights into the relations between the President and his military advisors during the critical early days of the Vietnam war.

BDM Corporation. *A Study of Strategic Lessons Learned in Vietnam.* Washington, D.C.: 1979. Volume I: *The Enemy,* Volume II: *South Vietnam,* Volume III: *US Foreign Policy and Vietnam 1945–1975,* Volume IV: *US Domestic Factors Influencing Vietnam War Policy Making,* Volume V: *Planning the War,* Volume VI: *Conduct of the War,* Volume VII: *The Soldier,* Volume VIII: *Results of the War,* and an Omnibus Executive Summary. This multi-volume work of more than 3500 pages gathers together under topical headings not only the literature on the Vietnam war but also discussions with many of the senior civilian and military decision-makers of the Vietnam era. Copies have been provided to the Army, Navy, and Air War Colleges, the National Defense University, the Army and Marine Command and Staff Colleges, and the U.S. Military Academy as an aid to Vietnam war researchers.

Bell, Coral. "The Asian Balance of Power: A Comparison with European Precedents." *Adelphi Papers No. 44.* London, England: The International Institute for Strategic Studies, February 1968. Somewhat dated because of the change in Sino-U.S. relations, this analysis still provides insights into the critical differences between European and Asian security issues.

Bell, J. Bowyer. *The Myth of the Guerrilla: Revolutionary Theory and Malpractice.* New York: Alfred A. Knopf, 1971. One of the first challenges to the counterinsurgency fad, it exposes how guerrilla war was transformed into "revolutionary war."

Betts, Richard K. *Soldiers, Statesmen and Cold War Scholars.* Cambridge, MA: Harvard University Press, 1977. Best analysis of role of JCS in Vietnam decisionmaking.

Bidwell, Shelford. *Modern Warfare: A Study of Men, Weapons, and Theories.* London, England: Allen Lane, 1973. A study of modern warfare by the editor of *RUSI.*

Blainey, Geoffrey. *The Causes of War.* New York: The Free Press, 1973. A source book on the causes of war that debunks current simplistic notions and illuminates the interrelationship between war and peace.

Blaufarb, Douglas S. *The Counter Insurgency Era: US Doctrine and Performance 1950 to the Present.* New York: The Free Press, 1977. The best single source analysis of the birth, life, and death of the counterinsurgency dogma.

Braestrup, Peter. *The Big Story: How the American Press and TV Reported and Interpreted the Crisis of Tet 68 in Vietnam and Washington.* (Two volumes) Boulder, Colorado: Westview Press, 1973. The landmark work on American media reporting on the Tet Offensive of 1968.

Brodie, Bernard. *War and Politics.* New York: MacMillan, 1973. A seminal work on U.S. civil-military relations by one of America's foremost strategists.

Bundy, McGeorge. "Vietnam, Watergate and Presidential Powers." *Foreign Affairs.* Winter 1979–1980. Analysis of why the U.S. failed to intervene in 1975 when North Vietnam flagrantly violated the 1973 "peace" accords by a former presidential national security advisor.

Byely, B., Colonel, Soviet Army, et al. *Marxism-Leninism on War and Army (A Soviet View).* Washington, D.C.: USGPO, 1972. Although turgid almost to the point of obscurity because of Marxist-Leninist jargon, the final chapter contains insights into the Soviet use of "the laws of military science and the principles of military art."

Clausewitz. See Von Clausewitz.

Cohen, Eliot. "Systems Paralysis." *The American Spectator*, November 1980, pp. 23–27. A critical examination of the effects of systems analysis on strategic planning.

Collins, John M., Colonel, USA. *Grand Strategy: Principles and Practices.* Annapolis, Maryland: Naval Institute Press, 1973. A source book on grand strategy by a former member of the National War College faculty.

_____, "Vietnam Postmortem: A Senseless Strategy," *Parameters: Journal of the US Army War College*, Vol. VIII No. 1. An analysis of our Vietnam strategy in terms of failure to properly apply counterinsurgency doctrine.

Cooke, James E., ed. *The Federalist.* Middletown, Connecticut: Wesleyan

University Press, 1961. The Founding Fathers' own commentary on the reasoning behind our Constitution.

De Tocqueville, Alexis. *Democracy In America*. New York: New American Library, 1956. An analysis of the American character made in the 1830s that still provides insights into the way we think and the way we act.

Don, Tran Van. *Our Endless War*. San Rafael, California: Presidio Press, 1978. A look at coalition warfare from the Vietnamese perspective by the former RVN Minister of Defense.

Dung, Van Tien, Senior General NVA. "Great Spring Victory." *Foreign Broadcast Information Service* (Volume I, FBIS-APA-76-110 7 June 1976; Volume II, FBIS-APA-76-131 7 July 1976). Remarkably readable and straightforward account of the 1975 North Vietnamese offensive that conquered South Vietnam by the NVA's field army commander.

Dunn, Joe P. "In Search of Lessons: The Development of a Vietnam Historiography." *Parameters: Journal of the US Army War College*. December 1979.

Eagleton, Thomas F., Senator. *War and Presidential Power: A Chronicle of Congressional Surrender*. New York: Liveright, 1974. An attack on the War Powers Resolution as a weakening of Constitutional principles.

Enthoven, Alain C., and Smith, K. Wayne. *How Much Is Enough: Shaping the Defense Program 1961–1969*. New York: Harper & Row, 1971. The definitive work on the impact of systems analysis on the Department of Defense during the McNamara era.

Erfurth, Waldemar, Gen., German Army. *Surprise* [Die Ueberraschung im Krieg (Berlin, 1938)] (translated by Dr. Stefan T. Possony and Daniel Vilfroy), Harrisburg, Pennsylvania: Military Service Publishing Co., 1943. Primary work on the principle of surprise.

Etzold, Thomas H., and Gaddis, John Lewis. *Containment: Documents on American Policy and Strategy, 1945–1950*. New York: Columbia University Press, 1978.

Fehrenbach, T. R. *This Kind of War*. New York: MacMillan, 1963. The best book written on the Korean war, it discusses the conduct of the war at every level from Washington to the front-line soldier and provides insights and perspective on leadership, training, morale, and combat operations.

FitzGerald, Frances. *Fire In The Lake: The Vietnamese and the Americans in Vietnam*. Boston, Massachusetts: Little, Brown & Co., 1972. By her own admission "not a scholarly work," this shallow analysis pandered to the prejudices of the anti-war movement in the early 1970s. Useful now primarily as a litmus test for discussions of the Vietnam war, it cries out for a sequel on those who have fled the society that this book extols. For a scholarly analysis of Vietnamese society see John T. McAlister, Jr. and Paul Mus's *The Vietnamese and Their Revolution*. New York: Harper & Row, 1970.

Foch, Ferdinand, Marshal of France. *The Principles of War* (translated by Hilaire Belloc). London: Chapman & Hall, Ltd., 1918. A French analysis of the principles of war, including Foch's four principles—Economy of Force, Freedom of Action, Free Disposal of Forces, and Security.

Freeman, Douglas Southall. *Lee's Lieutenants: A Study in Command.* New York: Scribners, 1942. The classic study of Southern leadership during the American Civil War.

Fuller, J. F. C., Colonel, D.S.O. *The Foundations of the Science of War.* London: Hutchinson & Co., Ltd., 1925. A British analysis of the principles of war by one of the world's foremost military theorists.

Gabriel, Richard and Savage, Paul. *Crisis in Command.* New York: Hill and Wang, 1978. A somewhat overdrawn but widely quoted critique of the Vietnam war emphasizing our overreliance on management at the expense of leadership.

Gelb, Leslie H., and Betts, Richard K. *The Irony of Vietnam: The System Worked.* Washington, D.C.: The Brookings Institution, 1979. An examination of the Washington bureaucracy emphasizing that the "system" accomplished all that it was asked to do and by inference highlighting the need for leadership to set bureaucratic goals.

Gittings, John. *The Role of the Chinese Army.* New York: Oxford University Press, 1967. Although now dated, a useful work on the PLA.

Haass, Richard. "Congressional Power: Implications for American Security Policy." *Adelphi Papers No. 153.* London, England: The International Institute for Strategic Studies, 1979. An excellent analysis on the role of Congress in American national security matters by a former Congressional staffer.

Hannah, Norman B. "Vietnam Now We Know." *All Quiet On The Eastern Front* (edited by Anthony T. Bouscaren). New York: Devin-Adair, 1977. A succinct critical strategic analysis of the Vietnam war by a former State Department foreign service officer with long experience in Southeast Asia.

Harrison, Selig S. *The Widening Gulf: Asian Nationalism and American Policy.* New York: The Free Press, 1978.

Hart, Liddell. *Thoughts on War.* London, England: Faber and Faber, Ltd., 1943. An analysis of the principles of war by a renowned British strategist.

Heiser, Joseph M., Lt. Gen., USA. *Vietnam Studies: Logistic Support.* Washington, D.C.: USGPO, 1974. An analysis of Vietnam logistics problems by the former commander of the 1st Logistical Command, Vietnam.

Herr, Michael. *Dispatches.* New York: Avon Books, 1978. A scatological and irreverent account of the Vietnam war that contains some of the best and most insightful writing on the war. His description of the 1st Cavalry Division moving to the relief of Khe Sanh, for example, captures in less than a page the Army at its best—as a kind of inexorable force that sweeps all before it.

Herrington, Stuart A., LTC, USA. *Peace with Honor? An American Reports on Vietnam, 1973–1975.* Novato, CA: Presidio Press, 1983. A firsthand account of the evacuation of Saigon by the last American soldier to leave Vietnam.

Honey, P. J. *Communism in North Vietnam: Its Role in the Sino-Soviet Dispute.* Cambridge, Massachusetts: The M.I.T. Press, 1963. An early account of North Vietnam's objectives in Indo-China.

Hoopes, Townsend. *The Limits of Intervention.* New York: David McKay Co., Inc., 1969. An account of Washington decision-making in late 1967 and early 1968 by a former Under Secretary of the Air Force in the Johnson Administration.

Hosmer, Stephen T., et al. *The Fall of South Vietnam: Statements by Vietnamese Military and Civilian Leaders.* Santa Monica, California: Rand Corporation, December 1978. A summary of oral and written statements by 27 former high-ranking South Vietnamese military officers and civilians on their perceptions of the causes of the collapse of South Vietnam.

Howard, Michael. "The Relevance of Traditional Strategy." *Foreign Affairs*, January 1973. An important article by a distinguished British strategist emphasizing the importance of conventional forces both in their own right and as legitimizers of the nuclear deterrent. Coinciding as it did with the Army's reevaluation of its role in national security it had a major impact on strategic thinking.

_____. "The Forgotten Dimensions of Strategy." *Foreign Affairs*. August 1979. An emphasis on the logistical, social, and technological dimensions of strategy as essential complements to the operational dimension.

Huntington, Samuel P. *The Soldier and the State: The Theory and Politics of Civil-Military Relations.* Cambridge, Massachusetts: The Belkap Press of Harvard University Press, 1967. The landmark work on U.S. civil-military relationships.

Javits, Jacob K., Senator. *Who Makes War: The President vs. Congress.* New York: Morrow, 1973. A detailed analysis of the conflict between the Legislative and Executive branches on the question of war powers by one of the framers of the War Powers Resolution.

Jessup, John E., Jr. and Coakley, Robert W. *A Guide to the Study and Use of Military History.* Washington, D.C.: Center for Military History, 1979. A collection of articles on the nature and use of military history as well as a series of bibliographic guides.

Johnson, Chalmers. *Autopsy on People's War.* Berkeley, California: University of California Press, 1973. An important critical analysis of "People's War" by a distinguished Asian scholar.

Johnson, Lyndon Baines. *The Vantage Point: Perspective of the Presidency 1963–1969.* New York: Popular Library Edition, 1971. An autobiographical account of the Johnson Administration.

Just, Ward. *Military Men.* New York: Knopf, 1970. An examination of the U.S. Army circa 1970.

Kalb, Marvin and Abel, Elie. *The Roots of Involvement: The US and Asia 1784–1971.* New York: W. W. Norton & Co., 1971. An account of our Vietnam involvement by two distinguished Washington journalists that is most useful in its analysis of decision-making at the national level.

Kautsky, John H. "Myth, Self-Fulfilling Prophecy, and Symbolic Reassurance in the East-West Conflict." *Journal of Conflict Resolution,* Volume IX, No. 1, March 1965. An important article that illuminates some of the causes of confusion in dealing with the Communist bloc.

Kearns, Doris. *Lyndon Johnson and the American Dream.* New York: Harper & Row, 1976. A biography drawn in part from personal interviews with President Johnson.

Kestor, John J. and Holloway, James L., III. "The Joint Chiefs of Staff: A Better System?" *AEI Foreign Policy and Defense Review,* Volume II, No. 1. An examination of the JCS system by a former Chief of Naval Operations and a former Special Assistant to the Secretary of Defense.

Kinnard, Douglas. *The War Managers.* Hanover, New Hampshire: University Press of New England, 1977. Results of a survey of more than 100 Army generals who had commanded in Vietnam.

Kissinger, Henry. *White House Years.* Boston, Massachusetts: Brown & Co., 1979. The memoirs of the former National Security Advisor to President Nixon and Secretary of State in the Nixon and Ford Administrations covering the period 1969–1973. The introductory chapters on the workings of the Washington bureaucracy are alone worth the price of the book.

Komer, R. W. *Bureaucracy Does Its Thing: Institutional Constraints on US-GVN Performance in Vietnam.* Santa Monica, California: Rand Corporation, August 1972. A landmark analysis of how bureaucratic *form* tends to shape and inhibit operational *substance.*

Kriete, Charles F., Chaplain (Colonel), USA. "The Moral Dimension of Strategy." *Parameters: Journal of the US Army War College,* Volume VII, No. 2, 1977.

Lung, Hoang Ngoc, Colonel, ARVN. *Strategy and Tactics.* Washington, D.C.: U.S. Army Center of Military History, 1980. An analysis of Vietnam war strategy by the former J-2, Joint General Staff, Republic of Vietnam Armed Forces.

Luttwak, Edward N. *The Grand Strategy of the Roman Empire: From the First Century A.D. to the Third.* Baltimore, Maryland: The Johns Hopkins University Press, 1976. Analysis of Roman strategy with disturbing parallels with NATO strategy today.

_____. "The American Style of Warfare and the Military Balance." *Survival,* March/April 1979. A warning about the dangers of an attrition strategy against a numerically superior adversary.

_____. "On the Meaning of Strategy . . . For the United States in the 1980s." *National Security In The 1980s: From Weakness to Strength* [W. Scott Thompson (ed.)]. San Francisco, California: Institute for Contemporary Studies, 1980. A critical look at military strategy today.

MacArthur, Douglas A., Gen., USA. *Annual Report of the Chief of Staff for the Fiscal Year ending June 30, 1935.* Washington, D.C.: USGPO, 1935. MacArthur told B. H. Liddell Hart that this report was prepared "as a doctrinal statement for study by officers of the American Army and as an educational document."

MacDonald, Charles B. *An Outline History of U.S. Policy Toward Vietnam.* Washington, D.C.: U.S. Army Center of Military History, April 1978.

Meyer, Edward C., Gen., USA. Chief of Staff, U.S. Army. *White Paper 1980, A Framework for Molding the Army of the 1980s into a Disciplined, Well-Trained Fighting Force.* Washington, D.C.: Department of the Army, 25 February 1980.

Momyer, William W., Gen., USAF, Retired. *Air Power in Three Wars.* Washington, D.C.: Department of the Air Force, 1978. An account of the air war in Vietnam by the former commander of the 7th Air Force and later commander of the Tactical Air Command.

O'Meara, Andrew P., Jr., Major, USA. *Infrastructure and the Marxist Power Seizure: An Analysis of the Communist Models of Revolution.* New York: Vantage Press, Inc., 1973. An analysis of the "explosive" and "implosive" models of revolution together with a critical examination of the Viet Cong organization and structure.

O'Neill, Robert J. *General Giap: Politician and Strategist.* New York: Praeger, 1969. An even-handed biography of the commander in chief of the North Vietnamese Army.

Osgood, Robert Endicott. *Limited War: The Challenge to American Strategy.* Chicago, Illinois: The University of Chicago Press, 1957. A seminal work on limited war theory.

_____. *Limited War Revisited.* Boulder, Colorado: Westview Press, 1979. A post-Vietnam reexamination of limited war theory.

Palit, D. K., Lt. Col., 9th Gurkha Rifles. *The Essentials of Military Knowledge.* Aldershot, England: Gale and Polden Limited, 1953. An excellent handbook on military strategy.

Palmer, Dave Richard, Brig. Gen., USA. *Summons of the Trumpet: U.S.-Vietnam in Perspective.* San Rafael, California: Presidio Press, 1978. The best single volume source on the conduct of the Vietnam war.

_____. *The Way of the Fox: American Strategy in the War for America 1775–1783.* Westport, Connecticut: Greenwood Press, 1975. An account of General George Washington as strategist.

Palmer, Gregory. *The McNamara Strategy and the Vietnam War: Program Budgeting in the Pentagon, 1960–1968.* Westport, Connecticut:

Greenwood Press, 1978. The most lucid account to date of the impact of PPBS on military strategy.

Phillips, Thomas R., Major U.S. Army. *Roots of Strategy*. Harrisburg, Pennsylvania: The Military Service Publishing Company, 1940. A collection of the works of Sun Tzu, Vegetius, De Saxe, Frederick the Great, and the military maxims of Napoleon.

Podhoretz, Norman. "The Present Danger." *Commentary*, March 1980. Although primarily concerned with America's present and future, the analysis of the evolution of containment theory is particularly valuable.

Ridgway, Matthew B., Gen., USA. *The Korean War*. New York: Doubleday & Co., Inc., 1967. An autobiography of the former Eighth Army commander and former Army Chief of Staff with emphasis on the Korean war but also some observations on limited war.

_____. *Soldier: The Memoirs of Matthew B. Ridgway*. New York: Harper & Bros., 1956. General Ridgway's observations on the responsibility of the Chief of Staff to the President and analysis of why the U.S. did not intervene in Indochina in 1954.

Sawyer, Robert K., Major, USA. *Military Advisors in Korea: KMAG in Peace and War*. Washington, D.C.: USGPO, 1962.

Schandler, Herbert Y., Colonel, USA. *The Unmaking of a President: Lyndon Johnson and Vietnam*. Princeton, New Jersey: Princeton University Press, 1977. A critical analysis of Washington decision-making after Tet 1968 based on both the official record and private interviews with the late General Earle Wheeler, then Chairman of the Joint Chiefs of Staff.

_____. "America and Vietnam: The Failure of Strategy" in *Regular Armies and Insurgency* (ed. by Ronald Haycock). London, England: Croom Helm, Ltc., 1979. An excellent analysis of our failure to set political objectives for the Vietnam war.

Sharpe, U. S. G., Admiral, USN and Westmoreland, William C., Gen., USA. *Report on the War in Vietnam*. Washington, D.C.: USGPO, 1968. A report on the Vietnam war for the period June 1964–July 1968 by CINCPAC and COMUSMACV.

Skirdo, M. P., Colonel, Soviet Army. *The People, The Army, The Commander*. Washington, D.C.: USGPO, 1970. A Soviet view of the political, economic, and moral factors of national power.

Summers, Harry G., Jr., Colonel, USA. "Army Strategy Today: Control War, Keep Peace." *Army*. October 1978. An analysis of Army strategy in the post-Vietnam period.

_____. "Politics and Culture of Southeast Asia." *Military Review*. June 1970.

_____. "What Did You Do In Vietnam, Grandpa?" *Army*. November 1978. A survey of changing American attitudes toward the Vietnam war.

Taylor, Maxwell D., Gen., USA. *Swords & Plowshares*. New York: Norton, 1972. The autobiography of the former Army Chief of Staff, Special

Advisor to the President, Chairman of the Joint Chiefs of Staff, and Ambassador to South Vietnam.

————. *The Uncertain Trumpet.* New York: Harper & Bros., 1959. An attack on the strategy of massive retaliation and the source of the strategy of flexible response.

Thomas, James A. *Holy War.* New York: Arlington House Publishers, 1973. An analysis of ideological factors in American public perceptions of war.

Thompson, Sir Robert. *Revolutionary War in World Strategy 1945–1969.* New York: Taplinger Publishing Company, 1970. One of the primary source books on counterinsurgency by the former British commander in Malaya.

Thompson, W. Scott and Frizzell, Donaldson D., eds. *The Lessons of Vietnam.* New York: Crane, Russak & Co., 1977. Excerpts from a 1973–1974 colloquium on the Vietnam war at the Fletcher School of Law and Diplomacy which included 31 distinguished military and civilian panelists.

Upton, Emory, Brevet Maj. Gen., USA. *The Military Policy of the United States.* Washington, D.C.: USGPO, 1917. A source book on the U.S. Army.

U.S. Congress. House. Committee on International Relations. *The War Powers Resolution.* 94th Cong. 2nd Sess. Washington, D.C.: USGPO, 1975.

————. Senate. Joint Committee on Armed Services and Foreign Relations. *Military Situation in the Far East.* 82nd Cong. 1st Sess. Washington, D.C.: USGPO, 1951. The so-called "Great Debate" on the Korean war which included testimony by Sec. of State Acheson, Sec. of Def. Marshall and Generals of the Army Bradley and MacArthur.

————. Senate. Committee on Foreign Relations. *Termination of Middle East and Southeast Asia Resolution.* 91st Cong. 2nd Sess. Washington, D.C.: USGPO, 1970.

U.S. Dept. of the Army. Field Manual 100–1: *The Army.* Washington, D.C.: August 1981.

————. Field Manual 100–5: *Field Service Regulations: Operations.* Washington, D.C.: August 1949.

————. Field Manual 100–5: *Field Service Regulations: Operations.* Washington, D.C.: September 1954.

————. Field Manual 100–5: *Field Service Regulations: Operations.* Washington, D.C.: February 1962.

————. Field Manual 100–5: *Operations of Army Forces in the Field.* Washington, D.C.: September 1968.

————. Field Manual 100–5: *Operations.* Washington, D.C.: July 1976.

U.S. Government Manual, 1979–1980. Washington, D.C.: USGPO, 1979.

U.S. Joint Chiefs of Staff, *JCS Pub. I: Dictionary of Military and Associated Terms.* Washington, D.C.: 1979.

U.S. War Department. Field Manual 100–5: *Field Service Regulations: Operations*. Washington, D.C.: June 1944.

_____. Field Manual 100–5: *Tentative Field Service Regulations: Operations*. Washington, D.C.: October 1939.

Vien, Cao Van, General, ARVN. "The Strategy of Isolation." *Military Review*. April 1972. A recommendation for isolating the Vietnam battlefield by a senior Vietnamese commander.

_____ and Khuyen, Dong Van, Lt. Gen., ARVN. *Reflections on the Vietnam War*. Washington, D.C.: U.S. Army Center of Military History, 1980.

Von Caemmerer, Lt. Gen., German Army. *The Development of Strategical Science* (authorized translation by Karl Von Donat). London, England: Hugh Rees, Ltd., 1905. An analysis of 19th century military thinkers including Jomini, Clausewitz, Moltke, Willisen and Archduke Charles of Austria.

von Clausewitz, Carl. *On War* (edited and translated by Michael Howard and Peter Paret with introductory essays by Peter Paret, Michael Howard and Bernard Brodie and a commentary by Bernard Brodie). Princeton, New Jersey: Princeton University Press, 1976. The basic theoretical work on war in a masterful new translation. Not only is the language more readable, the essays by Paret, Howard and Brodie, as well as Brodie's reader's guide, turn this classic into an understandable and usable guide to modern strategy.

von der Goltz, Colmar, Baron. (Lt. Gen., German Army) *The Conduct of War: A Brief Study of its Most Important Principles and Forms* (translated by 1st Lt. Joseph T. Dickman, 3rd Cavalry, Asst. Instructor in the Art of War, U.S. Infantry and Cavalry School). Kansas City, Missouri: The Franklin Hudson Publishing Co., 1896. A treatise on war particularly useful for its examination of offense and defense in both their strategic and tactical dimensions.

_____. *The Nation In Arms: A Treatise on Modern Military Systems and the Conduct of War* (translated by Philip A. Ashworth). London, England: Hugh Rees, Ltd., 1906.

Weigley, Russell F. *The American Way of War: A History of the United States Military Strategy and Policy*. New York: MacMillan, 1973. The source book on the evolution of U.S. military strategy.

Westmoreland, William C., Gen., USA. *A Soldier Reports*. Garden City, New York: Doubleday, 1976. General Westmoreland's autobiographical account of his service as COMUSMACV and Chief of Staff U.S. Army.

Weyand, Fred C., Gen., USA. "Serving the People: The Basic Case for the United States Army." *CDRS CALL*. May/June 1976. An analysis of the relationship between the Army and the American people.

_____ and Summers, Harry G., Jr., Colonel, USA. "Serving the People: The Need for Military Power." *Military Review*. December 1976. An analysis of how military power serves U.S. national interests.

———. "Vietnam Myths and American Realities." *CDRS CALL.* July/August 1976.

Whiting, Allen S. *The Chinese Calculus of Deterrence-India and Indo-China.* Ann Arbor, Michigan: University of Michigan Press, 1975.

Willoughby, Charles Andrew, Lt. Col., USA. *Maneuver In War.* Harrisburg, Pennsylvania: Military Service Publishing Co., 1939. An outstanding work on maneuver that derives a maneuver theory through analysis of the principles of war. This book also contains the text of *War Department Training Regulations 10–5*, 23 December 1921, the first official codification of the principles of war.

Wolfe, Tom. *Mauve Gloves and Madmen, Clutter and Vine.* New York: Farrar, Straus, and Giroux, 1976. Although it might not seem so from the title, this is an important book on American social attitudes by one of America's more observant commentators.

Index

Biographical Note

Colonel Harry G. Summers, Jr., Infantry, a designated Army strategist, holds bachelor's and master's degrees in military arts and science. An infantry squad leader in the Korean war, he served as a battalion and corps operations officer in the Vietnam war and later as a negotiator with the Viet Cong and North Vietnamese in Saigon and Hanoi. Now on the faculty of the U.S. Army War College, he has served as an instructor of strategy at the U.S. Army Command and General Staff, a member of General Creighton Abram's strategic assessment group, and, from 1975 to 1979, in the office of the Army Chief of Staff. His articles on strategy have appeared in *Army*, *Military Review*, and the *Naval Institute Proceedings*. Among his decorations and awards are the Combat Infantry Badge for both Korea and Vietnam, the Silver Star, the Legion of Merit, the Bronze Star for valor, and two Purple Hearts for wounds received in action. He is an associate member of the International Institute for Strategic Studies.